Baku

timeout.com

Time Out Guides Ltd
Universal House
251 Tottenham Court Road
London W1T 7AB
United Kingdom
Tel: +44 (0)20 7813 3000
Fax: +44 (0)20 7813 6001
Email: guides@timeout.com
www.timeout.com

Contents

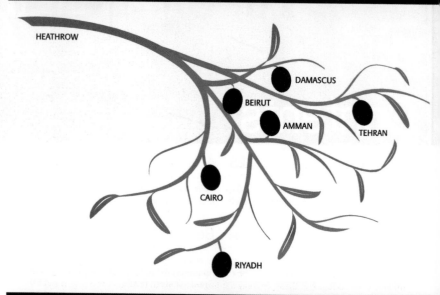

Introduction

When Ell & Nikki danced down the catwalk in Düsseldorf to celebrate their shock Eurovision Song Contest win for Azerbaijan, many TV viewers may have wondered exactly where Azerbaijan was. The answer is that it's a country that stands at the crossroads of Europe and Asia, an ex-Soviet republic set on the shores of the energy-rich Caspian Sea.

Today, Azerbaijan – and its capital Baku – are enjoying an economic boom on a much larger scale than the one that transformed Baku a century ago. After all, what other city would throw up a whole new venue, almost overnight, for the specific purpose of fulfilling its duty to host the Eurovision event a year after the 2011 triumph? And that's not all that's new in Baku. There are also three huge tower blocks fashioned in the tapering shape of flames, five five-star hotels and a new carpet museum gleaming gold and designed in the form of a rolled-up rug. And these are only the flagship projects to be unfurled over a six-month period before Europe descends on Azerbaijan in May 2012. Obviously, all had been planned long before 'Running Scared' swept the board in Germany but for Azerbaijan, the timing could not have been better.

When Robert Nobel turned up in this backwater of the Caucasus in 1875, it was in search of walnut trees to make rifle butts, his father having won and then lost the family fortune in the Crimean War. What he found instead was Baku in the grip of oil fever, a boom that would create untold wealth for the Nobels, the Rothschilds and visionary local philanthropists who built sumptuous mansions along grand boulevards. This development expanded Baku beyond the walled citadel created by the Shirvanshah dynasty in the 1400s. Their palace and the Old City around it are still Baku's key historic sight for tourists.

Again, oil has been the lubricant for today's rapid expansion, and it hasn't been limited to Baku alone. A new ski resort at Shah Dag opens in 2012, amid the majestic beauty of the Great Caucasus. Elsewhere, are remote mountain villages, stunning birdlife and bizarre Zoroastrian remains. Look hard enough and you can find Roman inscriptions carved in rock, petroglyphs dating from before 1,000BC, golden jackals and jungle cats. The ride there might be bumpy, the food and accommodation simple, but the welcome and the experience will be authenticity itself. Peterjon Cresswell, *Editor*

Baku in Brief

IN CONTEXT
Our In Context section examines the development of Baku and Azerbaijan from medieval kingdom of the Shirvanshahs to booming independent oil centre. We also examine the economic success of Baku and Azerbaijan today, while taking in the elegant architecture of the first oil boom a century ago, Azeri cuisine, and the rare wildlife protected in National Parks across the country.
▶ For more, see pp15-46.

SIGHTS
Baku's most definitive sights are the historic walled citadel of the Old City, and the elegant sweep of the Caspian waterfront, so impressively renovated in recent years. Around them is a busy capital that shows evidence of the 19th-century oil boom in its graceful mansions, the Soviet era in its metro stations and grand institutions, and post-independence prosperity in its skyscrapers and luxury hotels.
▶ For more, see pp48-83.

CONSUME
Baku's restaurants cater to a discerning international clientele, often with prices to match. Visitors of more modest resources may take advantage of the set-price lunches all around town, and foreigner-friendly bars in easy-to-find hubs in the city centre. We cover the best for all budgets, along with a rundown on the city's shopping scene and its outstanding hotels, from the historic to the sky-high.
▶ For more, see pp85-140.

ARTS & ENTERTAINMENT
Azerbaijan is the home of *mugham*, an indigenous form of music later adapted to incorporate another local speciality, jazz, and Baku has venues and festivals of international renown, in music and other art forms. Add a notable art scene, best taken in at the impressive Museum of Contemporary Art, then you'll find plenty to glean in terms of contemporary culture.
▶ For more, see pp141-149.

BEST OF AZERBAIJAN
From Baku, an improved road system leads north towards Russia and the dramatic mountain slopes of the Great Caucasus; south towards Iran and the gazelles and stunning birdlife of the Shirvan National Park; and west towards Georgia and the little-known communities of Avars, Udi and Molokans. The more adventurous can board a plane for the beautiful, landlocked exclave of Nakhchivan.
▶ For more, see pp151-201.

Baku & Around in 48 Hrs

Day 1 The City: Prime Sights and Panoramas

8AM Rise early for breakfast and then head to the Old City for a guided walk (*see p61*) through the narrow alleyways, taking in the **Maiden's Tower** (*see p56*). Head towards the waterfront, past the **Hadjinski Mansion** (*see p45*), the most ornate example of Baku's oil-boom architecture.

10AM Stroll down the **Bulvar** (*see pp70-76*). Spend a while window-shopping in Baku's first modern mall, the **Park Bulvar** (*see p127*). Walking towards the new harbour terminal, pick up a boat (*see p73* **Inside Track**) for a view of the city from the sea. Once back on land, wander a few blocks north to the **Landmark Building**, and take your pick for lunch between Spanish, Japanese or Chinese at La Bodega, Seto or Shin Shin.

2PM Time to explore the city's best modern cultural attraction, the **Museum of Contemporary Art** (*see p81*), a 15-minute walk or easy taxi journey east. Allow a good couple of hours, invest in a knowledgeable, English-speaking guide and bear in mind that the **Art Café Expression** (*see p115*) on the first floor does outstanding coffee, cakes and snacks.

4.30PM From here it's another 15-minute walk or north-west to Baku's Tsarist-era **railway station** (*see p79*), also the site of the city's main metro hub. Plunge deep underground on the Soviet-era escalator. Ride the blue line from 28 May two stops to its western terminus at Iceri Sheher, the newly revamped Old City station with the Louvre-like pyramid exterior.

7PM Take a gentle stroll downhill to focal **Azneft Square**, and along to the **funicular**. From the top station you'll get a brilliant panorama. A ten-minute climb will bring you to **Martyr's Hill** (*see p66*). Take the funicular back down to sea level for pan-Asian delights at **Chinar** (*see p111*), destination dining with a difference. A classic teahouse in former times, Chinar has kept its name but has been transformed by a London-based team of expert designers and chefs. (Make sure you book a table.)

NAVIGATING THE CITY

Baku is a great city to enjoy on foot, provided you bear in mind that crossing the major streets can sometimes be pretty daunting. Underground pedestrian walkways are becoming more common, particularly beneath Neftchilar (Bulvar) from the seafront to the city. Certainly walking is the best option to get to and from focal Fountains Square, with no metro station close by. There is a system of buses, but no timetables or maps to guide you once you find a stop. The metro is extremely cheap but poorly signposted once you get inside. If you get the hang of it, it's handy for the Tofik Bakhramov football stadium (*see p149*) and the railway station (*see p79*) – but the network is lined in a ring far from the very centre of town. There's no station at the hub of hotels and restaurants near the Hyatt, for example.

Taxis are parked all around town but it's a good idea to negotiate a price first.

Day 2 Out of the City: Cave Drawings & the Coast

8AM Get a good early start and head south out of Baku towards Gobustan, the first stop of a packed and varied agenda. Though Gobustan town itself is unremarkable, you're here for the unique petroglyphs, prehistoric carvings etched at least 20,000 years ago that are found in the **Gobustan Rock Art Cultural Landscape** (*see p159*) in the hills above.

11AM Pressing on south, after about ten kilometres (six miles) you'll come to an area of **mud volcanoes** (*see p156*), a distinct feature of Azerbaijan. To get a good view, turn off the main road at the sign for Dashghil, on a hilltop towards Alat, close to the shore. These are invariably gryphon variety volcanoes, steep-sided cones some two metres (6.5 feet) in height.

NOON For lunch, stick to something cheap and simple at a roadside grill. Lamb tail is always a popular dish.

1PM Push on further south beyond Alat to the **Shirvan National Park** (*see p194*), home to a large population of jeyran, or goitered gazelles. Some 200 species of birds can also be seen in the park – as well as bee-eaters, black francolins and pygmy cormorants, you might see an Egyptian vulture circling above. If you're lucky, you may also spot a jungle cat or golden jackal. Cheap, simple accommodation can be arranged if you don't fancy the drive back to Baku straight away.

6PM In the warmer months, you can round off the perfect day by heading back up the M3 highway towards Baku, past Gobustan, for a late dip at the beaches of **Shikhov** (*see p153*).

9PM Take your pick of one of the beach bars or restaurants on the strip, order a cold Xirdalan beer, leave the car and sort yourself out a taxi back to Baku whenever the mood takes you. Better still, call 189 and your mobile will bleep once the driver approaches.

SEEING THE SIGHTS

Many of Baku's museums close on Monday. Sometimes there are two admission prices, a higher one for foreigners, and there may be a fee for taking photographs. At some museums, English-speaking guides are available – the one at the Museum of Contemporary Art (*see p81*) is particularly recommended.

PACKAGE DEALS

The bulk of visitors to Azerbaijan – from the UK and the West in any case – come here on business. As Baku has diversified, there has been a concerted effort to groom the capital for tourism, to create a kind of Caucasian Dubai. The flurry of high-end hotel openings and staging of international events have certainly helped matters, but there are no special deals or passes for visitors in place as yet.

Best of Azerbaijan

ABSHERON & THE CASPIAN COAST

Jutting out into the Caspian Sea, the Absheron peninsula is both the location of Baku and home to unusual and attractive sights, both natural and historic, most within easy reach on a day trip from the capital. Leaving early in the morning, you can first head for the **Gala Historical Reserve** and its archaeological finds from around the region, before setting out for the historic sites of **Ramana Castle** and the **Ateshgah Fire Temple**, and the natural phenomena of the 'burning mountain' of **Yanar Dag**. The petroglyphs and mud volcanoes around **Gobustan** provide further drama, while the beaches of **Novkhani** and **Shikhov** come into their own in summer, when Baku residents head here for waterside relaxation.
▶ For more, see pp153-159.

GREAT WESTERN ROUTE

To see the most of Azerbaijan, drive out along the Great Western Route, one of the country's finest journeys. It's about five hours from Baku to the second city and former capital of **Ganja**, and six hours to the bucolic destination of **Sheki**. Beyond Sheki are the lovely villages of **Gakh** and **Zagatala**, set in a dramatic mountainous landscape dotted with Albanian ruins. An older road leads to **Gabala** and its Historical Museum, **Ismayilli** and its vineyards, and **Lahij**, a pretty town of artisans and craftsmen.
▶ For more, see pp179-186.

NAKHCHIVAN

This landlocked exclave is the most remote of Azerbaijan's destinations – but arguably the most beautiful. Accessible only by air, Nakhchivan is an ancient land with Biblical associations: legend has it that its first citizens were direct descendants of Noah. **Nakhchivan City** is home to ornate mosques, medieval mausoleums and museums dedicated to the many key cultural personalities who were born here. Salt caves, hot sulphur springs and the lemon trees of Ordubad are the stand-out features of trips beyond the city.

▶ For more, see pp179-186.

HEADING NORTH

Towards the borders with Russia and Georgia is the dramatic mountainous terrain of the Greater Caucasus. Here, ancient villages perch precariously on crags overhanging deep gorges. Their populations are a fascinating patchwork of ethnicities. Highlights include the impressive ruins of **Chiraz Castle**, the seaside resort of **Nabran**, and **Guba**, an administrative centre in Tsarist times and home to striking minarets and an ancient hammam. A more contemporary attraction can be found at the new ski resort of **Shah Dag**, beyond the glorious **Cloudcatcher Canyon**.

▶ For more, see pp187-193.

HEADING SOUTH

Past the rows of sunflower and watermelon fields south of Baku, heading towards Iran, the **Talysh** region is known for its verdant landscape, stellar cuisine and outstanding hospitality. The main features here are the hot springs of **Masalli Istisu**, the provincial capital and tea hub of **Lankaran** and the quirky border town of **Astara**. Closer to Baku, allow time to discover the rare birdlife and indigenous gazelle population of the **Shirvan National Park**.

▶ For more, see pp194-201.

Time Out Baku

Editorial
Editor Peterjon Cresswell
Deputy Editor Ros Sales
Listings Editor Peterjon Cresswell
Proofreader John Shandy Watson
Indexer Holly Pick

Editorial Director Ruth Jarvis
Editorial Manager Holly Pick
Management Accountants Margaret Wright, Clare Turner

Design
Art Editor Pinelope Kourmouzoglou
Senior Designer Kei Ishimaru
Group Commercial Designer Jodi Sher

Picture Desk
Picture Editor Jael Marschner
Picture Desk Assistant/Researcher Ben Rowe

Advertising
New Business & Commercial Director Mark Phillips
International Advertising Manager Kasimir Berger
International Sales Executive Charlie Sokol

Marketing
Senior Publishing Brand Manager Luthfa Begum
Guides Marketing Manager Colette Whitehouse
Group Commercial Art Director Anthony Huggins

Production
Group Production Manager Brendan McKeown
Production Controller Katie Mulhern-Bhudia

Time Out Group
Chairman & Founder Tony Elliott
Chief Executive Officer David King
Chief Operating Officer Aksel Van der Wal
Editor-in-Chief Tim Arthur
Chief Technical Officer Remo Gettini
Group Financial Director Paul Rakkar
Group General Manager/Director Nichola Coulthard
UK Chief Commercial Officer David Pepper
Time Out International Ltd MD Cathy Runciman
Cultural Development Director Mark Elliott

Contributors
Introduction Peterjon Cresswell. **History** Peterjon Cresswell. **Baku Today** Ben Illis (*Making Your Mind Up* Peterjon Cresswell). **Food & Drink** Ben Illis. **Wildlife** Ben Illis, Jane Mott. **Oil-Boom Architecture** Ben Illis. **Sightseeing** Peterjon Cresswell (*Caspian Controversy* Jane Mott). **Hotels** Peterjon Cresswell. **Restaurants & Cafés** Peterjon Cresswell, Jane Mott, Natalya Marquand. **Bars & Nightlife** Peterjon Cresswell, Jane Mott, Johanna Cronin. **Shopping & Services** Peterjon Cresswell, Steve Hollier (*Where the Stalls Have No Name, Cutting A Rug* Jane Mott). **Calendar** Peterjon Cresswell (*Novruz Bayrami* Jane Mott). **Arts & Entertainment** Peterjon Cresswell (*Fore!* Jane Mott, *Jazzerbaijan* Ben Illis). **Best of Azerbaijan** Ben Illis. **Directory** Peterjon Cresswell

Maps John Oakey. johnoakey1@gmail.com

Cover photography by Corbis
Back cover photography by Ben Illis

Photography by Ben Illis; except page 5 Four Seasons Baku; pages 7 (bottom left), 10 (bottom), 15, 16, 30, 31, 40, 43 (bottom left), 57, 141, 142, 145, 159 (left), 172 (top), 173 (top and bottom), 189, 203 Mamed Rahimov; pages 22, 25, 33 Corbis; page 26 Getty Images; pages 78, 79, 143, 146, 147 Ministry of Culture & Tourism; page 80 Peterjon Cresswell; page 86 Chirag Plaza; page 95 Soenne, Aachen; page 121 Alys Tomlinson.

The following images were supplied by the featured establishments: pages 24, 69, 90, 91, 93, 94, 97, 98, 128, 129, 130, 131, 144

The editor would like to thank Ben Illis, Jane Mott, Richard Rainbow, Dr Nazim Samadov.

Ministry of Culture and Tourism
of the Republic of Azerbaijan

About the Guide

GETTING AROUND

The back of the book contains street maps of Baku, as well as overview maps of the city and its surroundings. The maps start on page 220, with a map of the Old City on p58; on them are marked the locations of hotels (❶), restaurants (❶), and bars (❶). The majority of businesses listed in this guide are located in the mapped areas; the grid-square references in the listings refer to these maps.

THE ESSENTIALS

For practical information, including visas, disabled access, emergency numbers, lost property, useful websites and local transport, please see the Directory. It begins on page 203.

THE LISTINGS

Addresses, phone numbers, websites, transport information, hours and prices are all included in our listings, as are selected other facilities. All were checked and correct at press time. However, business owners can alter their arrangements at any time, and fluctuating economic conditions can cause prices to change rapidly.

The very best venues in the city, the must-sees and must-dos in every category, have been marked with a red star (★). In the Sights chapters, we've also marked venues with free admission with a FREE symbol.

PHONE NUMBERS

The area code for Baku is 012. You don't need to use the code when calling from within Baku: simply dial the number as listed in this guide.

From outside Azerbaijan, dial your country's international access code or a plus symbol, followed by the Azerbaijan country code (994), 12 for Baku (dropping the initial zero) and the seven-digit number as listed in the guide. So, to reach the Azerbaijan State Museum of History, dial + 994 12 493 3648). For more on phones, including information on calling abroad and details of local mobile-phone access, see p210.

FEEDBACK

We welcome feedback on this guide, both on the venues we've included and on any other locations that you'd like to see featured in future editions. Please email us at guides@timeout.com.

Time Out Guides

Founded in 1968, Time Out has grown from humble beginnings into the leading resource for anyone wanting to know what's happening in the world's greatest cities. Alongside our influential weeklies in London, New York and Chicago, we publish more than 20 magazines in cities as varied as Beijing and Beirut; a range of travel books, with the City Guides now joined by the newer Shortlist series; and an information-packed website. The company remains proudly independent, still owned by Tony Elliott four decades after he launched *Time Out London*.

Written by local experts and illustrated with original photography, our books also retain their independence. No business has been featured because it has advertised, and all restaurants and bars are visited and reviewed anonymously.

ABOUT THE EDITOR

Peterjon Cresswell spent a significant part of his errant student life in the former Soviet Union. A Russian-speaker now based in slightly saner Budapest, he has been covering the region for Time Out for nearly two decades, also writing guides to Croatia, Zagreb and Krakow.

A full list of the book's contributors can be found opposite.

In Context

Government House. *See p71.*

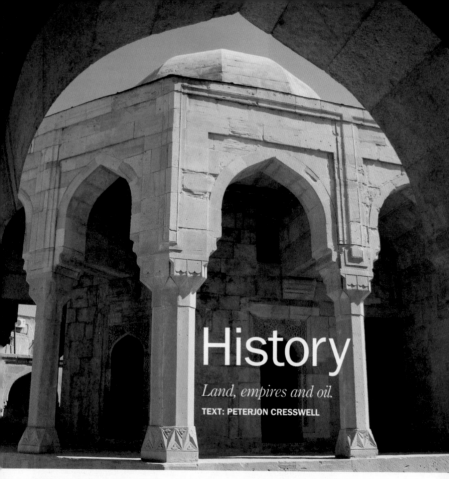

History

Land, empires and oil.

TEXT: PETERJON CRESSWELL

The location of what we know today as Azerbaijan – beside the Caspian Sea, coveted by Arab, Persian, Turk and Russian alike – has dictated its fate. This patchwork history, and coming and going of sundry tribes, rulers, regimes and religions force any writer of local history to qualify the term 'Azerbaijan', which didn't appear on the map as a nation until the short-lived, post-Tsarist democratic republic of 1918.

For the few thousand years of civilisation before then – this area being one of the world's oldest in terms of human history – the south Caucasus attracted Alexander the Great, the Romans, Genghis Khan and Tamerlane. Most notably, it brought the Shirvanshahs here to establish a kingdom in medieval times, with Baku as its capital. The Old City you see today is centred around their palace. But historians and archaeologists have found evidence of human endeavour that dates back long before this. In fact, Azerbaijan is the location of some of the oldest proto-human remains ever found.

'The Maiden's Tower, for example, is thought to have its roots in Zoroastrian culture.'

AZYKH AND ALBANIA

Sadly off-limits to most visitors to Azerbaijan as it lies within the disputed territory of Nagorno-Karabakh, the Azykh cave complex near Tugh was the subject of two significant excavations, one in the 1960s, and the other in the 1990s. What was found there was a jaw bone, around 300,000 years old, and stone tools. Azykh Man, as this relic came to be known, is one of the earliest such discoveries in the world.

Tourists can visit the **Gobustan Rock Art Cultural Landscape** (*see p159* **Rock of Ages**), some 40 miles (65 kilometres) south of Baku, an area of some 6,000 carvings, or petroglyphs, that date back to the Mesolithic period, or Middle Stone Age, of at least 6,000 BC. They illustrate a whole range of human activity that took place here. Other evidence from the later Neolithic time includes proof that irrigation was used to grow crops.

The most well-known civilisation of the Bronze and Iron Ages was that of the Albanians – no relation to Albania in the Balkans. Albania stretched across most of modern-day Azerbaijan and adjoining southern Dagestan. The Albanians lived here from halfway in the first millennium BC to soon after the Arab invasion of the 700s. When the Romans came here between 60 BC and 90 BC (a legionnaire's inscription – the easternmost evidence of a Roman presence – is another historical treasure worth looking out for at Gobustan, *see p159* **Rock of Ages**), it was the Albanians they conquered.

Those in the western part of the area adopted Christianity around 325 AD, while those in the east would come under the influence of Islam. Rare written evidence of Caucasian Albania has links with Udi, the language of what is perhaps the world's oldest Christian community (*see p172* **Family Tree**). Their spoken language, shares similarities with Lezghic (*see p191* **Family Tree**).

We know quite a lot about the Albanians thanks to the *Avesta*, a series of legends and scriptures passed down over several generations. They may be originally attributed to Zoroaster, father of Zoroastrianism, one of the great religions of the Ancient World. Its cornerstones were the promotion of good deeds, the concept of a moral duty and free will – and the worship of fire. Temples were built across the region, particularly in Iran, but evidence of Zoroastrian influence in Baku is more circumstantial. The **Maiden's Tower** (*see p59*), for example, is thought to have its roots in Zoroastrian culture, while the annual spring rites celebrations of **Novruz** (*see p143* **Novruz Bayrami**) have a definite fiery element.

The invasion of Alexander the Great in 330 BC stemmed the rise of Zoroastrianism, thanks to the burning of Persepolis and the ever-growing influence of Greek religion. The arrival of Islam ten centuries later finally killed off its dominance.

SASSANIDS, ARABS AND SELJUKS

Spanning the period of Late Antiquity between the Roman Empire and Muslim conquest, the Sassanid dynasty enjoyed a number of golden ages during its 400-year reign of Iran, Afghanistan, Iraq and this part of the Caucasus. With its capital near Baghdad, the Sassanid Empire embraced Zoroastrianism, making it the state religion. As well as founding many cities and building dams, the Sassanids created literary classics still popular in Iran today and invented the sport of polo.

Despite regular clashes with the Romans and skirmishes with Arab and Turkic tribes, the Sassanids enjoyed a high standard of education, and left behind remarkable

IN CONTEXT

Time Out

EXPLORE FROM THE INSIDE OUT

Time Out Guides written by local experts

Our city guides are written from a unique insider's perspective
by teams of local writers.

Covering 50 destinations, the range includes the official
London 2012 guide.

visit timeout.com/shop

Petroglyphs. *See p17.*

examples of pottery, tapestries and carpets. Known as Eran, later bastardised to Iran, theirs was the last great empire in the region before the arrival of the Arabs.

United under the newly burgeoning religion of Islam, the Arabs eventually conquered the area in the seventh and eighth centuries – Albania is officially considered to have been seized in 705. There continued a series of dynastic struggles and rebellions until the tenth century, when Albania fractured into a number of fiefdoms, including Shirvan, based at Shamakha. A terrible earthquake destroyed much of Shamakha in 1192, so the head of the Shirvanshahs, Akhsitan I, moved his court to Baku. He also began to build up a navy.

In the meantime, Turkic herdsmen under the dominant Seljuk dynasty took over the Caucasian plains, including much of Albania, leaving the remaining Christians to flee to the hills. Their generally unobtrusive rule allowed for trade to develop despite the various feudal differences. This period, during the 11th and 12th centuries, is known as one of relative peace, which allowed for the flowering of a golden age in Georgia, and soon Azerbaijan, too.

A local variety of architecture developed, in Shirvan and Absheron, even if little survives today. In Baku's Old City, part of the walls and the minaret of the Muhammed Mosque are evidence of this flourishing culture. The Maiden's Tower was also rebuilt during this time. Silk was produced, the Great Silk Route renovated and bridges built. Progress was made in medicine and astronomy, and paper was manufactured in significant amounts. This was the Caspian region that Marco Polo would have visited in the later part of the 13th century. The writer Nizami Ganjavi, whose statue can be found in Fountains Square (and in most other Azeri towns), composed his five, long narrative poems, studied and revered a millennium later. His mausoleum stands in his home town of Ganja (*see p162*).

TAMERLANE AND TURKIC TRIBES

The 13th century was marked by regular, destructive invasions by Mongols, who laid waste to much they saw in the region. The sons of Genghis Khan came to Azerbaijan in waves, first in 1220, and later taking the heavily defended Baku with difficulty. The key leader was Hulagu Khan, who named Tabriz as his regional capital, part of East Azerbaijan Province, just over the border in today's north-western Iran.

Baku was already known for its oil, as Marco Polo observed, and local taxes had already been levied on it by the previous regime. This made the city particularly

Maiden's Tower. *See p17.*

attractive to the Mongols, also keen for access to its harbour. Tamerlane, subject of the famous epic poem by Edgar Allen Poe, was the great military leader of the day, leading many campaigns in and around Azerbaijan fighting with and against the Mongol hordes and Turkic tribes. He died in 1404, leaving Azerbaijan to feuding khanates and the ever-encroaching Ottoman Turks.

SHIRVANSHAHS, SAFAVIDS AND OTTOMANS

The man to emerge in the aftermath of Tamerlane was Shirvanshah Ibrahim I, founder of the Derbendi dynasty of Shirvanshahs. Having led and cleverly avoided a number of military skirmishes in the region – at one point siding with Tamerlane and preserving Shirvan's independence – Ibrahim I was declared governor of Shirvan and Shamakhi.

Ibrahim I aimed to unite the various feuding dynastic forces of Azerbaijan but failed to conquer the key town of Tabriz in 1406, beaten back by the so-called 'Black Sheep Turkomans', or Kara Koyunlu. These Shi'ite Oghuz Turkic tribes had been defeated by Tamerlane in 1400, only to return stronger and more numerous. Ibrahim I allied with Constantine I of Georgia but was again defeated at the pivotal Battle of Chalagan in 1412, in today's Nagorno-Karabakh. Constantine was beheaded, Ibrahim I imprisoned. He would die soon afterwards. A mosque in his name still stands in Baku's Old City.

Baku at this time was pretty much laid out as the Old City is today, a warren of narrow, twisting alleyways and low houses, divided into neighbourhoods, each with a mosque, a market and public baths. There were caravanserais, a primitive system of water pipes, and everything lay behind two sets of defensive walls. Within them lived artisans, traders and merchants. The upper quarter, to the north-west, just above where the modern-day Icheri Sheher metro station now stands, was where the noble Shirvanshah family resided.

'Shah Abbas I died without a successor, the paranoid ruler having had three sons either killed or blinded.'

Son of Ibrahim I, Khalilullah I was head of the Shirvanshah dynasty from 1417 to 1465, and it was under his rule that much of the **Palace of the Shirvanshahs** (*see p62*) was developed, as was the Old City in general. His son, Farrukh Yassar, was one of many of the Shirvan clan to be wiped out by Safavid forces in 1500.

It was another Ismail I, this one the founder of the Safavid dynasty, a poet soldier descended from the Sufi order of Safaviyyas, fluent in Persian and Azeri, who conquered Baku after a long siege in 1501. He found a significant cache of Shirvanshah treasure at the grave of Khalilullah I. Basing himself at Tabriz, he proclaimed himself Shah of Azerbaijan and, a year later, Shah of Iran.

Under him were tens of thousands of Gizilbash soldiers, mainly Turkic-speaking Azeris in crimson headgear (*gizilbash*) and adherent to the Shi'a doctrine. They met their comeuppance at the Battle of Chaldiran, today in the West Azerbaijan Province of Iran, in 1514. Not only did the army of Ottoman Sultan Selim I outnumber them, but the overwhelming Ottoman victory eradicated all sense of Gizilbash invincibility. Ismail I was no longer divine – in fact, it is said that following this defeat, he simply took to the bottle.

Ismail I's son, Tahmasp I, headed the Safavid line for most of the 16th century but is best known for his kowtowing to Gizilbash command – and for his encouragement of the carpet industry, the silk trade suffering from the regular regional conflicts. Military engagements and peace negotiations with the Ottomans characterised his time in charge, and towns such as Baku changed hands several times. The most effective of the Safavid rulers was Shah Abbas I, who liberated Baku from the Ottomans in 1607. He is best known today for the wealth of caravanserais and mosques built around the Old City during his reign of four decades.

ENTER THE RUSSIANS

Shah Abbas I died without a successor, the paranoid ruler having had three sons either killed or blinded. But he did have the foresight to enter discussions with the East India Company, the King of Spain and the Tsar of Russia – anything to discourage any further Ottoman development in the region, in fact. Although the Safavids would die out a century or so after Shah Abbas I, they are thought to have laid the foundations for modern-day Iran.

During the 1500s and 1600s, while Baku was laid siege to several times, a significant a number of European travellers and diplomats visited the city and subsequently wrote travelogues. Underpinning almost every one of them was a detailed description of oil production here. This precious commodity continued to attract Ottoman attack and the interest of international trading concerns.

Azerbaijan, with the Safavids in decline and moving their powerbase further east to Iran, was divided into a number of autonomous khanates. These were run along the lines of a feudal aristocracy, with beys, sultans and naibs in a descending order of subordination. The khanates were similar to the regions that comprise the nation today, and the underlying ethnic movements of the early 18th century would have later echoes in the 20th century.

Looking for new trading routes, Russia annexed the northernmost khanates and later allowed for an influx of their compatriots, Armenians and Germans into Azerbaijan. Baku, the hub of the Baku Khanate, contained about a quarter of its 20,000

IN CONTEXT

Early oil drilling.

'At one point, quite incredibly, Baku was exporting half the world's oil, on the very eve of mass production of the car.'

population. With its harbour a particular attraction, Baku was the prime site when Peter the Great had his military commanders draw up a campaign to take the Caspian coast. The Baku nobility settled on surrender to the Tsar rather than have their city put under siege, but the request got lost in the confusing local chain of command. A furious Peter had Major-General Matushkin besiege the city from sea and land, and his troops entered Baku on 26 July 1723. A Russian garrison was set up in the Old City.

NADIR AND THE FIGHT AGAINST THE TSARISTS

But this time the Russians wouldn't stay for long. Following Peter's death, Russia's Caspian adventure was considered too costly, and there was growing local resistance to Tsarist rule. Amid the chaos appeared Afghan-born commander Nadir Afshar, whose soldiers took Shirvan and Shamakhi. On the back of this success, he persuaded the Russians to return their new conquests to Persia. Nadir was engaged in a dangerous game, playing off the Russians against the Ottomans and the Persians.

After gaining more territory, Nadir was assassinated in 1747 and rule reverted to the khanates. These grew in power, seeing a flourishing of literature and the creative arts in Ganja and Shusha, now Nagorno-Karabakh. Baku, within the Baku Khanate under former garrison commander Mirza Muhammed Khan I, his son Melik Muhammed Khan and later his grandson Mirza Muhammed Khan II, enjoyed relative stability and a gradual economic recovery over the last half of the 18th century.

At the end of the 18th century, though, the Russians turned their attention to the region once again. Eventually, despite a clash led by Baku governor, Hussein Gulu Khan, in 1806, in which local noblemen killed the Russian regional commander in chief and other khanates rose up, Baku succumbed to a century of Tsarist rule.

THE BOOM YEARS

The Treaty of Gulistan in 1813 ensured a temporary peace between Russia and Persia, and set in writing the inclusion of eight Azeri khanate states, Daghestan and eastern Georgia into the Russian Empire. The later Treaty of Turkmenchay saw Nakhchivan, Talysh and other khanates signed over to the Russians. The international borders outlined in these two treaties are, more or less, those in place today.

Russian colonisation had several effects. The old Azeri khanates became a network of provinces and districts. Azerbaijan as a whole, and Baku in particular, became more Europeanised, and the influence of Islam waned. Everything would be in place for the biggest influx of foreigners Baku would ever see – and a complete transformation of this Caspian backwater, thanks to the untold wealth that arose from the development of one commodity: oil.

The key date in this revolutionary development is 1872. Up until then, the Russians had run the burgeoning oil industry as a state monopoly. The first deep oil well had been tested in 1846 and drilled in Baku in 1848. Within a decade, the first refinery had been built in Surakhana and, within 20 years, there were more than 20 in Baku and surroundings.

But the decision by Alexander II to allow private individuals to extract oil on a long-term concession basis transformed a cottage industry into a huge, multinational, global concern. Before the decree, Baku consisted primarily of its Old City, its

IN CONTEXT

Ali & Nino

Who was the mysterious 'Kurban Said', author of this cult romance?

For a sense of the political and ethnic undercurrents rife in Baku towards the end of World War I, and an entertaining love story, head to a branch of Ali & Nino (*see p128*) and pick up a copy of the novel of the same name, which the store has helped to turn into a cult. Look beyond the story to its purported author, and you'll discover that *Ali & Nino* has a history as patchwork as its subject matter.

This star-crossed love story of an Azeri schoolboy and a Georgian princess is credited to one Kurban Said. There are many disputes as to his identity, but all parties are agreed that 'Kurban Said' is a pseudonym. There are three main contenders for authorship. One school of thought has it that 'Kurban Said' was Yusif Vazir Chamanzaminli, born simply Yusif Vazir in Shusha in 1887, who died in a Russian gulag in 1943. A recent special edition of the esteemed periodical *Azerbaijan International*, after six years of extensive research in ten languages, expounded this theory. The prolific Vazir attended the same school as the novel's hero Ali Khan Shirvanshah. The writer's last address in Baku, at Bunyad Sardarov Street 20, is marked with a plaque in Cyrillic. The nearby Institute of Manuscripts on Istiglaliyyat Street holds a number of his works, all of which use different and symbolic pseudonyms. 'Kurban Said' conveys the idea of 'joyful sacrifice', an ironic nod to the novel's climax, in which Ali dies defending Baku from the Bolsheviks.

An older theory had pointed to the Austrian Baroness Elfriede Ehrenfels von Bodmershof (*Ali & Nino* was first published in Vienna in 1937 – in German) and Lev Nussimbaum. The latter was a Kiev-born Jew who also

KURBAN SAID

wrote under the name Essad Bey, and who lived in Baku at the time of the events described. Nussimbaum died in Italy in 1942. He had first fled Hitler's Berlin for Austria, where he became good friends with Ehrenfels, and the novel was said to be a collaboration between the two. The Nazi records of the time, according to research by the *New Yorker* in 1999, pointed to Ehrenfels, who died in the early 1980s, as the author. That first version was copyrighted to the niece of the baroness, Leela Ehrenfels.

Finally, there is the bizarre case of Tripoli-born Vacca Bello, Nussimbaum's drug dealer, who, as Ahmed Giamil Vacca-Mazzara, had published the first Italian edition of *Ali Khan* in 1944. Vacca was responsible for a lengthy obituary of Nussimbaum in *Oriente Moderno* in 1942. Vacca is now thought to have been fishing for posthumous royalties through flimsy claims of familial ties to Nussimbaum.

Whatever the case, what is certain is that the novel has since been published in more than 100 editions, and in more than 30 languages. And the movie version? When *Ali & Nino* was becoming an international *cause célèbre*, plans were afoot for filming to take place in and around Baku's Old City – only for funding to fall through. Whoever picks up the baton will find a lot of the settings still in place: the Philharmonia Concert Hall, City Hall and, just inside the Old City walls near the Sabir statue, the house where Ali lives. Other scenes from the book take place in Dagestan, Iran and Shusha, locations that should give considerable headaches to any producer looking to shoot there in the 21st century.

300 buildings and few thousand residents. By 1883, swollen by the significant number of foreigners drawn by the oil industry, this population was 45,000. By 1913, when Baku had become one of the biggest industrial hubs in the Russian Empire, its population was up to 200,000. Azerbaijan's whole economy was gradually changing from a purely agricultural one to a partly industrial one, and society from rural to urban.

The opening up to foreign investors coincided almost exactly with Baku's first huge oil gusher and a rapid change to large-scale, mechanised production. This was concentrated in what became known as the Black City, in the far east of Baku, past what is today's modern harbour terminal. This morass of derricks, noise and black smoke was where fortunes were made, most notably for the Rothschilds and the Nobels. At one point, quite incredibly, Baku was exporting half the world's oil, on the very eve of mass production of the car.

The most dynamic players in this new, lucrative market were Ludvig and Robert Nobel, who had arrived in Baku by chance and saw the opportunity to improve on the primitive production techniques then in use. By 1877, they developed the world's first oil tanker, named *Zoroaster*, after Azerbaijan's fire cult, to export on a large scale. In 1882, they began oil production round the clock. Ludvig himself headed the influential Baku Council of Oil Industrialists, while the Rothschilds from Paris formed the Caspian-Black Sea Society for Commerce & Industry (*see p75* **Dallas of the Caucasus**). During this relatively short period of time, Baku was transformed. New quarters were thrown up almost overnight to cope with the demand for housing, though the infrastructure to service them – water, transport, lighting – was not as swift in arriving.

Nevertheless, the great local magnates of the day, most notably Zeynalabdin Taghiyev and Mammad Hassan Hajinski, reinvested much of their riches back into Baku's economy, improving its architecture and infrastructure. Taghiyev financed a horse-drawn tramway, parks, paved streets, houses of culture, schools, factories and mosques. His roubles allowed for the completion of a water pipeline from Guba. Hajinski was the driving force behind the landscaping of the waterfront Bulvar into

IN CONTEXT

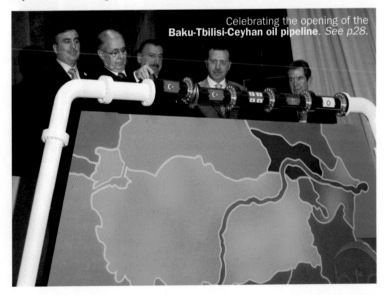

Celebrating the opening of the **Baku-Tbilisi-Ceyhan oil pipeline**. *See p28.*

a fine promenade and public park. Most of all, these men built opulent mansions, either overlooking Bulvar or in what was now the new city centre, its wide avenues leading east from the original urban hub of the Old City. The most impressive of them, Hajinki's, set at a corner of the Old City where it meets the Caspian Sea, now contains a branch of upscale fashion chain Tom Ford (*see p131*); Taghiyev's houses the Azerbaijan State Museum of History (*see p53*).

At the same time, the considerable amount of funds allocated to culture by local philanthropists gave rise to impressive theatres and venues for the classical arts. For the first time, European-style plays – by the likes of Mirza Akhundov – were written in Azeri, operas were performed and orchestras founded. This was an era of literary and linguistic blossoming. A local-language press came into being, including the influential satirical periodical *Molla Nasraddin*, an outlet for the burgeoning intelligentsia. Nariman Narimanov established Baku's first public library.

Steamships were built, a railway, and a grand train station in the east of town, with a direct link to the Black City. All this took manpower, finance, loans, bureaucracy, and the social composition of Baku also changed rapidly. Europeans, Persians and Jews from various countries flocked here, with Russians and Armenians taking up the best positions.

Given the poor conditions that many workers and their families toiled and lived in, and the revolutionary fervour in St Petersburg in 1904 and 1905, there arose great social unrest in and around Baku. Workers began to rise up against their foreign masters, partly prompted by prime agitator Koba, later known as Stalin, who served time in a Baku prison. Swedish workers were attacked and killed. Russian *agents provocateurs* set poor against rich, Azeri against Armenian, and interracial conflict boiled over into bloodshed. Against a backdrop of strikes and demonstrations, ethnic clashes broke out all over Azerbaijan.

IN CONTEXT

Soviet military intervention, 1989. *See p28.*

CONFLICT, CONFUSION AND INDEPENDENCE

As World War I broke out, Baku continued to produce oil, serving both German and British forces as warfare became ever more mechanised. In 1918 General Lionel Dunsterville led the so-called Dunsterforce to capture Baku's oilfield and strategic port ahead of the Germans. He found a city in chaos. In 1917, Russia had descended into civil war and Azerbaijan, Armenia and Georgia had formed the Trans-Caucasian Federation that November, based in Tbilisi. Shortly afterwards, the Armistice of Erzincan effectively ended conflict in the Caucasus between Russia and the Ottoman Empire. Russia formally exited World War I the following March with the Treaty of Brest-Litovsk. Matters between the Turks and Trans-Caucasian were far from closed, however, and Ottoman troops had to be held back at a series of battles in eastern Armenia in May 1918. That month, within three days, all three Trans-Caucasian nations declared independence. Enshrined in Azerbaijani lore, the date of 28 May marks the establishment of the world's first Muslim democratic republic. Its first capital was Ganja, though the new national government also met in Tbilisi.

That March, the Soviets had also sent a team of 26 commissars to Baku to nationalise the oilfields for the Bolsheviks. The so-called Baku Commune was immensely unpopular and inter-ethnic violence, the so-called 'March Days', saw many die on the streets of Baku. The 26 landed in jail as Turkish forces laid siege to the city. Amid the chaos, the 26 commissars escaped by ship but, in scenes straight out of a plot from a Tin-Tin cartoon, instead of Astrakhan they were fooled into having it steered to Turkmenistan. There they were summarily executed.

Baku was awash with spies, fifth columnists and rumour. Each of the three constituent new republics formed separate military units and skirmishes broke out between them. The Dunsterforce occupied Baku for six weeks until mid September, slipping out under cover of night for Turks and Azeris to enter the city and exact revenge on remaining Armenians, considered guilty for the 'March Days' massacre.

Baku took over duties as capital of Azerbaijan, and the Armistice of Mudros on 30 October between the Ottoman Empire and Allied Forces saw the Turks withdraw from the city. Peace-keeping Commonwealth soldiers, under General Thomson, re-occupied Baku and a state of martial law was declared. To the west, open conflict soon broke out between Azeris and Armenians in Nagorno-Karabakh, particularly in the key town of Shusha.

Given the hostilities, it is a wonder that the Azerbaijan Democratic Republic got any business done at all, but the head of the ruling National Council, Mammad Rasul-Zadeh, helped establish the Baku State University, among other positive measures.

ENTER THE SOVIETS

Preparing the way with a propaganda campaign and behind-the-scenes shenanigans that helped spiral inflation, the Soviets invaded again, taking Baku on 28 April, 1920. This time the Turks could barely help, given the collapse of the Ottoman Empire. By 1922, Azerbaijan had become integrated within the USSR. It was a situation that was to last for the greater part of the 20th century.

Soviet Azerbaijan's first leader was Nariman Narimanov, who had helped found Baku's first public library two decades before. Narimanov is considered to have at least tried to negotiate the best deal for his country, first with Lenin and then with Stalin, but for his pains he was poisoned in 1925 in Moscow.

Worse was to follow when the Stalinist purges saw the exile and/or death of key figures from Baku's cultural and political life. A walk up Istliglaliyyat today reveals a number of plaques erected in their honour. Poet and playwright Huseyn Javid, with his own memorial museum there, is one such example. Stalin also tampered with Azerbaijan's borders, giving territory to Armenia and thus splitting the country in two.

Although no fighting took place within its newly drawn borders, Azerbaijan was heavily involved in World War II, with Hitler keen on getting his paws on Baku's oilfields. Hundreds of thousands of Azeris lost their lives fighting for the Soviet Union, and Baku became a city of intrigue and rumour as the Nazis attempted to woo its influential personalities over to the German side. But Azerbaijan remained tied to the Kremlin, which sent thousands of German prisoners of war to construct railroads and many of Baku's post-war buildings. The Tofik Bakhramov football stadium is one such structure.

After 1945, Azerbaijan lost much of its political clout in Moscow and the focus of the Soviet oil industry shifted to Siberia. The rise of local party high official Heydar Aliyev through the ranks helped redress this balance, and by the 1980s he had become the first Muslim in the Politburo.

INDEPENDENCE AND NAGORNO KARABAKH

Tensions brewing in and over the disputed region of Nagorno-Karabakh between Armenia and Azerbaijan spilled over into civil unrest and violence in early 1988. Soviet military intervention was required on a number of occasions but on 20 January, 1990, Gorbachëv's troops shot 132 nationalist demonstrators on the streets of Baku. For more on the issue of Nagorno-Karabakh, *see p176*.

Four days later, Moscow appointed Ayaz Mutallibov as First Secretary of the Communist Party of Azerbaijan. In December 1990, Mutallibov manoeuvred to have the 'Soviet' name dropped from the Republic of Azerbaijan and sovereignty declared. Full independence would come a year later, with the dissolution of the Soviet Union.

Following the Armenian massacre of Azerbaijanis at Khojaly and losses in Nagorno-Karabakh, Mutallibov resigned over the military failure. Given also the economic difficulties in the immediate post-Soviet period, and the shortcomings of interim president Abulfaz Elchibey, the scene was set for someone to come in and take the reins: Heydar Aliyev.

ENTER THE ALIYEVS

From his powerbase in Nakhchivan, former Politburo member Heydar Aliyev was in a better position to reverse the losses in Nagorno-Karabakh and appease the military. He swept to power with an overwhelming majority in the presidential election of October 1993. After territorial gains in Nagorno-Karabakh, a ceasefire was signed in the spring of 1994, shortly before Aliyev's biggest political success: the so-called 'Deal of the Century', a $7.4 billion investment in the oil industry, opening Baku and its Azeri-Chirag-Guneshli oilfield to consortium led by BP, and exporting oil to the West in significant amounts. This was followed by the discovery of the Shah Deniz gas field, the opening of the Baku-Tbilisi-Ceyhan oil pipeline and Baku-Tbilisi-Erzerum gas pipeline, combining to make Azerbaijan a major player in the field of international energy.

The rapid influx of capital and expat workers began to change the face of Baku, which was emerging from its ex-Soviet shell to accommodate new high-end hotels and office blocks. After a dip in 1998-99, a newly booming economy began to manifest itself around the city.

In 2003, Heydar Aliyev's son, Ilham Aliyev, was elected as President of the Republic of Azerbaijan, and re-elected five years later. Considered the father of the nation, Heydar Aliyev didn't live to see the results of the oil boom. Severely ill throughout most of 2003, he died that December.

Spiralling revenues from the oil and gas industries have seen the transformation of Baku, with traces of its Soviet past removed, the Old City and Bulvar overhauled and luxury international boutiques and five-star hotels opened. In 2012, Azerbaijan takes up its position as a non-permanent member of the United Nations Security Council, and Baku hosts the Eurovision Song Contest while also bidding to stage the Olympic Games of 2020.

Baku Today

The pace of change is breathtaking.

TEXT: BEN ILLIS

Ben Illis is a travel writer and photographer who has spent much of the past three years travelling in Azerbaijan.

Over the first decade of the 21st century, the international face of Baku – and through Baku, the international face of Azerbaijan – has changed beyond belief. Many capital cities have come to be defined both by growth and development and, by the speed at which this occurs. In the case of Baku, perhaps more than any other capital in the world, this fluidity and focus on the future and the futuristic has come to be more than just a casual descriptor, but, rather, a definition of the city today.

'In Baku, big is good, bigger is better, but biggest is definitely best.'

ANOTHER GOLDEN ERA

Of course, rapid change is nothing new to Baku. In the latter half of the 19th century, the first oil boom resulted in Baku's population increasing almost 15-fold over five decades, as a desert town grew to become one of the world's major players in the new oil industry – as well as being one of the world centres of wealth and wealth production.

The energy boom – oil and gas – of the late 20th and early 21st century may not have resulted in such a dramatic increase in population, but in terms of how it has affected the face of the city, the change has been no less dramatic. With a current estimated population of just over two million, almost a quarter of the population of Azerbaijan, Baku is the undisputed hub of the nation in every arena – government, culture, media, business, industry and much more besides. The boom that the city is currently experiencing has left its mark on all of these and has changed the city's infrastructure at every level.

RECONSTRUCTING THE CITY

In 2003, work began on reconstructing much of the city's Downtown area at vast expense. From the stretch of Nizami known in Soviet times as Torgova, to Fountains Square and the Bulvar, great areas of the city have been systematically boarded off, sand-blasted, torn down, replaced, shined, rubbed and polished, and revealed to be component parts of a modern city that has embraced its future with arms wide open and a firm grip. Steel and glass jostle with sandstone and marble, complemented by sculptures and public art, and a real focus on usable public space.

IN CONTEXT

TV Tower.

Eternal Flame.

The city's skyline has also been altered dramatically, the iconic thrust of the **TV Tower**, opened in 1996, and at 310 metres (1,017 feet) Azerbaijan's tallest structure, has been joined by the equally dramatic, icon in the making of **Flame Towers**. Three gently undulating, tapering skyscrapers rise to over 200 metres (655 feet), covering a ground area of some 28,000 square metres. The towers are set around communal space, featuring parks and retail centres, and have been designed to emulate flickering tongues of flame, in homage to Azerbaijan's fire-worshipping history. One of the towers is to be home to the new Fairmont Hotel, one of the six major international hotel brands opening large properties in Baku in 2011 and 2012, creating some 1,600 new luxury guest rooms. For more on these developments, *see p90* **The Fab Five**.

The towering Soviet behemoths of the Absheron and Azerbaijan hotels, which defined the Bulvar area for decades, are gone, replaced by a Hilton and a Marriott, which both opened in 2011. Dubai-based Jumeirah have joined the game, with their super-deluxe offering lying outside the city on the beach at Mardakan. The Four Seasons has constructed an elaborate palace on the edge of the Old City and throws open its doors in early 2012, while Kempinski plies its trade from up on the hilltop near the Flame Tower complex. Not to be left behind, work is also well under way in the Hyatt district on the Park Plaza complex – yet another ambitious urban regeneration design, which will combine three skyscrapers and yet more well-designed public space. But the ambitious construction does not end here. Other projects, such as the Crescent Tower, Full Moon Rising, Sky Park and SOCAR Tower, are in various stages of planning and development, lending their own brand of the futuristic to a city whose buildings already have a touch of science fiction about them.

2012 AND BEYOND

The Bulvar extension is one of the most pivotal projects in Baku's ongoing process of renovation and rejuvenation. It already stretches beyond the Old City from its other extremity near Government House, tucked in next to the old commercial port – itself being moved to a new location around 30 kilometres south of the city, leaving its husk free for further metamorphosis into the sparkling new Port Baku complex. By the time Baku plays host to the Eurovision Song Contest in 2012 (*see below* **Making Your Mind Up**), the Bulvar is expected to reach all the way beyond the Old City to National Flag Square, home to the world's tallest flagpole, making it the world's longest waterfront promenade. In Baku, big is good, bigger is better, but biggest is definitely best.

Along the Bulvar, other new buildings have made their mark. The **Park Bulvar** mall and entertainment complex (*see p127*) is a great pull for both shoppers and leisure seekers; while the wedge of the contemporary Bulvar Business Centre features conferencing facilities with a sought-after waterfront location. Further on, the space-age **International Mugham Centre** (*see p148*) capitalises on the status of *mugham* as a rediscovered and revitalised form of traditional Azeri music.

Making Your Mind Up

And soon you will find there comes a time… for hosting Eurovision.

For all the grandiose projects such as museum buildings in the shape of carpets and towers in the form of roaring flames, there's one event that will do more to raise the Baku's international profile than anything else: having won the Eurovision Song Contest in 2011, Baku will host the contest in 2012.

Cheesy, sanitised, politicised, rigged – you name it, the Eurovision Song Contest gets accused of it. But despite the slurs, an estimated 175 million TV viewers tune in every year, bringing an international media circus to the event.

When Baku-born Ell & Nikki (in fact Enfield, London, housewife Nigar Jamal and her co-singer Eldar Gasimov) danced in triumph around the Düsseldorf stage after winning the 2011 event, it signalled the start of a new era and a new mindset for Azerbaijan. Waving a Turkish flag in thanks for the 12 votes allocated from Istanbul, the pop duo of newly found 'Running Scared' fame were not only celebrating an unlikely victory – Azerbaijan having only first participated in this 50-year old kitsch-fest as recently as 2008 – but beckoning Europe to come out to the edge of the Caspian Sea on 26 May 2012.

In the meantime, not only would a suitable events venue have to be provided but, in an example provided by Ukraine, which found itself a similar position in 2005, draconian visa processes would have be radically reconsidered. The prize: a successful Eurovision 2012, a positive global image for Azerbaijan and an international realisation that Baku's bid to host the 2020 Olympic Games is a realistic and viable one.

So far, so good. Austro-German company ALPINE Bau, responsible for Bayern Munich's Allianz Arena and several other football stadia used for Euro 2008 in Austria and Euro 2012 in Poland, are on schedule with the building of the **Baku Crystal Hall**. Set on Flagpole Square, named after the world's tallest flagpole, unveiled in 2010, this spanking new arena has a capacity of 23,000 and a state-of-the-art media centre capable of accommodating 1,500 journalists and broadcast crews. As for Azerbaijan's visa regulations, this matter was undergoing serious consideration as the scaffolding was being put up.

The conduit for this radical turnaround, Ell & Nikki, were last-minute entries to the 2011 contest. Each a vocalist in their own right, both took part in singing contests as children before attending university. Nigar Jamal then met her future husband, Englishman Luke, and moved to north London to raise a family. Eldar Gasimov continued to study music.

The Mugham Centre is one of the pet projects of First Lady Mehriban Aliyeva, who has proved herself a force to be reckoned with in Azerbaijan's recognition of its unique cultural landscape. In addition to the Mugham Centre, the **Museum of Contemporary Art** (*see p81*) was endowed by Mrs Aliyeva and houses work by more than 800 of Azerbaijan's most significant artists of the past century, in a bright, impressive, two-storey complex.

Azeri art is also well supported by the Art Ex East Foundation, established to bring both Azeri and international contemporary artists to the attention of both Bakuvians and visitors to the city. Art Ex East maintains an exciting and vibrant gallery in the Old City, **Kiçik Qalart** (Kiçik Gala 58), which hosts exhibitions from up-and-coming artists from Azerbaijan and other countries of the former Soviet Union, as well as shows that demonstrate a particular relevance to the Azeri people.

Eli & Nikki.

Each entered the contest to represent Azerbaijan at Eurovision 2011 separately, and were joint winners. It was decided that these two winners should become a duo, and so Eldar & Nigar became the catchier Ell & Nikki. The song was provided by Iain Farquharson and Swedish duo Stefan Örn and Sandra Bjurman, aka Sandra di Amante, who were also responsible for Azerbaijan's entry in 2010, 'Drip Drop'.

'We got a call the day before the final saying that it would be great if you could come over to Düsseldorf,' said Sandra. 'There was already a real buzz about the Azerbaijan entry.' On the night of the victory, crowds in Baku took to the streets to dance about in the rain. Sandra and Stefan caught up with the duo at four in the morning at the after-party in Düsseldorf but couldn't go with them on the special flight laid on to whisk them to the waiting crowds at Baku airport.

'We'll definitely be there in 2012,' said Sandra. 'We've heard so much about Baku.' Also there will be Ell & Nikki themselves, after a year of personal appearances across Germany, Russia and Turkey, where they enjoy cult status. Ambassadors for Azerbaijan, the pair might not fully appreciate the enormity of the part they could be playing in raising the profile of their country from that of an ex-Soviet backwater to a modern European nation.

The genuinely worthwhile collection of the **State Carpet Museum** (*see p76*) is due to move to its new home, a revolutionary seafront building shaped in the form of a rolled-up rug, in 2012. By then, a new museum of Azeri metalwork and handicraft will be open at the **Gala Historical Reserve** (*see p154*), just outside Baku. Meanwhile, the enormous and curvaceous **Heydar Aliyev Cultural Centre** (*see p174*) is growing at a rate of knots, courtesy of an ambitious design by Zaha Hadid's team of international architects. This centre comprises a new state library, a conference centre and museum, as well as a network of other facilities and public space.

Azerbaijan's flourishing arts scene is well-represented also in its festivals. The more significant annual ones generally take place in the autumn and include the Rostropovich Classical Music Festival; the Start International Festival of Student Film; the International Jazz Festival and the Hajibayli Music Festival. The Puppet and Mugham Festivals are both currently staged every two years.

Sport has not been overlooked, either, and an extensive programme of stadium construction has been planned, ahead of Azerbaijan's bid to host the 2020 Olympic Games. Baku is one of six cities currently in the frame.

Meanwhile, Downtown is the hub of the city's nightlife, which, a decade or so ago, was mainly restricted to billiard bars lit by a single strip light, attracting a rather seamy clientele composed mainly of rig workers and their pursuant ladies of the night. These days, designers and architects from the world's most glamorous cities compete for contracts to build and design truly world-class bars, nightclubs and restaurants, whose chefs, themselves drawn from the crème de la crème of international cuisine, craft menus and signature dishes that would more than hold their own in London, Tokyo or New York.

OUTSIDE THE CITY

The extensive renovation of Azerbaijan is not restricted to Baku. Roads have been reconstructed and are being improved across the country, with the highways to the Iranian border to the south, the Georgian border to the north-west and the Russian border to the north forming the arteries around which a web of smaller re-constructed thoroughfares are spidering their way. Azerbaijan's cultural gems in the provinces are also being extensively renovated and refreshed, with the **Khan's Palace** (*see p164*) in Sheki, the **Historical Reserve at Gobustan** (*see p156*), the **Historical Museum of Ordubad** (*see p184*) in Nakhchivan and the all new open air Visitors' Centre of the **Gala Historical Reserve** (*see p154*) leading the way in presenting the historical and cultural highlights of the regions.

So, what's next? Well, the design and implementation of ambitious building projects reaches its zenith with the ongoing construction of the **Shah Dag** ski area (*see p192* **Taking to the Slopes**) near Gusar, in the north of the country.

IMPROVING THE INFRASTRUCTURE

Back in Baku, more skyscrapers, hotels and restaurants are set to join those already in existence to serve the many foreign tourists the authorities are hoping to attract in years to come. Transport links are improving apace, with a planned extension to the city's metro rumoured to include a complete overhaul of the current system – and, one would hope, much-needed clear signage. Other mooted plans include a carbon-neutral floating city in the harbour; the largest bridge in the world, to span Baku Bay, and a whole host of other grand schemes.

Eurovision 2012 will be without doubt the largest single tourist-oriented challenge Azerbaijan will have had so far – and one that the International Olympic Committee will be watching with great interest to see how the city handles itself as it considers Baku's 2020 Olympic bid. Thereafter, the sky's the limit in this vibrant, eclectic and indefinable city.

Food & Drink

From dolma to doghramach, Azerbaijan offers a feast for the senses

TEXT: BEN JLLLIS

As a glance at a map would suggest, Azeri cuisine has both Turkish and Persian influences. A typical Azeri meal consists of bread, greens, fresh cheese and/or butter, meze, soup, and something from the grill – most likely a permutation of mutton – or a *plov* (pilaf). Alongside the salt and pepper in a table-top cruet set, the crimson grains are *sumakh*, a citrus-flavoured condiment made from the dried and crushed petals of the *sumakh* plant, which is often seen growing wild by the roadside in the Talysh region and cultivated in many a European garden too. *Sumakh* is commonly used as a garnish and sprinkled over almost any dish, which may also be studded with pomegranate seeds, sprinkled with chopped parsley or finely sliced onion and decorated with little cones of rolled *lavash* bread. Azeri fruit and nuts are delicious, with pomegranates, persimmons, watermelons, honeydew melons, apples, lemons, cherries, strawberries, grapes, apricots, almonds, walnuts, hazelnuts and pistachios grown across the country and served seasonally.

BREAD

Bread in Azerbaijan is likely to be one of three main types: *chörek* is the generic name for brick-shaped loaves and is the least tasty variant; *tandir* is named after the eponymous wood-fired oven in which it is baked and is moist, chewy and flavoursome, very like an Indian naan; *lavash* is a wafer-thin flatbread, rather like a wheatflour Mexican tortilla and very good for making sandwich wraps.

GREENS, SALADS AND MEZE

Salad, or *salatlar*, usually refers to the German or Russian style of salad – cubes of potato in mayonnaise, enlivened with diced egg, vegetables or cheese. Salads in the leafy sense only really exist in westernised eateries in Baku, while greens – *göy* (which confusingly means 'blue') – are served whole, stacked on a plate rather than cut and tossed together. It has been suggested that this practice, common across the Middle East, dates from a time when the wealth and generosity of a host could be measured by the variety and abundance of his greens. Thus a rich man could afford the irrigation necessary to grow a profusion of greens and herbs, and would demonstrate his standing by offering mounds of greenery to his guests. Common greens served include parsley, coriander, dill, tarragon, spring onions, garlic leaves (also rolled and inserted into the nostril to stem nosebleeds) and purple basil. In the north-west, a peppery leaf, *kir salat*, is often offered and is rather like a fiery kind of wild rocket. Sliced cucumbers, tomatoes and radishes may be served on the same plate or separately. Wild herbs, stems and vegetables, such as fennel and cow parsley, are often salted to preserve them and taste delicious with fresh cheese.

'In rural eateries, ordering chicken will likely mean someone butchering, plucking, drawing and prepping one of the birds clucking around in the garden.'

Meze is not an Azeri term, but is the easiest way to describe the various pastes and dips often served, as across the eastern Mediterranean, Levant and Middle East, with the bread and greens at the start of a meal. *Adzika* is a spicy tomato paste, brought to life with diced greens, lots of raw garlic and herbs, and delicious scooped up with *tandir* bread. *Haydari* is a Turkish dish and rather like the Greek tzatziki, made from strained yoghurt, or *gatig*, with fresh herbs – most often dill. *Mangal salat* is a delicious mix of finely chopped grilled vegetables, blended with herbs, olive oil and lemon juice.

SOUPS

Thick, gloopy *dovgha* and its thinner equivalent *doghramach* (often served cold) are two soups made of thinned yoghurt, which in the case of *dovgha* is then thickened up again over a slow flame. Both are served with diced cucumber and onions, and rice is sometimes stirred in. *Dushbara* is a thin mutton broth containing tiny ravioli-like twists of pasta filled with spiced meat.

MAINS AND HOT DISHES

The undisputed champion of the Azeri kitchen is more often than not located outside it – the *mangal,* or grill. Options are often restricted to grilled mutton and precious little else, served as a minced meat *lule* kebab or in whole chunks as a *tike* kebab. Collectively, these grilled goodies are known as *kebablar* and are presented on a platter topped with chopped raw onion and herbs, wedges of lemon and dusted in *sumakh*. Other options might include chicken or fish, which is usually one of the five sub-species of sturgeon. If you're eating sturgeon – or, indeed, most Azeri fish – be sure not to skimp on *narsharab*, a wonderfully tart pomegranate sauce routinely served as an accompaniment. Farmed trout is also increasingly widespread and is usually served fried or grilled. Quail is also common. A meal from the *mangal* usually comes accompanied by grilled potatoes, tomatoes, aubergines and sometimes even apples.

Sadj is served served sizzling at your table in a cast-iron skillet atop a cast-iron stand. Sadly, the skillet can all too often be swimming in oil, but when it's done right it really is delicious. *Sadj* may contain any of the same meats or fish listed above, coupled with potatoes, aubergine and tomato. A mixed *sadj* will probably contain chicken and mutton, though rarely mixes meat with fish.

Lavangi is a traditional chicken dish from the Talysh region, now also found in Baku. It is traditionally a whole bird stuffed with a paste of walnuts, although some smarter restaurants in Baku take the flavours of *lavangi* but serve them in delicious bite-sized rolls, sometimes even replacing the chicken with strips of sturgeon. *Tabaka*, meanwhile, is a style of cooking chicken that is a bit like spatchcocking, only the meat is pounded flat. Note that in rural eateries, ordering chicken will likely mean someone butchering, plucking, drawing and prepping one of the birds clucking around in the garden.

Plov is the Russian name for pilaf and is the most common term for what is actually known in Azeri as *ash*. There is a bewildering array of more than 40 traditional *plov*

IN CONTEXT

dishes in Azerbaijan, but most are, in essence, buttered basmati rice, sometimes flavoured with saffron or herbs and topped with either dried berries or nuts. *Plov* is usually served with a stew of some description on the side – particular favourites include *govurma*, which is mutton cooked with onions and sometimes fruit. *Govurma* is sometimes transcribed as korma, but has nothing to do with the creamy north Indian curry. *Fisinjan* is mutton with a rich sauce of ground walnuts and pomegranate, and *sabzi govurma* is mutton cooked in greens.

A delicious winter speciality that should be snapped up when available is *syudlyu plov* – smoked or salted fish served with buttered rice cooked with roasted sweet pumpkin. Also popular in winter are the many regional versions of the fatty meat and spud stew known as *bozbash*. *Piti* is made from the fatty tail of the sheep, with chickpeas and tomatoes, and is especially well liked, although likely too fatty for most western palates.

Dolma are, like their Greek or Turkish equivalents, vegetables or leaves stuffed with mutton, lightened on occasion with rice. Unlike in Greece, however, *dolma* are as likely to be stuffed aubergines, tomatoes or green peppers as vine leaves and are served hot. *Gurza* are little pasta twists, rather like the contents of *dushbara*, and are usually served either in broth or deep-fried. They are filled with mutton and often served in Baku restaurants as a starter.

SNACKS

Tum are toasted pumpkin seeds, served as street food in newspaper cones. *Nokhud*, or chickpeas, are often served boiled and salted as an accompaniment to beer; squeeze them gently to pop them out of their seed casings. *Sasharkhli pendir*, literally 'hairy cheese', is not as unappetising as it sounds. A stringy variety of cheese, it is served with a squeeze of lemon, again as an accompaniment to beer. *Qutab* are folded pancakes of wheatflour, traditionally filled with finely chopped greens or minced mutton, with a dollop of sour cream and a dusting of *sumakh*. Although traditionally served as street food, they are often also served as a starter in restaurants. *Kuku* are small, thick omelettes, stuffed with finely chopped herbs and often served cold.

SWEETS

A platter of prepared fruit is the most common way to finish an Azeri meal. On occasion a range of sherbets may also be served, which are in essence chilled cordials, made the old-fashioned way from steeping some fruit or spices in hot water for several hours, then filtering the result and sweetening with pounds of sugar. *Halva* is generally the Sheki version of the famous sweetmeat and is much like Greek or Turkish baklava. Elsewhere in the country, *halva* may refer to the more familiar baked paste of nut flours and honey common across the Islamic world.

BREAKFAST

A traditional Azeri breakfast consists of bread served with butter, cheese, cream and honey. Tea is the breakfast drink of choice – coffee-drinking visitors planning to spend time in the provinces should bring their own and bear in mind that milk is likely to be off the menu. Eggs are also increasingly popular – 'omelette' is pretty universally understood. Oddly, for a nation with such astonishingly good fruit, fresh juice is uncommon at the breakfast table.

DRINKS

An oft-quoted saying has it that 'Allah forbade us to drink wine, so we drink vodka', and it is certainly true that alcohol is both freely available and commonly drunk by Azeris, especially in Baku. The resurgence of Azeri viticulture continues apace with some wines, especially the dry reds of Ganja and Ismayilli, offering remarkably good quality and value. Semi-dry and sweet reds are a tad on the syrupy side for the vast majority of western palates, though, while the whites are not generally recommended. For more information on visiting a winery and finding out about the Azeri wine trade, see p175 **Château Monolit**, Vodka, or *arag*, is widely available at a bewildering range of prices. The more expensive brands are surprisingly smooth and well worth shelling out for, but steer well clear of the cheaper stuff. Delicious Tutovka, or mulberry vodka, is syrupy and more of a liqueur. Local beer Xirdalan and Turkish import Efes are found pretty much everywhere, along with a range of other regional brews and imported Russian and other former CIS brands of varying quality. Nakhchivan brand beer is also recommended, but rarely on sale outside the exclave (*see pp179-186*). Delicious fresh pomegranate, persimmon and quince juices are commonly made in homes across the country during autumn and winter, but they are rarely commercially available.

OTHER CUISINES

Baku has an impressive array of restaurants serving various international cuisines, with Turkish, Japanese, Chinese, Asian fusion, Persian, Tex-Mex, Italian and German proving especially popular. Georgian restaurants also feature strongly on the culinary map and are, along with Turkish ones, the only international cuisine likely to feature outside Baku. Georgian hospitality – and wine – has a justly excellent reputation, and Georgian restaurants are popular venues for celebratory dining.

Marketing a Monster

With stocks dwindling, caviar is becoming rarer and more expensive.

Caviar, the silvery-grey roe of the sturgeon fish, is one of the world's most popular and expensive delicacies. But the sturgeon itself is anything but delicate – with bony plates along its back, this bizarre, Stone Age throwback of a creature was understandably first taken for a sea monster when presented to the ancient Azeris.

There are five sub-species of sturgeon native to the Caspian. Three of these sub-species are collectively known as osetr or osetrina, and are the cheapest and most widespread, producing the lion's share of caviar and, indeed, sturgeon meat. More highly prized is the caviar of the sevruga and, especially, the beluga, which has nothing to do with the white whale by the same name. Beluga can live as long as humans and don't reach fertility until their third decade. The largest specimen ever caught was nine metres long.

With many sturgeon being fished before they are sexually mature, stocks have dwindled. There are now strict quota controls and much attention is being put into farming fry to re-stock the Caspian. In the old days of the USSR, the Caspian fishing quota was split 50/50 with Iran. Since the fall of the Soviet Union, the four Caspian coastal states of the former USSR – Azerbaijan, Kazakhstan, Turkmenistan and, of course, Russia – have each been pushing for a 20 per cent share of the haul, a move which, unsurprisingly, Iran has strenuously resisted. Caviar exports from Azerbaijan are strictly controlled, with an allowance of one 125g jar per person. Note that the deals of old that could be found in the bazaars of Baku are a thing of the past and the only secure way to buy good caviar nowadays is through a trusted source, such as the management of **Paul's** restaurant (*see p104*) in Baku. As of 2011, 125g goes for about $110. This is more than ten times the price of a decade ago, but still around a quarter of the price in a European duty-free shop.

IN CONTEXT

Wildlife

Fabulous birds of prey and rare mountain mammals.

TEXT: BEN ILLIS, JANE MOTT

One particular aspect of Azerbaijan that has the potential to attract significant numbers of western tourists is wildlife. If you're only in Baku for a few days, it's worth heading out of town to visit the Shirvan National Park (*see p194*) and its stunning array of birdlife. Other treasures of the natural world here include the jeyran gazelle and the East Caucasian tur.

With 363 recorded species, Azerbaijan is high on the list of regions soon to be catalogued by the Ornithological Society of the Middle East. *Birdwatching in Azerbaijan* (£19.99, order online at www.nhbs.com), by Schmidt, Gauger and Agayeva, provides a thorough and readable guide to local birdlife, along with practical information for tourists. Alternatively, most standard European guides to birds will suffice for the identification of most species. More information on Azeri birdlife can be found on the website of the Azerbaijan Ornithological Society (www.aos.az).

Birdlife

Common all over the country are golden orioles, rosy starlings, hoopoes, two types of brilliantly coloured bee-eater, and the equally brilliant heavier-set European roller. Brown and grey shrikes often join them on telephone wires, along with marsh harriers and two species of kestrel. European storks are also widespread, their clumsy, messy nests perched precariously atop telegraph poles or purpose-built nesting poles at many provincial restaurants, which also provide homes for myriad smaller birds.

An hour's drive south of Baku, the most popular day trip is to the petroglyphs and mud volcanoes of **Gobustan** (*see p156*). Both venues are significantly enlivened by a little birdwatching on the side. Around the petroglyphs there are rock nuthatches flitting about alongside pied wheatears, while in the undergrowth blackcaps, chiff-chaffs and Menetries's warblers are not uncommon. These small birds attract both merlin and hobbies, and catching sight of these small falcons chasing their prey is a thrilling spectacle. Looking upwards, there may be both ravens and choughs on the cliff line, and perhaps an Egyptian vulture or two circling above. Those interested in wildflowers might look for the endangered variable iris tucked snugly beneath the wormwood scrub; the latter scents the air with a wonderful fragrance as it is trampled underfoot.

Leaving the main road in search of the mud volcanoes, look for marsh harriers, the most common raptor of the region, hunting low over the reed beds and cultivated areas. Lesser kestrels, more abundant and less solitary than the common kestrel, sit patiently on the power lines, their eyes focused on the ground below and the possibility of a kill. In the less-stagnant, less-polluted pools, the striking black-winged stilt high-steps through the water on bright red legs, while graceful pratincoles swoop in small flocks above.

The **Shirvan National Park** (*see p194*) offers more opportunities to see species that are not often encountered in Britain. The park is not only renowned for its jeyran gazelles (*see p42*), but also for flamingos and the black francolin, a rare, shy member of the partridge family. In addition, there are many bee-eaters and rollers, three species of lark, cuckoos, hoopoes, pale Isabelline wheatears, stone and common curlews, whimbrels and little owls. In the lagoons and reed beds nearer the Caspian sit pygmy cormorants sunning their wings, ferruginous ducks, red-crested pochards, little grebes, egrets, purple and grey herons, Kentish plovers, sand plovers and sand martins. Look out too for bitterns, though they are more commonly heard than seen, with their deep booming calls. The privileged may even spot sacred and glossy ibises, Eurasian spoonbills and common pelicans.

Winter sees flocks of tens of thousands of migrants at **Flamingo Lake**, the park's large reservoir, and up to a thousand eagles and other large raptors coming in for the kill. Large birds of prey are also worth searching out as they soar over higher ground all across the country. Star sightings may include bearded, Egyptian, griffon and black vultures; and Bonelli's, booted, steppe, imperial, white-tailed and golden eagles. Up in the mountains you may also be lucky enough to see the rare Caucasian snowcock, while the Zagatala region is the best place to spot the vulnerable Caucasian black grouse.

The endemic Guldenstadt's redstart and its smaller cousin, the common redstart, are a bright and widespread addition to many a day's birding in the north-west of the country, while the Caucasian variant of the yellow wagtail – the black-headed yellow wagtail – is often encountered in the south, especially in **Nakhchivan** (*see pp179-186*). Also in Nakhchivan, chukar partridges, common quails and Caucasian pheasants may put in an appearance among the clumps of headily scented wild thyme, camomile and little orchids on the slopes of **Alinja citadel** (*see p182*), preyed upon in turn by the magnificent booted eagles that make their home on top of the dramatically craggy peak.

Mammals

In addition to hundreds of smaller mammals, many of which will be familiar to European wildlife watchers, Azerbaijan is home to several uncommon species of both prey animals and predators. Of the former, the most renowned is undoubtedly the jeyran (*see below*), or goitered gazelle, which can easily be seen in large numbers in **Shirvan National Park**. Also of note are the wild sheep, or *mouflon*, now restricted to remote areas of **Nakhchivan**; and the East Caucasian tur, a mountain goat antelope restricted to the very high mountains of the greater Caucasus. Both of these creatures are extremely shy and only exist in small numbers, so are unlikely to be encountered. Also present are chamois, as well as both red and roe deer.

On the predatory front, the Caucasian leopard maintains a precarious existence, largely in the **Talysh mountains** (*see p194*), although it has also been recorded in the mountains above Ilisu in the **Gakh** region (*see p167*). The Shirvan and **Hirkan National Park** (*see p199*) both also have populations of the elusive jungle cat, grey wolf and golden jackal, although all are more likely to be heard than seen. In Shirvan, the fortunate might just catch the odd flash of a reflective retina in torchlight or car headlights at dusk. Grey wolves, European lynx and brown bear are still relatively widespread throughout the dense forests of the Caucasus, although in dwindling numbers and strictly protected. Their main habitat lies in the **Ilisu State Reserve**, although their scarcity means the likelihood of a sighting is slim.

The Caspian seal is one of the world's smallest and can usually only be seen in spring and summer in quieter parts of the **Absheron peninsula** (*see pp153-159*), although they have also been recorded in busier parts of the region – and even in Baku bay on occasion.

JEYRAN

For Azerbaijan, the local recovery of the jeyran, variously known also as the goitered, black or Persian gazelle, is an ecological success story. Petroglyphs dating back to the fourth millennium BC depict hunts for the jeyran, known to have been a principal prey for the primitive men of the region.

Today, the jeyran is the most widespread of any gazelle in the world but is still listed by the World Wildlife Foundation as a vulnerable species, with a world population numbering somewhere between 40,000 and 120,000. Azerbaijan is home to the only viable wild population left in the Caucasus. In the 1920s, an estimated 40,000 jeyran lived in huge flocks across the whole Transcaucasian region. By the 1960s and '70s, extensive hunting across the region led to them becoming extinct in Georgia and Armenia, with only a handful left in Turkey and Iran. In 1961, when Shirvan National Park was established to protect them, the Azeri population was already cut off from other populations of the species in central Asia and thought to number only around 200. The establishment of reserves such as Shirvan National Park allowed the population to stabilise and then increase dramatically. In Shirvan alone, there are now an estimated 4,000 jeyran, which can be easily viewed in their small family groups in summer, and in herds of up to several hundred in winter.

EAST CAUCASIAN TUR

The Caucasian tur is a dramatically muscular species of mountain goat antelope with curved horns that can measure up to almost two metres (six feet) from tip to tip. There are two sub-species of Caucasian tur, East and West, the former native to Azerbaijan. Unfortunately, the tur's dramatic horns have made it a target for trophy hunters, despite it being protected and listed as near threatened by the WWF. Some traditional subsistence hunters in remote villages still hunt tur for food and hides, although this practice is being discouraged by a combination of legal action and education.

'There are thought to be only about 1,000 Caucasian leopards left in the wild across the world, with only around a dozen in Azerbaïjan.'

CAUCASIAN LEOPARD

The Caucasian leopard is a particularly large sub-species of leopard, first described in 1914 by the Russian explorer and naturalist Konstantin Satunin. Around a decade later, the British naturalist Reginald Innes Pocock described the Persian leopard, now thought to be a variant of the same sub-species. The Caucasian leopard has a range stretching from eastern Turkey through to western Afghanistan, with the greatest density now concentrated to the west of that span. Food shortages and an increase in the amount of land brought under cultivation during the Soviet era led to increased competition between leopard and man, with leopards – and, indeed, wolves and bears – hunted as a perceived threat to livestock. This led to a dramatic decline in numbers. There are thought to be only about 1,000 left in the wild across the world, with only around a dozen in Azerbaijan, most of which live in the Talysh mountains.

The species was thought to be locally extinct until one was caught on camera in **Hirkan National Park** in 2007. An ambitious plan by the WWF is now under way to protect the northern population and link it up again to the gene pool of the southern population, which is much larger (around 500 individuals) and located in Iran. Only time will tell if these efforts have come soon enough.

IN CONTEXT

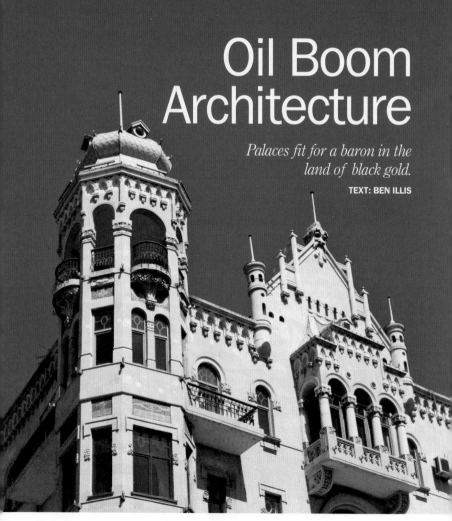

Oil Boom Architecture

Palaces fit for a baron in the land of black gold.

TEXT: BEN ILLIS

In among the gleaming, contemporary skyscrapers built on the riches of the energy trade over the last ten years, striking architectural evidence survives of the previous oil boom of a century ago. Now mainly restored, the mansions built by the oil barons of the pre-Soviet era are one of the capital's great tourist attractions. The discovery of oil in the mid 19th century transformed Baku, which at the time was a sleepy little desert town with a port and a population of around 5,000. Afterwards, Baku – and Azerbaijan – were never the same. In the last quarter of the 19th century, the denationalisation of the oil industry (in 1872) and increased technology in both the drilling and extraction industries led to a massive rise in regional output.

'Within a relatively short time, a ring of grand palaces surrounded the centre and even sprang up within the walls of the Old City.'

KLONDIKE ON THE CASPIAN

As with the Klondike gold rush, happening around the same time, the oil boom in Baku attracted a massive influx of chancers, desperately hoping to make a fast buck. Nobel, Rothschild and local heroes such as Taghiyev, Hadjinski and Mukhtarov all made good and drafted in teams of architects, engineers and builders to help them show off their wealth. Between about 1880 and the outbreak of World War I, these men would give Baku the largest facelift the city had ever experienced – and would ever experience until, arguably, the second oil boom of the post-Soviet era. The architects they employed were fresh from building the rich palaces and grand avenues of Europe. They came from Paris and Budapest, Rome and Moscow, to put Baku firmly on the map with elaborate confections, in which the Italian Renaissance rubbed shoulders with German rococo.

Baku barely knew what had hit it. Contemporary paintings from the early 1870s show the walled city of Baku surrounded by bare earth, studded with derricks and spurting oil wells. Within a relatively short time, a ring of grand palaces surrounded the centre and even sprang up within the walls of the Old City. Despite being chopped up into apartments and thoroughly neglected throughout the Soviet era, these mansions remain to this day and, with their mish-mash of architectural styles and influences, have given Baku much of its character. The following five buildings give arguably the best overview of oil-boom architecture (with some of the most interesting back stories), and are accessible in a half-hour stroll around the outside of the old city wall, heading clockwise from the Maiden's Tower (*see p59*).

HAJINSKI MANSION

The Hajinski Mansion was built for oil baron Isabey Hajinski in 1912 and is among the most ornate of Baku's mansions, as well as being one of the first to be wholly renovated. Its hanging balconies and architectural flourishes demonstrate its hybrid pedigree, with Islamic touches on a European framework that delights some, while sending architectural purists into apoplexy. Its most famous guest was General de Gaulle, who stayed here en route to a meeting with Stalin in Moscow in 1944. De Gaulle did not want to cross enemy air space and so a secret route via Iran was devised, with a stopover in Baku to take in the opera. There is a bas relief of him at ground-floor level on the outside of the mansion, which overlooks the boulevard right next to the Maiden's Tower. Today, the ground-floor space is occupied by a Tom Ford boutique. The shop is the only public access to the mansion.

PHILHARMONIC HALL

Around the corner from the Hajinski Mansion, at the top of Niyazi, and now overshadowed by the large, impenetrable-looking block of the Presidential Offices, the Philharmonic Hall (*see p149*) was initially built in 1910 as a casino. The original design of the building was reputedly sketched on the back of a napkin with a cigar stub in a fit of inspiration by its architect, Mikhailov, its design a homage to the casino at Monte Carlo. Its gilt roof and twin yellow towers give it an unmistakable silhouette, its dome slightly Islamicised, exactly as per the architect's original intent. In 1937, it was extensively renovated and named after the great Azeri composer, Muslim Magomayev.

IN CONTEXT

MUKHTAROV PALACE

A block back from Istiglaliyyat, on Mukhtarov, the 1912 Mukhtarov Palace (*see p53*) is perhaps Baku's most ornate oil-boom mansion. Currently undergoing extensive renovation, this pile has as its crowning glory a statue of a very British-looking medieval knight, standing proudly atop a plinth. The knight was added by master builder Gasimov, the man behind the mansion, who tragically slipped and fell to his death as he put it in place. The tragedy didn't end there, as his widow, unable to contemplate a life without her love, ended her own life too, and was buried with her husband. The wedding-cake architectural style and frothy exuberance of the Mukhtarov Palace hint at its history as one of the most popular wedding palaces of the 20th century. Indeed, to many a Bakuvian, it is known simply as the 'Wedding Palace'. But this moniker is not just due to the romantic legacy of the Gasimovs, but also to that of its original owner, Murtuza Mukhtarov.

Mukhtarov was born to a lowly family and, despite already being married, fell in love with Lisa, the daughter of an Ossetian aristocrat. Knowing his pedigree was not sufficient to gain the approval of Lisa's father, Mukhtarov set about impressing the man with his devout nature, building a series of mosques and, bit by bit, winning his favour. When at last they were united, Lisa and Mukhtarov embarked on a grand tour, where the new Mrs Mukhtarova fell in love with an Italian palace. Returning to Baku, Mukhtarov commissioned the city's most fashionable architect and master builder, Gasimov, to build the palace as a surprise Valentine's Day love token. When the Communists stormed the palace in 1920, Mukhtarov is said to have leapt to the building's defence, screaming at them to 'get off his damn carpet', before being shot for his troubles. Lisa escaped, but the romantic legacy of the building was sealed.

FANTASIA HAMMAM

When it was constructed back in 1887, the Fantasia Hammam (*see p136*), three blocks north of the main fountain in Fountains Square, was the first hammam in Baku to be built with private cabins for bathing, thus allowing men and women to bathe on the same day. Largely untouched since, it avoided the sometimes over-enthusiastic renovation that has dramatically cleaned up much of the rest of the city and destroyed a lot of its old world charm. The waters were, and still are, piped in from the Shollar springs in the Caucasus mountains, and the main tea salon features astonishingly ornate plasterwork mouldings on the ceiling and some original painted tiles dating from 1896.

AKHUNDOV OPERA & BALLET THEATRE

In 1909, the magnificently rich Mailov brothers were captivated by a performance by the great Russian soprano Nezhdanova, or so the story goes (some accounts have Nezhdanova replaced by an unnamed Argentine or Italian singer). The soprano declared she would never return to Baku unless one of its wealthy citizens proved philanthropic enough to build an opera house worthy of her talents. The Mailov brothers rather ambitiously vowed to do so within a year and Nezhdanova agreed to return to perform. Fellow oil baron Taghiyev, doubting such a rapid construction was possible, bet them they could not succeed within the time frame, offering to foot the entire construction bill should they come good. A year of overtime and double pay, and the Opera & Ballet Theatre, now named after Akhundov, the 'Caucasian Molière', stood proud. Taghiyev, good to his word, reached deep into his pocket and picked up the tab. How Nezhdanova's resulting performance went is sadly not recorded, but Baku had gained another piece of notable architecture and another story to boot. The building was gutted by fire in the 1960s, but has recently been restored to its former glory and stands opposite the ugly, modern-build Young Spectators' Theatre on Nizami.

IN CONTEXT

Sights

Philharmonia Concert Hall. *See p149.*

Introduction

Your key to the city.

For the casual visitor, Baku has obvious attractions. First, there's the **Old City** (*see p55-64*), the walled citadel that held most of what was Baku before the oil boom of the late 19th century, and which contains its two most historic sights: the **Maiden's Tower** (*see p59*) and the **Palace of the Shirvanshahs** (*see p62*). Like most of the Old City itself, the palace has been significantly renovated over the years. Secondly, there's the **waterfront** itself, transformed into a public park during the boom years and being (generally) tastefully modernised of late.

Of the city's other attractions, a number of the main museums are currently closed for renovation – the Azerbaijan State Museum of History, for example, while the Rustam Mustafayev National State Museum of Arts is partially closed. The focal **Museum Centre**, which contains the **Letif Kerimov State Museum of Carpets & Applied Arts** (*see p76*), will probably close in 2012, the Carpet Museum moving to a dramatic, purpose-built construction on the seafront. It is not clear what will happen to the other museums in the complex.

OTHER MUSEUMS

Baku also specialises in house museums, modest but personal institutions set in the former home of the subject matter. The best lies in the Old City, the **Museum of Vagif Mustafa-Zadeh** (*see p54*), former home of the musical genius who revolutionised the music scene here by fusing jazz with traditional mugham.

Mention must also be made of the **Museum of Contemporary Art** (*see p81*), which shows the best Azeri art, much of it avant-garde, produced in the last seven decades, in surroundings fitting of a cutting-edge institution in any modern-day metropolis.

A number of Baku's museums can provide an **English-speaking guide**. The charge varies, but is usually around AZN5. The quality of the guide can vary too, from those with a genuine passion for and rounded knowledge of their subject, and an excellent grasp of English – as in the case of the Museum of Contemporary Art (*see p81*) – to ones who give a textbook spiel by rote and seem reluctant to provide in-depth background. Either way, given the often poor documentation at many museums and sights, hiring a guide should be worth the money. Taking photographs can also entail an extra fee. Be aware that Monday is generally, but not exclusively, the day of closure for city attractions.

Only two metro stations serve the downtown area: Icheri Sheher at the western wall of the Old City, and Sahil a 15-minute walk east of Fountains Square. Most of the city centre is otherwise walkable.

THE BEST SIGHTS

Best historic landmark
Palace of the Shirvanshahs
(*see p62*).

Most moving sight
Martyrs' Alley (*see p66*).

Best modern attraction
Museum of Contemporary Art
(*see p82*).

Most charming house-museum
Museum of Vagif Mustafa-Zadeh
(*see p54*).

Most unusual memorial
Richard Sorge (*see p79*).

Baku by Area

Orient yourself.

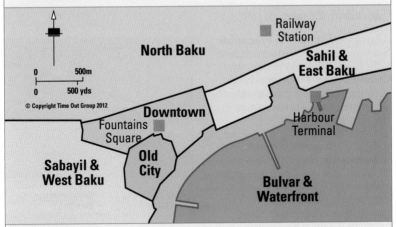

North Baku

Railway Station

Sahil & East Baku

Downtown

Fountains Square

Harbour Terminal

Old City

Sabayil & West Baku

Bulvar & Waterfront

0   500m
0   500 yds
© Copyright Time Out Group 2012

SIGHTS

DOWNTOWN

Baku's Downtown area is centred on the pedestrianised plaza of Fountains Square. The streets immediately to its east and south-east are packed with shops, restaurants, bars and theatres. Just north runs the city's main throughfare, Nizami Street. Oil-Boom mansions and the odd museum also feature.

OLD CITY

This self-contained medieval hub is a maze of narrow alleys, renovated caravanserais, ornately carved portals and restored mosques. Some hotels and restaurants take advantage of their roof terrace to provide panoramic views, particularly out to sea, as the south wall of the Old City was knocked down in the late 1800s. The area contains Baku's two essential sights: the Maiden's Tower and the Palace of the Shivanshahs.

SABAYIL & WEST BAKU

Overlooking the Old City from on high, this prominent area features key landmarks such as Martyrs' Alley, the National Cemetery and, as of 2012, the Flame Towers. Much of Sabayil allows for a splendid vista of sea and city and is best accessed, when it is up and running again, by funicular.

BULVAR & WATERFRONT

This relatively thin strip of landscaped greenery and fin-de-siècle façades currently runs from just west of the Old City to the harbour building at the edge of Black City in the east – but plans are afoot to extend it further. Bulvar is where the city has come to relax, en famille, since the oil barons collaborated with the city government to reclaim land from the sea and have it landscaped in the early 1900s. You'll still find old-style funfair rides, and authentically retro terrace cafés. Here also is the Museum Centre and, further west, the building its main attraction, the Carpet Museum, will move to.

NORTH BAKU

The area north of Nizami is a criss-cross of main streets lined with shops, official buildings and hotels. Stretching from Yasamal in the west to Narimanov and Ganjlik in the far north-east, it is centred on the extensive and significant district of Nasimi. Hubs include the Hyatt area, named after the hotel in question, Fizuli Square and the main railway station, where another mall is due to be built.

SAHIL & EAST BAKU

Baku at its busiest and most grid-locked, this relatively small area behind the Museum Centre and Government House is quickly coming into its own thanks to the arrival of five-star hotels. Here, too, stands the city's best modern-day attraction: the Museum of Contemporary Art.

Downtown

The hub of the modern city.

All roads in Baku lead to **Fountains
Square**. This newly renovated plaza
is the heart of the modern-day city.
Under wraps for a long period until
2011, the square now gleams with
new statuary and a contemporary
feel. To the south is a hub of Baku
bar life, shopping and general social
activity. To the north, **Nizami**, lined
with shops and one of the city's main
axes, runs east–west the whole length
of the city centre. Downtown is also the
location for city green space Molokan
Park and some interesting 'house
museums' set up in homes once
occupied by illustrious predecessors.

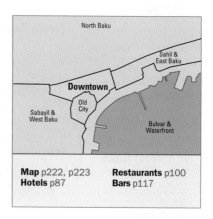

Map p222, p223	**Restaurants** p100
Hotels p87	**Bars** p117

Map p222, p223 Hotels p87 Restaurants p100 Bars p117

SIGHTS

FOUNTAINS SQUARE & AROUND

Not so much square as an oddly shaped
rectangle, Fountains Square is an expansive,
pedestrianised space, much of which is
modernised and lined with shops selling high-
street brands. However, in its south-eastern
corner, bordering the Old City and Azerbaijan
Prospekt, a sense of history and decorum is

INSIDE TRACK
NIZAMI AND SLOWHAND

Most rock fans may know that Eric
Clapton's classic song 'Layla' was inspired
by his unrequited love for Pattie Boyd, then
George Harrison's wife. What they probably
don't know is that the title itself came from
Leyli & Majnun (or Layla & Majnun), a
tragic love story by Azerbaijan's best-loved
literary figure, medieval poet Nizami
Ganjavi. In Nizami's version, Layla's father
has her married to someone else, leaving
her loving admirer Majnun in spiritual and
mental distress – *majnun* means 'mad' in
Arabic. While Clapton took his anthem from
the 12th century, poet Nizami in turn had
based his take on something that had
occurred 500 years before that.

granted by a wide parade of steps alongside
a delicately landscaped area of descending
fountains. On each side, little jets of water
create a burbling sound cherished in the Islamic
world, and benches allow courting couples
a remarkable feeling of peace and solitude,
considering this is the epicentre of a noisy,
gridlocked, booming metropolis.

The focus of this south-eastern part of the
square is a statue of poet **Nizami Ganjavi**
(1141-1209), known as the Azeri Shakespeare,
whose 'Leyli & Majnun' and 'Seven Beauties'
are considered as masterworks. 'Nizami' actually
means someone who writes, and was a *nom
de plume*. There are Nizami statues all over
Azerbaijan, including in his home town of Ganja.
Here, not only is he standing on a hexagonal
plinth featuring scenes from his works, he is
looking down upon centuries of Azeri writers
following in his footsteps, whose statues and
portraits surround the façade of the **Nizami
Ganjavi National Museum of Literature**.

The north side of the museum faces the
shining attractions of Fountains Square,
maintained by a veritable army of cleaners
from early every morning. A bright, fully
functional, traditional carousel provides a
colourful and pleasingly old-style backdrop
to diners on the terrace of the **Café City** (*see
p101*) and in the **Favvara** (*see p102*), beside a
faux-historic colonnade that lends the square
a film-set feel. Mock Easter Island statues,

Fountains Square.

SIGHTS

several fountains – one surrounded by large ball-bearings, another by little hippos with their mouths gaping open – and greenery the size of half a football pitch, meet the eye as local pedestrians criss-cross the square arm in arm or gabbling into their mobiles. As if to emphasise contemporary customs, one of a number of statues recently installed here and on the Caspian seaboard shows a trendy young girl in cut-off jeans talking into her phone.

She is talking, suitably enough, outside McDonald's, which sits below one of the square's better terrace options, the rooftop **Dalida** (*see p102*). From here, clearly visible is the **Armenian Church**, its windows bricked up but its lights on – it is remarkable enough that it is even standing, given the all-too-recent war between the two countries.

Nizami Ganjavi National Museum of Literature

Istiglaliyyat Street 55 (492 1864). All buses to Fountains Square. **Open** 11am-5pm Mon-Sat. **Admission** AZN10. **No credit cards.** **Map** p222 G3.

Thousands pass by this impressive building on the main square – surrounded by statues and colourful portraits of Azeri literary giants – every day without going in. Those curious enough to pay the hefty AZN10 admission can look forward to a chronological walk through the history of Azeri literature, from medieval poets to modern-day novelists. Poorly documented in English, its interest to the foreign visitor is quite limited, although some of the manuscripts are undoubtedly beautiful. Look out too for copies of *Molla Nasreddin*, the influential satirical publication from the early 20th century. Coins, carpets and ceramics are also on display.

Although it provides a pretty and historic counterpoint to the brash consumerism elsewhere around the square, the Museum of Literature is an expensive disappointment for foreigners. Still, there's no charge for admiring the lovely statuary and delicate portraits of the nation's greatest writers outside of the building. Most figures are from the medieval era, and each is honoured with a couple of lines of their writings. More modern personalities include Mirza Alakbar Sabir (1862-1911), Huseyn Javid (1882-1941) and, with a customary cigarette at his brow, Muhammed Huseyn Shehriyar (1906-1988).

NIZAMI & AROUND

On the north side of the square is a bank of cashpoints, near the Soviet-era bookstore going under the snappy title of the **Book House of the Administration Department of the President of the Republic of Azerbaijan** (*see p128*). Behind here is a pretty and peaceful unnamed square centred on an Italianate fountain, overlooked by the friendly little bar **Tequila** (*see p119*). You'll also see a plaque, one of scores of delicately carved likenesses around the city, marking the previous residency of a notable personality – in this case, here lived the academic Zeynalov.

This stretch is a part of the pedestrianised drag **Nizami**, one of Baku's shopping hubs and main axes, running east–west parallel with Bulvar and the waterfront 15 minutes' walk south. Running the entire length of the city centre, from opposite the imposing Narimanov monument in the west through to the Museum of Contemporary Art (*see p81*) in the east, Nizami rarely varies from arrow-straight. The section here by Fountains Square was once characterised by the Soviet era **MUM** department store (*see p127*), Baku's equivalent of Moscow's GUM and opened the year Gagarin went into space. Fifty years later, Nizami offers a contemporary take on cosmopolitan retail.

One street north of Nizami is the narrower street of **Tolstoy**, whose junction with **Rasul Rza** further along is another little bar hub.

PASAZH & EASTWARDS

Back at McDonald's, Fountains Square tapers down eastwards to a characterful walkway called **Pasazh**, lined with arcades whose ceilings are decorated with attractive, colourful frescoes showing scenes from Baku. A couple of more interesting souvenir shops, with Soviet-era artefacts, can be found around this little area.

INSIDE TRACK
MOLLA NASREDDIN

You'll find the attractive cartoon covers of *Molla Nasreddin* mounted in the **Nizami Ganjavi National Museum of Literature** (*see above*), in the **Ali & Nino** café (*see p100*) and in the **Museum of Azerbaijani Independence** (*see p76*) in the imposing Museum Centre on the Bulvar. *Molla Nasreddin* was founded by Azeri writer Jalil Mammadguluzadeh at the turn of the last century, when Azerbaijan was under Tsarist rule. Originally published in Tbilisi, this Azeri-language magazine, written in Arabic script, poked fun at snobbery, corruption and religious dogma by means of humorous columns and striking cartoon art – the UK's *Punch* or the Soviet *Krokodil* would not be bad comparisons. It saw its last publication in Baku in 1931, at the start of Stalin's worst purges. Mammadguluzadeh died a year later, after countless run-ins with the authorities.

SIGHTS

Pasazh leads to **Khagani**, another important thoroughfare, which begins with the lovely urban space of **Molokan Park**. Featuring a large fountain and a popular playground with all kinds of rides and climbing frames, it is almost permanently lined with parents and grandparents watching over their young charges. Here is where you'll also find Baku's two most central, 24-hour internet cafés, offering all kinds of printing services.

A little further along Khagani is Baku's theatre district, with the **Russian Dramatic Theatre** (*see p149*) the main venue for Russian-language productions. Around here you'll also find the **MF Akhundov Opera & Ballet Theatre** (*see p147*), the **Young Spectator Theatre** (founded in 1928) and the **Mahni Theatre**.

RASUL RZA & SOUTHWARDS

On the southern side of Fountains Square, an area bordered to the east by Rasul Rza and to the west by Mammadamin Rasul-Zadeh, is a hub of bar life, shopping and general social activity. This is where downtown really feels like downtown.

Among the cafés, you'll find **Ali & Nino** (as well as the bookshop of the same name, opposite; *see p100* and *p128*) and the **Café Mozart** (*see p102*); among the restaurants, **Beyrut** (*see p101*), **L'Oliva** (*see p104*), **Zakura** (*see p105*), and the **Sunset Café** (*see p105*). You'll also find the the **Azerbaijan State Museum of History**, set in a beautiful mansion created by oil magnate Hadji Zeynalabdin Taghiyev but currently closed for renovation.

Perhaps more notably, though, also here is the city's main bar area, where **Tarlan Aliyarbeyov** meets **Ali-Zadeh**. Taxis line pavements crossed by a constant flow of barhoppers, and imbued with aromas from a popular kebab spot. Key venues include **William Shakespeare** (*see p120*) and **Otto** (*see p119*), while **808** (*see p117*) and the **Phoenix** (*see p119*) number among the lesser-known establishments.

If you're passing during the day, take a look at the ornate **shopping arcade** that fills half the block between Rasul-Zadeh, Ali-Zadeh and Zarifa Aliyeva: it was built in Italianate style in 1898 by the great oil baron and benefactor of the day, Zeynalabdin Taghiyev.

Azerbaijan State Museum of History

Z Taghiyev Street 4 (493 3648). All buses to Fountains Square. **Open** 10am-6pm Mon-Sat. Currently closed for renovation. **Map** p223 H4.
Founded in 1920, this is thought to be the largest museum in Azerbaijan, though sadly this impressive property owned by the oil magnate who gave his name to the street it stands on – Hadji Zeynalabdin Taghiyev – is currently closed for renovation. Its collection is equally impressive, numbering around a quarter of a million items, some dating right back to

SIGHTS

Fountains Square. *See p50.*

SIGHTS

the Palaeolithic period. Many artefacts were found during post-war archaeological trawls of the Caspian Sea, and the museum remains a centre for historic research.

WEST OF FOUNTAINS SQUARE

Downtown, focus very much falls on the area south-east of Fountains Square, and Nizami just north of it. To the west of Azerbaijan Prospekt, tucked in between the outer edge of the Old City and the residential stretches of Yasamal further north, there are far fewer attractions. Heading west, you come across a couple of oil-boom mansions worth investigating – **Mukhtarov's Wedding Palace** and the **Mitrofanov Residence** – and a couple of modest museums set up in houses occupied by illustrious former residents. The **House-Museum of Leopold & Mstislav Rostropovitch** probably has the most appeal for foreign visitors, while the **Apartment-Museum of Abdulla Shaig** spotlights one of Azerbaijan's best-known children's writers.

Apartment-Museum of Abdulla Shaig
Abdulla Shaig 21 (492 2961). All buses to the Narimanov monument. **Open** 9am-6pm Mon-Sat. **Admission** AZN3. **No credit cards**. **Map** p221 B5.

An eternally popular writer of children's literature, plays and folk tales, Shaig is also known for his translations of Shakespeare and Daniel Defoe into Azeri. During his long stint as a teacher in Baku, Shaig lived in this street, since named after him. Here you'll find photographs, manuscripts and school textbooks he created. This collection is not of immediate interest to the foreign visitor but some of the editions on display are beautiful.

★ House-Museum of Leopold & Mstislav Rostropovitch
Rostropovitchlar 19 (492 0265). All buses to the Narimanov monument. **Open** 10am-5pm Tue-Sun. **Admission** AZN3. **No credit cards**. **Map** p221 B5.

Of all Baku's so-called 'house museums', this is one of the most attractive. Mstislav Rostropovitch was one of the great cellists of the modern age, as well as a conductor of world renown. This is the house he lived in as a boy, before he went up to the Moscow Conservatory as a 16-year-old. When he was 22, Prokofiev wrote a cello sonata for him. A radical voice in the Soviet Union, he later lived and worked in America. He returned to Baku to give master classes, and this museum opened in 2002, five years before his death. Mstislav's father Leopold is given equal credit in the museum's title as one of the two rooms has been put together just as it would have looked in the pre-war days, when Leopold was head of the household. You can also see Leopold's last letter to his son. There are awards, programmes and photographs, but more substantial English documentation would be surely be appropriate for such a giant of the international classical-music world.

Oil-Boom Mansions

Baku's 19th-century oil barons put their wealth into opulent houses.

The area around Fountains Square changed dramatically in the boom years following the discovery of oil from the second half of the 19th century. As well as a distinctly Parisian air of wide boulevards, this is where you'll find a number of the oil-boom mansions built by millionaires who made their fortunes almost overnight in Baku.

Cross busy Azerbaijan Prospekt and head west up steep Ahmad Javad and the third corner you come to is Mukhtarov. Named after the entrepreneur who built a palace here to please his wife, the street is currently a hive of activity as **Mukhtarov's Mansion** –

also known as the Wedding Palace – is being renovated. You should be able to make out the statue of a knight, though, added by the master architect of the day, Gasimov, who slipped and died as he put it in place.

At the far end of Ahmad Javad, the **Mitrofanov Residence** was the lavish creation of the oil baron of the same name, whose inclusion of bare-breasted women, people's faces and animals would not have gone down well with the Islamic authorities when it opened in 1898.

For more on the architecture of oil-boom mansions, see *pp44-46*.

The Old City

Traces remain of medieval Baku.

If any part of Baku has its own identity and easily definable parameters, it's the Old City, Icheri Sheher. Occupying a brain-shaped area close to the Caspian seafront on the western side of the modern capital, Icheri Sheher contained practically the entire city until it began to spill beyond its confines from the Tsarist era onwards in the earlier part of the 19th century. If you're only in Baku for a day, this is the must-visit.

Surrounded by high city walls and accessed via main entrances near Icheri Sheher metro station on the western side, and the double gates on the north side close to Fountains Square, the Old City also flanks the Caspian Sea that used to lap close to the base of the **Maiden's Tower**, one of its two main attractions. The other is the **Palace of the Shirvanshahs**, a self-contained complex within a complex, close to the north-west corner.

North Baku

Sahil &
East Baku

Downtown

Old
City

Sabayil &
West Baku

Bulvar &
Waterfront

| **Map** p223 | **Restaurants** p107 |
| **Hotels** p89 | **Bars** p120 |

HISTORY OF THE OLD CITY

There is some debate among historians as to whether the Palace of the Shirvanshahs was really constructed by the Shirvanshahs, who came here in the 12th century after an earthquake flattened their former base at Shamakha, or by Zoroastrians, who may have been responsible for the erection of the Maiden's Tower.

What is known is that Baku's first city walls were put up in the 12th century. They were set out in two rows, some 15-20 metres (49-66 feet) apart, with a ditch between them. Before it receded, the Caspian came right up to the edge of the Old City, allowing ships to dock, as the walls then reached the water. The outer walls were later dismantled at the onset of the oil boom in the 1880s, allowing room for the modern city to develop.

Inside, the town was separated into quarters, each with its own mosque and hammam, and some with a caravanserai. What you'll find today is a warren of alleyways and main streets, most of them signposted, dotted with mosques and minarets, modestly sized hotels and guesthouses, a couple of caravanserais, a dozen beautifully carved portals, half a dozen

INSIDE TRACK
CARAVANSERAIS

Looking from the outside as they would have done 600 years ago, the caravanserais of Baku's Old City would have accommodated traders passing through on their way to or from the East. Some would have been dealing in silk, although Baku was not as major a stop-off on the famed Silk Road as Samarkand or Kashgar. Nevertheless, laid out in classic rectangular or square style with an open central courtyard surrounded by two floors of alcoves, the caravanserais you see today would have been put to good use over many centuries. Downstairs would have accommodated the traders' animals, provided storage space for their goods, as well as tea, food and space to bathe; sleeping quarters were upstairs. These historic spaces now provide sustenance in the form of restaurants: the **Mugham Club** (see p108), **Caravanserai** (see p107) and the **ART Garden** (see p107).

foreign embassies, and sundry carpet and souvenir shops, their traders gently persuading you to enter. The hassle factor is considerably less than in other similarly historic hubs across the Muslim world – tourist groups are relatively small in number, the only walking tour regularly available hardly advertised (*see p61* **Walk**). Renovations are widespread – you may be unable to walk down a certain alley for the plethora of planks and huddles of busy workmen – while the sound of hammering drowns out the rare car that can traverse only the very widest streets.

MAIDEN'S TOWER & AROUND

Blending in with the skyline near the Hajinski Mansion on the open, sea-facing side of the Old City, the **Maiden's Tower** is Baku's most iconic sight, the one featured on fridge magnets and in miniature form at the souvenir stalls around its base. Around the corner of the horseshoe building set between the tower and the sea, a tucked-away information office proffers audio-guide walking tours (*see p61* **Walk**), with the tower as their starting point.

Also around the base, amid extended families of hungry cats, you'll find scaffolding and a sign indicating that restoration work is currently being carried out by Remmers and Atelier Erich Pummer. The sign suggests that 'the ultimate appearance of the Maiden's Tower following restoration will be determined by input from the relevant expert community and public consultation' – although the work appears to be more structural than cosmetic in nature following earthquake damage in 2000.

The form and function of the Maiden's Tower have been matters of intense academic conjecture. It is ideally located to operate as a watchtower, and dates back perhaps even hundreds of years before the birth of Christ, but it's the shape of its base that has caused the most debate. That shape has been interpreted either as a number 6, key to the sexagesimal numerical system used by the Babylonians, or something more akin to the sign for fire, fundamental to Zoroastrian worship. Its alignment with the sun at the equinox may also point to some kind of astronomical use.

Alongside this is the legend told to tourists about a king's daughter flinging herself from the tower to save her maidenhood from unwanted marriage – as reflected in the local name of Qiz Qalasi ('Maiden's Tower' or 'Virgin's Tower').

Historians concur that what we see today is the result of a 12th-century rebuild, as also indicated by the sign in Kufic script, the oldest of Arabic scripts, on the outside of the south wall, easily visible with the naked eye, referring to the 'Tower of Masud', a noted architect of the day.

The Old City.

INSIDE TRACK POOR ST BART

One of the 12 disciples, the Apostle Bartholomew, also known as Nathaniel, was born in the first century AD in Cana, Galilee. Although details are scant, he is said to have travelled as a missionary to India and around Asia Minor, before arriving in what was then Caucasian Albania. His visit to Albanopolis, thought to be present-day Baku, was not a happy one, however. On the apparent orders of the local pagan king Astyages, Bartholomew was flayed alive and crucified head down, perhaps at the very spot beside Maiden's Tower where a chapel was built nearly two millennia later.

What is also sadly evident is that, as what should be a prime tourist attraction, the Maiden's Tower is chronically under-visited. True, the admission fee of 2AZN is modest enough, but so are the attractions that fill the various storeys as you climb up, each display seemingly more random than the last, roped off from close view and hardly featuring any kind of documentation. Most visitors are satisfied, though, with the climb up the tower and the commanding view from the top – those slightly shaky with heights should visit on a day when the strong Baku winds drop.

Over a little bridge from the Maiden's Tower, is the 15th-century **Haji Bani Hammam**, uncovered during archaeological excavations in 1964, which would have served the community of this quarter of the Old City. Here also are the remains of **St Bartholomew's Chapel**, erected in 1892 but demolished by the Soviets in 1936. In 2003, the Ecumenical Patriarch Bartholomew I of Constantinople, of the Eastern Orthodox Church, came to Baku with sacred relics of the Apostle Bartholomew to meet with the then Azerbaijani President Heydar Aliyev and propose the reconstruction of the chapel. As yet, though, the remains are untouched. Every 24 June, a Christian ceremony takes place here in memory of the saint's deeds.

On the north side of the Maiden's Tower stands an attractive row of businesses along **Gulla**, including the characterful second-hand (mainly Russian-language) bookstore, **Kitab Magazasi Elman** (*see p129*), a good source of cheap city maps. Here also is the **Giz Galasi** art gallery (Gulla 6, 012 492 7481, www.qgallery.net), set up by private owners in 1999, with an adjacent outlet for gifts and souvenirs.

Recently opened beside the Haji Bani Hammam, you'll find a little branch of the **Ali & Nino** book chain (*see p128*), selling English-language books and guides. Running west of this picturesque former market square uncovered in the 1960s, the wide thoroughfare of **Asaf Zeynalli** is lined with carpet outlets and their respective barkers. When trade is slack, the older men sit here and while away an hour or so over a game of *nard*, a regional form of backgammon. An impressive caravanserai contains the **Mugham Club** (*see p108*), possibly the most atmospheric spot in Baku to eat out, hosting traditional live music and dance. Further along, a more modernised caravanserai contains the **ART Garden** (*see p107*), another restaurant.

Ten minutes' walk further west, the wild hair and striking profile of Vagif Mustafa-Zadeh dominates the corner of the street named after him. Turn right at this bust of Baku's best-loved jazz musician and you'll come to his house, now the **Museum of Vagif Mustafa-Zadeh** (*see p62*).

Walking east from the Maiden's Tower and Haji Bani Hammam, you'll pass a religious burial place dating back to the 1300s, then after a slight upwards slope, you'll come to two facing caravanserais, Multani and Bukhara, that now comprise the **Caravanserai** (*see p107*) restaurant.

Maiden's Tower. *See p59.*

SIGHTS

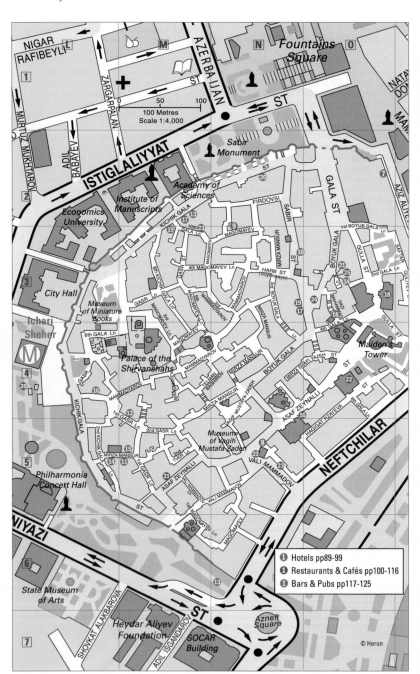

Carry on walking north-east, along broad **Böyük Gala**, and you'll arrive at the **Shamakhi** double gates, the main entrance for vehicles admitted by permit, and a short walk from Fountains Square. Above the gates are carved symbols of a lion and a bull, symbols of the Shirvanshah dynasty that ruled it. Here once stood a customs building and sanitary station, where incoming animals would have been groomed, their hooves slathered in antiseptic tar oil. The gates also acted as a security system, funnelling any would-be band of attackers into two separate streams that would be easier to control.

Here also was the site of the gruesome murder of Pavel Tsitsianov, a Georgian Imperial Russian military commander known for his firm and bloody hand in the Caucasus at the turn of the 18th and 19th centuries. Arriving boldly at these double gates in 1806, and expecting to be presented with the keys to the city, he instead met with a hail of gunfire, beheading and the chopping off of his hands. The garden just outside was named after him by later Tsarist rulers until pre-Soviet Azeri independence in 1918.

Today, there is little evidence of any bloody misdemeanour – only a kiosk selling Soviet-era souvenirs and football badges (*see p134*).

★ Maiden's Tower

Neftchilar Prospekt (492 8304). All buses to Bulvar. **Open** 10am-6pm Tue-Sun. **Admission** AZN2; AZN0.20-AZN0.60 reductions. **No credit cards. Map** p58 04.

Baku's most distinctive landmark, overlooking the Old City and Caspian Sea that once lapped it, is a fortified lookout post eight storeys and nearly 30 metres (98 feet) high. The current structure dates from the 12th century, but the building's origins are mysterious and a matter of much debate. Accessed via a series of stone staircases (watch your head on the way back down), each storey seems to feature a random display of artefacts or souvenirs, not all of them documented and most of them roped-off from a closer view.

Having bought your ticket from the little booth opposite, you enter via a winding metal staircase and trapdoor that were added in recent times – for centuries beforehand, someone would drop a ladder down, thus deterring any would-be foe from ascending. The first storey has maps and early photographs of Baku and the Old City, with carriages awaiting Oil-Boom-era visitors at the base of the Maiden's Tower. At the next level are ceramic finds and the top of a well 21 metres (69 feet) deep, while somewhat underwhelming displays of weapons, including swords and shields, souvenirs and carpets feature further up. The view from the top, though, is what you're after. *Photo p57.*

Mugham Club. *See p57.*

PALACE OF THE SHIRVANSHAHS & AROUND

Constructed by the ruling Shirvanshahs escaping after an earthquake in Shamakha, this palace complex overlooked Baku from on high. Today, this major landmark continues to provide commanding views of the Old City, sea and surroundings, its *divankhana* pavilion, mosque, mausoleum and baths lending a sense of an enclosed, elite community.

The **Palace of the Shirvanshahs** (*see p62*) was commissioned by Sheikh Ibrahim I in the early part of the 15th century. Historians disagree as to whether it was actually built as a palace – which, thanks to significant modern-day reconstruction, it certainly looks like – or as a place of memorial and worship for a Sufi saint. What is clear is that within a century, the Safavids had conquered Baku, the palace fell into disuse and disrepair, and it was later occupied by Tsarist forces.

Having been excavated and restored over the past two centuries – the hammam ruins were only discovered in 1839 – the Palace of the Shirvanshahs is now one of Baku's prime tourist destinations. Much like the Maiden's Tower, however, it is woefully short on documentation. A must-visit, nonetheless.

This higher, north-western section of the Old City sees the greatest concentration of embassies – the Greek, Slovenian and Italian

SIGHTS

Palace of the Shirvanshahs. *See p62.*

embassies among them – the steepest climbs and finest views, not including those from the roofs of the many hotels and restaurants dotted around the walled, historic quarter.

Hidden down a narrow street a short walk from the palace, the **Museum of Miniature Books** (*see p62*) provides a short if entertaining diversion, free of charge. It's not so much a museum as an expanded room in a private house but there are some 3,000-plus examples on display here. Most would be of interest to Russian speakers (note the photograph of Boris Yeltin's visit in 2005), but this relatively new attraction also features a modest section of works in English.

As you head towards the Icheri Sheher metro station from here, you'll pass a pleasant patch of greenery centrepieced by an imposing **bust**

INSIDE TRACK LOCALS FIRST

Some of Baku's museums operate a two-tier system of admission prices, one for Azeris and one for foreigners. In some cases, the difference is significant – say, in the case of the Nizami Ganjavi National Museum of Literature, of limited interest to outsiders in any case, where the ticket price of AZN1 for locals is literally one-tenth of that demanded of foreign visitors. Levies for Turkish nationals are often half that of other foreigners.

of Vahid. Another example of Baku's detailed statuary, this likeness shows the lined forehead and concentrated gaze of one of Azerbaijan's best loved poets of the 20th-century. Born Aliagha Mammadgulu oglu Isgandarov, Vahid ('Unique') is credited with bringing the medieval meter known as *gazal* into the post-war poetry of the Soviet era. This laid the groundwork for spoken-word, freestyle yet rhythmic *meykhana*, an alternative form of story-telling, itself the base for domestic Azeri rap.

Just the other side of the fortress walls from the palace complex is the large open square featuring Icheri Sheher (formerly Baki Sovieti) metro station, with a bizarre glass pyramid outside, not unlike the one at the Louvre in Paris. From here, you can be at downtown Sahil or Baku's main railway station in next to no time.

Heading down towards the sea, halfway to the Maiden's Tower, you'll arrive at one of the dozen mosques dotted around the Old City. The **Mohammed Mosque** is known for its antiquity, its construction in 1078 making it one of the oldest in Azerbaijan, and for the **Sinig-Gala Minaret** alongside. Its appearance differing from the intact, renovated nature of its nearby counterparts, the Sinig-Gala was given the name of 'Broken Tower' as a symbol of defiance. Bombardment by Peter the Great's army in 1723 caused the damage, the subsequent capture of the city shortly before the Tsar's death giving Bakuvians ample excuse to leave the tower as it was.

Close by the Mohammed Mosque is one of Baku's most endearing yet little-known

Walk The Old City

An audio tour takes you around the best of the Old City.

With other city tours absurdly priced at over €20, the audio walking tour available from the information office (Gulle Street, 417 7933, www.icherisheher.gov.az, open 9am-6pm daily) on the Caspian side of the Maiden's Tower, is a bargain at AZN5. Don't forget to take your passport, to be used as collateral. The tour has 16 points, starting at the Maiden's Tower, featuring the Palace of the Shirvanshahs twice, and including a jazz-*mugham* medley at the end. The 23 push-button entries on your pocket-sized, grey audio guide, correlate to red-square headphone signs around the Old City, and a notional 60-minute limit on your tour. Each extra hour is another AZN1.

Of the three-language options, the English one produces an American-accented voice and a knowledgeable, enjoyable jaunt around Baku's main tourist destination, with plenty of interesting asides that touch on a range of subjects, from Stalin's prison term in Baku to the social function of wells in medieval society.

The text begins with a condemnation of the Soviet attitude towards Baku's priceless architectural heritage, and the little-known threat from Moscow of the Old City being razed to the ground in the post-war era.

After a walk around the **Maiden's Tower**, and a brief run through the conjecture over its purpose, the tour moves opposite to the **Haji Bani Hammam**, and the role

bathhouses played in medieval Bakuvian society: they were the place where women picked their son's future wife. After a look at the ruins of **St Bartholomew's Chapel**, your walk takes you past the arcaded burial place nearby, the twin caravanserais of **Bukhara** and **Multani**, and on to the **Sailor's House** (1909) with its ship-like exterior. This brings in the architectural expansion during the Oil-Boom years, allowing for some quite jaw-dropping facts to be spieled out. In 1863, the population of Baku was 14,000; by 1920, it was 250,000. In between, at a certain point in 1898, Baku was responsible for half the oil used in the world.

You'll then learn more modern history as, after the remains of the **Baku Khan's Palace**, you come to the once-elegant **National Encyclopaedia Building**, and talk turns to the doomed independent republic of Azerbaijan of 1918, the first democratic and secular one in the Muslim world.

After passing by the gates, city walls and **Palace of the Shirvanshahs**, you are led to four of the Old City's dozen mosques – **Chin**, **Mohammed**, **Juma** and **Ashur** – before a stop at the two-storeyed caravanserai of the **Mugham Club** music venue.

An hour should easily have you back at the Maiden's Tower, the start and end point of a tour that will have guided you almost completely around the inner circumference of the Old City.

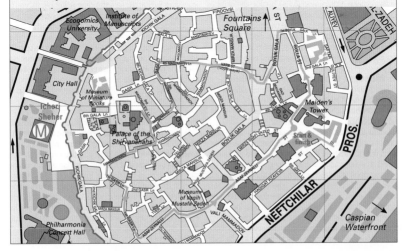

Vagif Mustafa-Zadeh

A musician ahead of his time.

As Dizzy Gillespie said, 'Vagif Mustafa-Zadeh was born before his time. His music is from another planet... It's music from the future.'

Born in 1940, Vagif Mustafa-Zadeh spent his boyhood under Stalin, secretly listening to jazz broadcasts on the BBC and Voice of America, and the equally banned indigenous form of rhythmic poetry, *meykhana*. He could also play piano from the age of three.

Rising up through the halls of musical academia, Mustafa-Zadeh quit the Azerbaijan State Conservatory to focus on his first love: jazz. And not just any jazz, but an improvised form that incorporated an indigenous cultural format, *mugham*, itself the fusion of classical poetry and traditional music.

He performed at festivals across the Soviet Union before gaining a reputation abroad, taking first place at a jazz composition competition in Monaco in 1978. He also formed a number of bands, including Qafqaz, Leyli and Sevil, where he met his second wife, Eliza. Their daughter, Aziza, is a jazz star in her own right, much as a daughter from his first marriage, Lala, is a prize-winning classical pianist. The piece that won him the award in Monaco was entitled 'Waiting for Aziza', composed shortly before she was born in 1969.

Sadly, Mustafa-Zadeh never lived to see his daughters' worldwide success – he died on stage, shortly after a concert in Tashkent, Uzbekistan, in 1979.

attractions: the **Museum of Vagif Mustafa-Zadeh** (*see below*). The father of *mugham*-jazz – a fusion of traditional and improvised jazz music – lived in a modest two-room flat here, now transformed into a two-room museum that's worth a quick look around.

FREE Museum of Miniature Books
Gala Street 1 (492 9464). Metro Icheri Sheher. **Open** 11am-5pm Tue, Wed, Fri-Sun. **Admission** free. **Map** p58 L4.

This unusual attraction opened on International Book Day in 2002 and is worth a look around for curiosity reason alone. Containing 3,750 books, the bulk of them in Russian (Pushkin, palindromes, Anna Akhmatova), this small venue of two adjoining rooms also displays volumes in Esperanto and Chinese, as well as a collection of poetry by Shelley, and sections for children's books and autographed copies.

★ Museum of Vagif Mustafa-Zadeh
Vagif Mustafa-Zadeh Street (no phone). Metro Icheri Sheher. **Open** 11am-5pm Tue-Sat. **Admission** AZN3. **No credit cards.** **Map** p58 N5.

There's something very personal about a visit to the remarkably modest flat where the master of *mugham*-jazz, Vagif Mustafa-Zadeh, once resided and practised. It's not just the piano in the corner or the photographs of his mother, who worked in music and theatre, and of his daughter, the current jazz star Aziza. It's the Soviet-era furniture that would have accommodated Mustafa-Zadeh's guests, probably also notable musicians of the day, and the Rossiya record player he would have played his vinyl on. With a little Russian, you might glean from the kindly lady

running the place that the woman on one of the album sleeves later became Mustafa-Zadeh's second wife.

★ Palace of the Shirvanshahs
Böyük Gala Street 46 (492 1073). Metro Icheri Sheher. **Open** 10am-7pm daily. **Admission** AZN2. **No credit cards.** **Map** p58 M4.

Climbing the incline to the staircase that leads to this outwardly impressive palace complex, the first-time visitor is immediately aware of its elevated vantage point and, as later investigation may uncover, the extent to which it has been completely renovated. After buying your ticket from the non-English speaking lady at the self-standing ticket booth, you'll find yourself in a pretty, petite courtyard, with a small hexagonal pool, beside a map indicating nine main points of interest. To your left is the *divankhana*, dating back to 1428, an octagonal pavilion five paces across, the wind blowing through its six little door openings. Its purpose may have been as a venue for state receptions or as a courtroom. Interesting-looking but undocumented stones dot the courtyard around it.

This frustrating lack of documentation extends to the two-floor main palace building. It is explained, however, that the building follows the classic pattern of Oriental palaces, with external and internal apartments, and household needs looked after on the ground floor. Maps of the Shirvanshah empire and a family tree help provide an introduction, as it was Sheikh Ibrahim I (1382-1417) who had the first stone laid here. Also on display in a large main room are beautifully crafted dresses, purses, bowls, swords, coins, *nard* boxes, tools and carpets. As you continue through the palace, you should enjoy the framed paintings of Baku by Hüseyn Alakbarov, and fabulous caricature models of local characters by Elmira M Abbas, but you'll leave the palace little wiser about the history surrounding it than when you entered.

Across the courtyard and down one level, the Shah Mosque (1441) offers a wonderful chance to see the two praying halls (the back one was for women), standing beside the Shirvanshah's mausoleum (1435), built for Khalilullah's mother. Behind and below this are the palace baths, or rather their ruins, but the hammam layout is easy to see.

Above, back at palace level, another mausoleum is said to have been built for sufi mystic Seyid Yahya Bakuvi, whom the Shirvanshahs hired as their children's tutor. Here also stands the somewhat plain Eastern Portal (1585) and, before it, copies of the cannons used in the defence of the Old City against Tsarist forces in the early 19th century.

The Palace of the Shirvanshahs is an essential visit, and easily worth its AZN2 admission fee. *Photo p60.*

AROUND THE OLD CITY

Encircling the fortifications of the Old City are three of Baku's major thoroughfares: , Niyazi, Istiglaliyyat and Neftchilar, also known as Bulvar. The last is covered in the chapter Bulvar & the Waterfront (*see pp70-76*). Landmarks close to the Old City, between Istiglaliyyat and Niyazi and the city walls, are described below in relation to the metro station of Icheri Sheher.

North from Icheri Sheher

Leading somewhat steeply north-east from the metro station, traffic-clogged **Istiglaliyyat** is lined with a number of imposing institutions.

INSIDE TRACK
OLD CITY MOSQUES

As you wander around the Old City, you'll pass a fair number of mosques and minarets, each serving what was once a neighbourhood community. Few can be visited but most have been furnished with a carved plaque giving the year of opening in Arabic and Latin script. The oldest is the **Mohammed Mosque** (*see p60*), its Sinig-Gala Minaret owing its unusual shape to the Russian invasion by Peter the Great. Close to it and also active is the **Gileyi Mosque**, dating back to the early 1300s while the other side of the Giz Galasi hotel from the Mohammed Mosque, the **Khidir Mosque** was built in 1301. To see the inside of one, the **Shah Mosque** in the Shirvanshah complex (*see p59*) is open to the public and an essential stop on any visit there.

First up is **City Hall**, built in the late 1800s, looking every bit as stern as its other title, Baki Sovieti, suggests that it should. Then comes the **Economics University**, of particular historical significance, for it was here that the parliament of the short-lived Azerbaijan Democratic Republic (1918-21) was convened after its move from Ganja. The grand avenue it stands on was given Russian names under Tsarist and Soviet rule but its current title of Istiglaliyyat ('Independence') is apt, given the

SIGHTS

Philharmonia. *See p64.*

events of 90 years ago. There are several plaques on either side dedicated to honourable individuals whose demise coincided with the Stalinist purges of the mid- to late 1930s. Between the two wings of the Economics University – one of which is the former Empress Alexandra School for Girls, the first such institution in the Islamic world – a stark **monument** lists the six points of Azerbaijan's declaration of independence, in Azeri, in Latin and Arabic script, and dated 28 May 1918.

Alongside stands the **Mohammed Füzuli Institute of Manuscripts** (Istiglaliyyat 8, 492 8333), containing priceless Korans and early works of Azeri literature, but open to researchers by appointment only. In the same building but with its own entrance, the **Huseyn Javid Museum** (Istiglaliyyat 8, 492 0657) is of limited interest to outsiders but features another beautifully detailed, carved likeness of this poet, playwright and novelist. Having lived in this house since 1920, Javid was arrested by Stalin's henchmen in 1937, exiled to Magadan, in Siberia's frozen east, where he died in December 1941. Exonerated in 1956, he was only repatriated in 1982, when his remains were transported from Siberia to his home town of Nakhchivan City, where his mausoleum can be visited (*see p181*).

Moving closer to Fountains Square, the impressive building next along, topped by

a striking band of gilt-edged writing against a bordeaux background, is the former Ismayilli Palace. Now, as this gilt writing suggests, home to the **Academy of Sciences**, it was built by Oil-Boom millionaire Musa Naghiyev in honour of his son Ismail, its design based on the Doge's Palace in Venice.

Facing Fountains Square from across the beeping cars and buses of the busy junction where Istiglaliyyat meets Azerbaijan Prospekt is a pretty patch of greenery with a statue of popular writer **Sabir**, an impoverished poet and satirist with a social conscience, he was a significant contributor to the influential periodical *Molla Nasreddin*. Born Alakbar Zeynalabdin oglu Tahirzadeh, this innovative philosopher wrote under several pen names, including Sabir, Hop-Hop and Fasil.

South from Icheri Sheher

Walking south towards the sea from the Old City metro station, you'll first come across the classic **Filharmonia Café** (*see p108*), Baku's best spot for ice-cream, set in the grounds of the same name. As you wander these pleasant surroundings, you may be struck by a certain sense of unreality, accentuated by the kitsch piped music ('I Just Called To Say I Love You', 'Theme From Love Story') that plays as lovers entwine around the bubbling fountains amid the Tsarist-era, landscaped, stepped gardens, in the shadow of the wedding-cake **Philharmonia concert hall** (*see p149*). If this looks like something from Monte Carlo, it's because that is what this former casino was modelled on when it opened in 1912. Designer Gabriel Ter-Mikelov used the Opéra de Monte-Carlo as his architectural example.

The Soviets not being ones for encouraging such entertainment among the wealthy, it then became the resident concert hall for the Philharmonic society, and a number of state orchestras, choirs and folk ensembles. It was converted in 1937, taking the name of Muslim Magomayev (*see left* **Inside Track**), the composer who died that same year. Today, it hosts an eclectic if mainstream range of folk and classical concerts, but it's worth visiting for the building alone.

The same year that the Philharmonia opened, so did the equally grandiose **Rustam Mustafayev National Museum of Arts** opposite, currently partly under renovation.

As you look down Niyazi on **Azneft Square** from here, with the SOCAR State Oil Company, Heydar Aliyev Foundation and President's Office on the Sabayil side, you might realise that the **Four Seasons** (*see p95*) could not have chosen a finer location for its five-star hotel. Due to open in early 2012, it will have the Old City behind it and the Caspian beyond.

SIGHTS

INSIDE TRACK
THE MAGOMAYEV DYNASTY

The grandiose **Philharmonia** (*see p149*) was opened as a concert hall in 1937, and took the name of a composer who had died that year: Muslim Magomayev. Unlike many of his contemporary luminaries, Magomayev had not fallen foul of Stalin's witch hunt – among his many populist operas and rhapsodies, he had written a propagandist piece in favour of the Communist victory over the Azerbaijan Democratic Republic the previous decade. Magomayev died of tuberculosis. His namesake grandson was one of the biggest singing stars of the Soviet Union, a baritone at home in both the pop and opera genres. A lifelong smoker, he died in 2008, his funeral attended by the good and great of Soviet and post-Soviet popular music. Grandfather and grandson occupy an ornate grave in the national cemetery of **Fakhri Khiyaban** (*see p68*) a short taxi drive west of the Philharmonia in Sabayil.

Sabayil & West Baku

Monuments, martyrs and landmark buildings.

The heights of Sabayil contain some of Baku's most notable landmarks: some long-established and others yet to open. Immediately overlooking the busy roundabout of **Azneft Square** and the main boulevards of Niyazi and Neftchilar, Sabayil feels a world away. Many of the people heading up here do so by car – perhaps chauffered car – for this is where you'll find the **Azerbaijani National Assembly**. It stands opposite the simply remarkable **Flame Towers**, due to open in 2012, the architectural project to end all architectural projects in new boom Baku (*see p69* **The Famous Flames**). Above all this, between here and the lower area of Bayil near the military harbour, stands the **Telecom Tower**, constantly changing colours from lime green to fluorescent blue to bright red up and down its 310-metre (1,020-foot) structure, the highest building in Azerbaijan. Up here, too, are two cemeteries, **Martyrs' Alley** (home to the Eternal Flame) and the national cemetery of **Fakhri Khiyaban**.

[Map showing areas: North Baku, Sahil & East Baku, Downtown, Old City, Sabayil & West Baku, Bulvar & Waterfront]

Map p221 **Restaurants &**
Hotels p95 **Cafés** p109

SIGHTS

When it is back in operation, the best way to scale Sabayil will be by **funicular**, a Soviet-era contraption whose lower station stands near the destination restaurant **Chinar** (*see p109*) and the tranquil square centred on a fountain depicting Bahram slaying the dragon, taken from the literature of Nizami. In turn, the statue gives its name to the **Dragon Lounge** (*see p125*), the fashionable cocktail bar and nightclub above Chinar. The scene is lent architectural gravitas by the **Useynov building**, a fine-looking façade behind which eminent professors and academics resided when the Chinar was a popular teahouse under the same name. Back then, there would have been no view of two contemporary landmarks: the **International Mugham Centre** (*see p148*), opened in 2008, and the **Carpet Museum** (*see p76*), set to move to new premises in 2012.

When it's running, the blue or red-and-yellow trains of the funicular (20q) trundle past the **Green Theatre** (*see p148*), a Soviet-era landmark that reopened in 2007, which now stages – as it did then – family-friendly shows and entertainment under the stars in summer.

Funicular.

Chinar.
See p65.

now home to skateboarders and canoodling teenagers, and is one of the few places in Baku completely festooned with graffiti.

Once an amusement park – and before that, a cemetery – **Martyrs' Alley** is a moving and tastefully conceived memorial to the 130-plus victims who died as a result of Black January (*see below* **Black January**), the massacre in Baku by Soviet troops of demonstrators seeking Azeri independence in early 1990. Each victim, including the woman who committed suicide after the loss of her husband, is honoured with a stark, marble slab with a likeness of their face etched upon it. Small rows of tulips add colour to the pathos.

This sombre and touching promenade leads to an archway below which flickers the **Eternal Flame**, before a panoramic view of the Caspian. If you look just above the flame, the arch creates the perfect frame for the blur of the blue, red and green of the Azeri flag fluttering in the distance, set atop the world's tallest flagpole, a 162-metre-high (531-foot) monument. It stands on the square named after it near the military harbour in Bayil.

MARTYRS' HILL

At the top, the funicular station overlooks what was once Kirov Park, a somewhat ironic name considering the function of this area, now known as **Martyrs' Hill**, today. Kirov was the Bolshevik pioneer pivotal in bringing Communism to Azerbaijan, later murdered in the Stalinist purges of the 1930s. His huge statue once stood near the station before being knocked down in 1991; the area around where it was is

BAYIL

Around the flag, at sea level in Bayil, is a perfect example of how Baku is changing almost overnight, a 23,000-capacity concert venue, the **Baku Crystal Hall**, is being built in six months by the same Germany company responsible for Bayern Munich's Allianz Arena football stadium. Time is of the essence, as this will be where the 2012 Eurovision Song Contest will be held. For more, *see p32* **Making Your Mind Up**.

Black January

The anniversary of the killing of Azeri citizens by Soviet forces.

Every 20 January, Baku stops. Solemn music plays in metro stations and ships out in the Caspian Sea honk mournfully across the water. The anniversary marks the brutal suppression by Soviet forces of demonstrators calling for Azeri independence in 1990. The tragedy came in the context of the gradual and bloody break-up of the Soviet Union, and in the rise of the Popular Front of Azerbaijan, who barricaded Baku while calling for freedom from Moscow.

The USSR defence minister, Dmitry Yazov, positioned outside Baku, had his men blow up the national television station and cut phone links with the city. On the night of 19 January, 1990, Soviet troops moved in to smash through the barricades, claiming the PFA had been firing on them. Crowds gathering in the main streets and squares of Baku to protest the Soviet aggression were shot at by Yazov's forces. A State of Emergency was declared by Mikhail Gorbachev in the Kremlin, but by then hundreds lay dead or injured. A mass burial began on 22 January, followed by 40 days of mourning. All told, it is thought that more than 130 citizens were killed and 700 injured. It is not clear how many Soviets fell. The exercise was seen as a warning to other Soviet republics seeking to break away – and Gorbachev would later refer to it as 'the greatest mistake' of his political career.

SIGHTS

Martyrs' Alley.

Flame Towers.

SIGHTS

The grand opening in Bayil of the world's tallest flagpole in September 2010 was perfectly timed. Not only did it take place in front of a gathering of distinguished onlookers, including Russian president Dmitry Medvedev, it set the bar at 162 metres (531 feet) in a bizarre flagpole war around the globe. First there was the face-off in the Demilitarised Zone of Korea, when North beat South in Kijong-dong, setting the record at 160 metres (525 feet). Meanwhile, in the Caucasus, Turkmenistan had long been boasting of the world's tallest flagpole, a massive spread of dark green fluttering outside the Presidency. Azerbaijan reaching new heights in 2010 was the ideal thumb-nosing exercise across the Caspian Sea – and required an overall cost of $32 million.

Tearing yourself away from the splendid Caspian panorama, your attention is drawn to the **Turkish Martyrs' Mosque**, also overlooking the sea. Another nearby Turkish monument expresses gratitude to the 1,130 troops who fell fighting for Azerbaijan in 1918. And World War II hero, Azeri tank commander Hazi Aslanov, who died in battle in 1945, is granted similar honour in plinth form. There is even a memorial to the British troops who were fighting the Turks in the chaotic finale to World War I, erected amid much controversy in 2003. All around are other graves, of Azeris who fell in the Nagorno-Karabakh conflict of the early 1990s.

From here, adventurous tourists can take a little side trip south to scale the **Telecom Tower**. But turn into Izzat Nabiyev behind the National Assembly, and you come to grand gates leading to **Fakhri Khiyaban**, the national cemetery something along the lines of Père Lachaise in Paris.

But not even Père Lachaise has gravestones like this, towering architectural monuments to Azerbaijan's great personalities. The first ones you come to, for singer Rashid Behbudov, composer Muslim Magomayev and his grandson, the singer of the same name, are ornate, grandiose creations – elsewhere, writers are depicted standing in a pensive mood and musicians pose beside grand pianos, all beautifully carved in stone and marble.

Pride of place goes to former president Heydar Aliyev, who died aged 80 in 2003, and who guided the new republic of Azerbaijan through the difficult years after independence from the Soviet Union. He is displayed standing tall in a suit and tie, before a backdrop of a carved map of Azerbaijan, between two rows of purple tulips; the family plot lies opposite.

Fringing the southern border of the cemetery, the **Botanical Gardens**, which opened in the mid 1930s, contains some 2,000 species but is more of a venue for scientific research than a major tourist attraction.

Walking back towards the **National Assembly** – be sure not to take any photographs – you'll be struck by one of the most unusual and ambitious architectural creations of the new millennium: the **Flame Towers**. On the site of the former Hotel Moskva, three vast buildings rise up, tapering as they do into the form of a flame, the national symbol of Azerbaijan. The project has constantly been set back by the fierce winds whipping off the Caspian, but is expected to be complete at some point in 2012. *See right* **The Famous Flames**.

Further out, another long-awaited hotel development overlooks Sabayil, the five-star **Kempinski** in the underused district of **Badamdar**. *See p90* **The Fab Five**.

Closed to the public until fairly recently, the **Telecom Tower** bears no little resemblance to its counterpart in Alexanderplatz, Berlin. This one, though, changes its appearance constantly, with lurid patterns of blues, greens and reds emitting from the 310-metre (1,020-foot) spike throughout the night. On national holidays, the tower becomes a vast, vertical flag of Azerbaijan, proudly displaying the blue,

red and green of the tricolour. Instigated as a project under the Soviets in 1979, Telecom Tower was shelved in the mid 1980s until then-president Heydar Aliyev took it up again and had the building opened with an elaborate ceremony in 1996.

In 2008, the **Telegulle** restaurant (*see p111*) opened on the 62nd floor, making the tower accessible to the public.

The Famous Flames

Baku catches fire with this unique architectural adventure.

It's an architectural undertaking that would beggar belief in Las Vegas or Dubai. Stand on Baku's downtown seafront or in the Old City, and you'll see them rising in the distance, three tapering towers reaching up, combining to form the shape of a vast fire.

Begun in 2008, at an initial cost of $350 million, the **Flame Towers** comprise a trio of buildings, each with a different function. The first, southern tower, 33 storeys high, will be residential and contain 130 apartments. The second, northern tower will come under the most scrutiny as this will be the site of the Flame Towers Fairmont Baku Hotel, a

30-floor luxury destination incorporating guest rooms, serviced suites, a spa and fitness centre. It's perhaps the most notable of the five major five-stars to open in the city in the space of six months. *See p90* **The Fab Five**.

The third, western edifice is the Office Tower, set over 28 floors grouped into four tiers, each with an atrium and sharing a sky garden. Altogether, this will contain more than 33,000 square metres (355,209 square feet) of commercial office space.

The whole will surpass anything built in this last decade of architectural superlatives in Baku. Now they just need to fill the place.

SIGHTS

Bulvar & the Waterfront

Baku's signature boulevard runs along the Caspian shore.

Baku's showcase seaboard mixes the best of Oil Boom, fin-de-siècle architectural style with contemporary, commercial savvy. Combining a family-focused promenade, a shopping hub and – in a recent development – a nexus for high-end hotels, what maps refer to as Neftchilar Prospekt and Bakuvians call 'Bulvar' is a broad avenue adjoining a tastefully relandscaped strip of parkland running alongside the murky waters of the Caspian Sea. It is currently being extended, at both ends. Once this is complete, it will be the world's longest waterfront promenade.

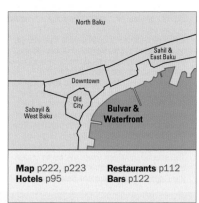

North Baku

Sahil & East Baku

Downtown

Old City

Sabayil & West Baku

Bulvar & Waterfront

| **Map** p222, p223 | **Restaurants** p112 |
| **Hotels** p95 | **Bars** p122 |

Hajinski Mansion.

A CHANGING BOULEVARD

Currently, most of the northern part of Bulvar also borders the city centre, which means that wherever you are downtown, you're always a stroll away from the sea. This, though, is changing, as the Bulvar is being extended beyond Government House and the new harbour terminal to the east, while to the west, past the new International Mugham Centre and yet-to-be-opened Carpet Museum fashioned in the shape of a rolled-up rug, a further new complex is emerging around the world's tallest flagpole (*see p72*). Once complete, the Bulvar extension will be key to the city's urban redevelopment. For more, *see pp29-34* **Baku Today**.

In the meantime, a number of notable developments have taken place over the last few years, including Baku's first proper shopping mall and leisure centre (**Park Bulvar**; *see p127*), two five-star hotels (the **Hilton** and the **Marriott**; *see p90* **The Fab Five**), and the city's first high-end restaurant complex, **Sahil** (*see p110* **From London with Love**).

This transformation comes a century after the first; when the original Oil Boom was attracting significant international interest and serious

Caspian Controversy

Sea or lake? This is no mere semantic quibble: ownership of resources is at stake.

The Caspian is the largest enclosed body of water on earth and a remnant of the ancient Paratethys Sea. Rivers such as the Volga flow into it but only evaporation allows the water to escape. As a result, it has on average one-third the salinity of the ocean, and the northern Caspian is less saline than the south. The sea, if, indeed, it is one, is so shallow in the north that it freezes over in winter. In the south, it reaches depths of more than 1,000 metres (3,280 feet).

A legal decision as to whether the Caspian is actually a sea or a lake will have profound economic and political consequences. Currently, international disputes over the status of the Caspian concern the bordering countries of Azerbaijan, Iran, Russia, Kazakhstan and Turkmenistan. If it is decided that the Caspian is a sea, then there are legal precedents that would allow the surrounding nations to divide it into separate national sectors. If it is legally defined as a lake, then all the resources might have to be divided equally. The latter scenario would be particularly advantageous to Iran in the south because it has a proportionately smaller coastline. If Iran could achieve an internationally recognised legal definition of a lake, then this would entitle it to claim far more of the marine environment as its sovereign territory and, therefore, the resources that lie within and below it – in particular, the vast oil reserves. Rattling in the closet is an old treaty signed between the Soviet Union and Iran dividing the spoils – which then meant fish – two ways. Naturally, the three republics that emerged after 1991 no longer see it this way.

The current situation is that Azerbaijan, Russia and Kazakhstan have signed treaties – that Iran does not recognise – to resolve their territorial disputes. Iran continues to pursue the equal division of resources dependent on the Caspian being defined as a lake. The position of Turkmenistan is unknown. However, as oil and gas exploration proceeds apace in the whole area, particularly in the relatively unexplored south, the dispute has the potential for holding back the economic development of the region to a significant degree and fomenting significant political unrest.

money, the Caspian was still lapping around the base of the Maiden's Tower. Partly thanks to the vision of influential city mayor RR Hoven and the dynamism of the newly rich entrepreneurs, the sea-facing city walls of the Old City were knocked down, a strip of land reclaimed from the sea and a boulevard created, which linked the city with neighbourhoods vital to the oil industry.

Grand houses were constructed, most notably the **Hajinski Mansion**, and trees planted along the once barren promenade, a result of Hoven's initiative that incoming ships should also bring in fertile soil as an import levy. The boulevard, **Bulvar**, was opened at some point in 1909, a pleasant thoroughfare for families to relax and partake of a kind of Caspian passeggiata.

Under the Soviets, some of the more bourgeois aspects of Bulvar's attractions were targeted toward social entertainment – the converting of the **Children's Puppet Theatre**, for example, and the introduction of amusement rides. There was an open-air cinema, cafés such as **Mirvari** (*see p112*), whose retro appearance is now part of their charm, and a **tower**, every bit like the one in Blackpool, for parachutists to dive off. A classic, Stalinist-looking edifice, once referred to as 'Dom Soviet' and now **Government House**, was erected at what was then the eastern extent of the promenade. Nearby, a stately building was named after Lenin, focusing on his life and works. The **Museum Centre** may have moved the spotlight from Communism to carpets, but for now at least, it still feels like one of those fusty old institutions of the post-war period. After nearly 50 years, one of its components, the **Carpet Museum**, will move in 2012 to impressive new premises on the waterfront.

After a long period of neglect, the Bulvar was given priority as part of Baku's dramatic regeneration. Newly opened underground walkways, some with toilets, mean that you can now cross Bulvar in safety. If you stride down the boulevard first thing in the morning, you'll be greeted by an army of sweepers in work clothes stamped 'Bulvar' who keep the pavement immaculately clean all day long. In a hangover from the days before everyone had a camera-phone, a smaller band in worktops marked 'Foto' will offer to take your picture for money.

Along with Fountains Square, Bulvar was singled out for the siting of a series of imaginative, contemporary statues – a ship's captain, an old fisherman, a painter, an elderly

SIGHTS

gentleman leaning forward to shake your hand. Alongside are dotted recently bedded trees and plants, notable enough to warrant labelling – 160-year-old olive trees from Pistoia, Italy; other examples from Argentina. Juice bars in the shape of sliced oranges provide freshly squeezed refreshment. At a dozen or so terrace cafés, old men gather over tea for entire afternoons, at tables taken by families at weekends. Kids have plenty to occupy them, with dodgem cars, fairground rides and giant transparent balls in which they can wade over water. For more, *see pp145-146*. There's also a little tourist train and boat rides out into the Caspian Sea (*see p73* **Inside Track**).

WESTERN SEABOARD

The development of the far western end of the seafront, as far west as **Bayil** (*see p66*), is a very recent phenomenon. One year after the raising of the world's tallest flagpole in September 2010 (*see p68* **Inside Track**), in a square now renamed after this unusual attraction near the military harbour, a German team of architects responsible for four major football stadia in central Europe is building an events venue, **Baku Crystal Hall**, in next to no time. This is where fans of Eurovision will gather in spring 2012 for one night of frivolous pop.

As far as the main section of the Caspian promenade is concerned, the first major building at the western end is the **International**

Bulvar.

Mugham Centre (*see p148*), a futuristic-looking building opened in 2008 and dedicated purely to the traditional music of Azerbaijan known as *mugham*. This impressive edifice is being joined later in 2012 by the new **Carpet Museum** (*see p76*), for which the term 'futuristic-looking' doesn't even scratch the surface. Its exterior fashioned in the shape of a rolled-up rug, with an exquisite carpet pattern to boot, the bright golden Carpet Museum comprises four floors and an interior flooded with natural light. Its contents will have been moved from the current Carpet Museum at the Museum Centre (*see p71*), a stately pile halfway down the seafront.

These shiny contemporary landmarks will impress visiting dignitaries whizzing back in chauffered cars around nearby **Azneft Square** and up to major institutions such as state oil headquarters SOCAR and the presidential buildings.

Officially, Neftchilar Prospekt, aka Bulvar, starts from Azneft Square, with the non-fortified side of the Old City behind it, and grandiose, turn-of-the-century façades setting the architectural tone. Although sadly and incongruously currently occupied by a Tom Ford fashion store, the **Hajinski Mansion** is the jewel in the crown, tastefully restored to its former glory. For more about Baku's oil-boom architecture, *see pp44-46*. As an attractive plaque, complete with a natty likeness of the Free French leader, describes, this was where De Gaulle stayed in 1944, en route to Moscow to meet Stalin. It is said he spent a night at the opera before taking off for the Kremlin.

The seafront promenade's park area is divided into pathways, patches of green and

SIGHTS

buildings dedicated to recreation – a centre for tennis and other ball games, for instance – and terrace bars such as the **Kafa Lala**. As the Old City gives way to the modern-day Downtown, another family-friendly attraction comes into view: the **Children's Puppet Theatre** (*see p71*). A beautiful confection of yellow and white, with a dramatic mural in the lobby, this is another fin-de-siècle creation, opened in 1910 as Baku's first cinema. It became a puppet theatre in 1931 and was later named after children's author Abdulla Shaig, who died in 1959.

INSIDE TRACK
CASPIAN CRUISE

Every hour in summer, a robust passenger boat leaves the quay just outside Baku's main harbour terminal to take tourists around the Caspian Sea for half an hour. There's no commentary, no bar or restaurant and nothing by way of any safety demonstration, but your chain-smoking captain will assuredly point the *General Kerimov* or the *Salatin Asgarova* towards Bayil. You won't go out too far, but far enough to make out structures and appreciate the ever-changing cityscape of Baku as you take it in from east to west. Tickets cost AZN2 (AZN1 for kids from five to 12, and 30q for toddlers) and are available from the *kassa* by the quay.

EASTERN SEABOARD

The seafront's pretty pattern of greenery, fountains and walkways is broken up by a modest walkway jutting into the sea, and a number of landmarks old and new. Familiar from Soviet times are the parachute tower, now reduced to being a somewhat elaborate stand for a digital clock, and the much-loved **Mirvari** (*see p112*) café-restaurant, modelled on the shape of a pearl. Nearby, the singularly ugly **Baku Biznes Merkezi** business centre is offset by the adventurous, pod-like exterior of the **Park Bulvar** (*see p127*), the city's first modern mall. With upscale restaurant **Zeytun** (*see p113*) and French-style **Kitchenette** (*see p112*) making best use of its elevated, sea-facing locations, as well as a large, prominent branch of **Debenhams** (*see p127*) on the ground floor, a cinema, planetarium and bowling alley, this is a retail, dining and entertainment hub in one, unlike anything Baku has ever seen. Soon it will be complemented by **Sahil** (*see p110* **From London with Love**), a restaurant complex also capitalising on the Caspian panorama, and including what promises to be the city's first contemporary Azeri restaurant. Behind the project is the Azerbaijan Hospitality Group, whose success with the downtown Zakura and Chinar has changed the face of Baku's hospitality industry.

Across the street on Neftchilar, over the road from a somewhat grandiose fountain, a stern-looking institution, the Museum Centre, currently houses the **Carpet Museum**, the **Theatre Museum**, the **Museum of**

SIGHTS

Azeribaijani Independence, and other attractions such as an art gallery and a Russian-language multimedia theatre.

All this is due to change at some point in 2012, when the main attraction, the Carpet Museum, moves to its impressive, purpose-built location (*see p76*) back along the seafront near the International Mugham Centre. No one is yet sure what will happen to the other museums in the building once the carpets are relocated – the most likely outcome being that the Museum Centre will house some kind of governmental institution, and the other museums will be moved elsewhere.

The Museum Centre itself was the Vladimir Ilyich Lenin Museum until 1992, when the Carpet Museum was relocated from the Juma Mosque in the Old City. For those wanting to export their newly bought carpet from Azerbaijan, this is the institution that deals with licences and permission slips (*see p138* **Cutting a Rug**).

Moving east from the Museum Centre, you'll approach a wide plaza invariably filled with parked cars, **Azadlig Square**, dominated by the imposing edifice of the **Government House**. This is the biggest public square in Baku and is soon to have its appearance and focus altered by the opening of two five-star hotels either side of Government House, the Hilton and the Marriott. It was landscaped at the height of the Soviet era and featured a large statue of Lenin, outside what was then Dom Soviet, and which gave the square its name. Hotels were later added, the **Azerbaijan** and the **Absheron**.

Little surprise, then, that the former Lenin Square was where demonstrators gathered in 1990 to protest the brutal Soviet massacre of 20 January (*see p66* **Black January**) and fly the banned flag of the Republic of Azerbaijan. Soon afterwards the statue had disappeared and the square was renamed Azadlig: 'Freedom'.

Planned as early as the mid 1920s, shortly after the Soviet takeover of Azerbaijan, Government House took two decades to construct, interrupted by World War II. Since occupied by several ministries of the newly independent Azeri Republic, Government House was renovated over four years from 1996 to 2000. It remains a monumental pile of huge, echoing corridors.

The easternmost section of the waterfront features the main **harbour terminal** and the **Port Baku Towers** complex, just north of it, which will gradually take over many of its responsibilities. The current harbour building feels modern enough, and features the **Sea Port Hotel** (*see p96*) and its sea-facing restaurant (*see p113*). In front of it is the ticket office for Caspian boat trips in sturdy old craft reminiscent of the Soviet days. Behind, the rising shape of the Port Baku Towers development is something very much of the 21st century.

The area is currently awash with construction and boarded-up plots of land, partly intersecting with an ugly estuary of railway lines reaching for the sea, and for an elongated industrial zone forever linked to the first oil boom: **Black City**.

Bisected by Nobel Prospekt, this whole area was a hive of back-breaking activity in the days of the first oil boom. Here stood a forest of oil derricks that made fortunes for the likes of the Nobels and the Rothschilds, creating a mass of black smoke and round-the-clock din. At the point when the 19th century became the 20th, Baku was extracting more oil than the entire United States. This success story ended with the chaos after World War I, and the subsequent Soviet expropriation of Baku's oil industry.

Today, the heart of Baku's oil industry is west of Bayil, and much of the former industrial zone to the east awaits redevelopment. The **Nobels' mansion** in the Black City has been restored and now contains a **museum** (*see right* **The Dallas of the Caucasus**) dedicated to their achievements in Baku.

INSIDE TRACK
PORT BAKU TOWERS

When it opens, there'll be no harbour building like it along the Caspian coast. The Port Baku Towers, a harbour-area complex being built by the UK architectural firm Chapman Taylor, is located a block inland from the current terminal. The current international marine trade port will move to Alat, while much of the ferry activities will be dealt with at the Port Baku Towers development. The original port, built in 1902, is already the largest and busiest on the Caspian. Now it will be the sleekest. Set above a platform of shops, the larger of the two new towers will be a 25-storey office block, featuring a spa, indoor and outdoor pools, and sports facilities, and the smaller tower will have the same contemporary look.

★ **Jafar Jabbarli State Museum of Azeri Theatre**
Museum Centre, Neftchilar prospekt 123A (012 493 4098). Metro Sahil. Due to move in 2012. **Open** 10am-6pm Tue-Sat. **Admission** AZN3. **No credit cards. Map** p222 J3.

It would be a great shame if this sympathetic collection illustrating the history and development of theatre in this part of the Caucasus, put together with such affection for the subject, were to be lost or relocated thoughtlessly. Currently set on an upper floor of the Museum Centre, the Theatre Museum covers a century of local drama, from its beginnings during the Oil Boom through the Soviet era and beyond.

The Dallas of the Caucasus

The Nobels were the dynasty and Villa Petrolea was their Southfork.

Most people know the Nobels for the annual prizes for global achievement and perhaps for the fact that Alfred Nobel, third son of Immanuel, invented dynamite. Few might appreciate that Baku made the Nobels. From a failing arms business in the mid 19th century, the Nobel dynasty was transformed by Baku's oil boom, which they ruled for three decades. During that time the money they made allowed them to invent the world's first oil tanker and create an ornate mansion set in stunning grounds.

Though the Nobels abandoned their Black City base after the Soviet invasion in 1920, their mansion, the **Villa Petrolea** (*see p76*), has recently been restored and now houses a museum covering their heritage.

Immanuel Nobel was an inventor and arms manufacturer who made his fortune during the Crimean War – then lost it. His well-connected son Ludvig took over, and used his influence in the Tsarist empire to send brother Robert to the Caucasus to find walnut trees to make rifle butts. Instead, he found Baku in the grip of oil fever. This was 1875. Noticing the primitive nature of the refineries then operating there, and taking advantage of a recent lifting of a Russian monopoly, Robert and Ludvig were soon neck-deep in oil and its profits.

By 1877, they had so much of the stuff to transport they had to invent the world's first oil tanker, *Zoroaster*, named after Azerbaijan's fire cult. By 1882, they began distilling oil around the clock. As an indication of the scale of the Nobel operation, at the very end of the 19th century it is estimated that the oil

company they had formed, Branobel, was Baku's largest, extracting nearly 18 per cent of Tsarist Russia's total production, which is to say nearly nine per cent of the world's. Alfred's shares helped finance his Nobel Prize awards, and expunge his guilt over the invention of dynamite.

Meanwhile the family built its mansion, set in an area of greenery dotted with 80,000 plants and fruit trees, conceived by eminent Polish botanist E Bekle. By now Ludvig's son Immanuel was involved in the day-to-day running of the family business, building two new tankers in 1903.

But in the turmoil surrounding the Russian revolution of 1905, workers began to rise up against their foreign masters, partly prompted by prime agitator Koba, later known as Stalin, who served time in a Baku prison. Swedish workers were attacked and killed. A decade later, the Bolsheviks took over Russia, then Baku. Having lost their assets, the Nobels fled to Stockholm, but Ludvig's son Gösta managed to salvage matters by selling half the company shares in New York.

Under Soviet rule, the Villa Petrolea fell into disrepair and most of the grounds, which used to run down to the sea, were built upon. Today, part of the area, on the north side of Nobel Prospekt, is Luna Park, as well as the seat of the Azeri Football Association. Much of the mansion has been restored, reopening in 2008 thanks to the work of the Baku Nobel Heritage Fund. It houses a museum dedicated to the Nobels and their work in Baku, and hosts official receptions and events linked to the Baku Nobel Oil Club based there.

Founded as early as 1934, the museum features models of famous playhouses, posters, handbills, set designs, costumes and stills. While some of the original publicity material was produced in Arabic or Cyrillic script, there is modest documentation understandable to the English speaker. Some of the lives led by the theatrical personalities featured here could not have been scripted in Hollywood: turn-of-the-century star of stage and screen Huseyn Arablinski took his name from a lady he fell for in the audience, and was killed on stage by his cousin. Jafar Jabbarli, after whom the museum is named, was a Communist sympathiser who translated *Hamlet* into Azeri, and who is considered the father of modern Azeri screenwriting. He died the same year that this museum opened.

★ Letif Kerimov State Museum of Carpets & Applied Arts

Museum Centre, Neftchilar Prospekt 123A (493 6685). Metro Sahil. Due to move in 2012. **Open** 10am-6pm Tue-Sat. **Admission** AZN5. **No credit cards. Map** p223 J3.

Whether housed in this stately home of more than four decades or at a wonder of contemporary architecture a kilometre away, the collection gathered together by researcher and carpet-maker Letif Kerimov is simply unique and a must-visit. It was Kerimov who categorised the 144 different styles of Azeri carpets, based on their region, city or village of origin. This museum is duly named after him, his bust standing in the doorway.

As you walk through each well-documented room, the various schools of local carpet-making are explained in detail: the artistic originality, dark blues and sedate colour combinations of the Baku School; the high density of knots and animal motifs in the Guba School; the depictions of shahs and sultans in the Tabriz School. Some 1,300 examples are on display at a time, from a collection numbering 6,000.

Manufacturing methods and tools are also shown, including looms and spinning wheels, and mat-making tools from thousands of years ago. This is a fascinating place to visit and offers a real insight into an age-old indigenous craft.

▶ *For more on the production of carpets in Azerbaijan, see p138 Cutting A Rug.*

Museum of Azerbaijani Independence

Museum Centre, Neftchilar Prospekt 123A (493 8382). Metro Sahil. Due to move in 2012. **Open** 10am-5pm Tue-Sat. **Admission** AZN2. **No credit cards. Map** p223 J3.

The third main museum in this seafront building comprises six rooms dealing in rough chronological order with the general notion of Azerbaijani independence. Beginning with a framed copy of the constitution and text of the national anthem, written by Ahmad Javad, who was later shot by the Soviets, the exhibition then focuses on the short-lived Azerbaijan Democratic Republic formed in 1918. A photograph of the proud members – moustached to a man – of the original cabinet complements a mock-up of a desk and photocopies of original documents. The subject matter then moves to the Soviet era, the massacre of 20 January, the Nagorno-Karabakh conflict, and the rapid development of infrastructure and the economy post-independence. In the last room stands a model of the Baku-Tbilisi-Ceyhan oil pipeline, surrounded by photographs of sundry ceremonial signings that helped bring Azerbaijan the riches it is currently enjoying.

▶ *For more on the 20 January massacre, see p66 Black January.*

★ FREE Villa Petrolea

Nizami Park, Nobel Prospekt 57/2 (424 4020). **Open** 11am-7pm Mon-Fri. **Admission** free. *See p75* **The Dallas of the Caucasus.**

Carpet Man

Letif Kerimov spent his whole life in carpets.

Letif Kerimov was born in 1906 in Shusha, Nagorno-Karabakh. His mother was a carpet-weaver and his father a milliner. Conflict forced the family to move to Iran, where, as a young boy, Kerimov studied weaving techniques. He moved back to Shusha, worked at a carpet factory and gave tuition to weavers. He became a master of the genre: the carpet he wove in honour of Persian poet Firdowski, which went on show at the Paris International Exhibition in 1937, displays his skill. In fact, Kerimov worked in many fields: he was also a jewellery maker and interior designer; you can see his handiwork in the **Nizami**

Ganjavi National Museum of Literature (*see p51*). His three-volume masterpiece on the history and development of carpet-making in Azerbaijan, published over two decades, is the definitive tome on the subject, and helped provide the framework for the **Carpet Museum** (*see above*) he founded, the first of its kind in the world, at the Juma Mosque in the Old City in 1967. Kerimov died in 1991, as his beloved Shusha fell under siege during the Nagorno-Karabakh conflict with Armenia. Some 600 priceless carpets had to be saved and transported from Shusha, where they found a home in the Carpet Museum's newly opened premises.

SIGHTS

North Baku

Shops, hotels, the zoo, football stadium and Baku's railway station.

The area north of Fountains Square and the main street of Nizami is a grid-pattern of streets filled with shops and offices, interspersed with main squares and clusters of upscale hotels. For every broad, traffic-filled avenue – Azerbaijan prospekt, Fizuli, Samed Vurgun – there are a dozen streets that are poorly paved and ill-lit. For the visitor on a short stay, unless your hotel is here, you're at a trade fair or there's a restaurant you want to visit, there's little reason to leave Downtown or the Old City.

To the west of the area, north of

North Baku

Sahil & East Baku

Downtown

Old City

Sabayil & West Baku

Bulvar & Waterfront

Map p220, p222	**Restaurants** p113
Hotels p96	**Bars &**
	Nightlife p122

Sabayil is residential **Yasamal**; two of Baku's most charming house- museums are located along along its southern fringe, House-Museum of Leopold & Mstislav Rostropovitch and the Apartment-Museum of Abdulla Shaig, both covered in the Downtown section (*see p54*).

To the east, **Nasimi** is named after the Turkic mystical poet of the late 14th and early 15th century, whose beliefs fell foul of the religious authorities, and who was skinned alive for his trouble. His statue stands between Nizami, Tolstoy and Samed Vurgun, at the southern edge of this large district of north-central Baku.

The area includes the nexus of hotels, restaurants and conference centres by the Bakikhanov roundabout, known to long-term expats as the **Hyatt area**, the **Teze Bazaar** (*see p132*), and family-friendly attractions such as the **circus**, **aqua park** and the **children's railway** (for all, *see pp145-146*).

Dominating the focal square of **Fizuli**, the **Azerbaijan National Drama Theatre** (*see p148*), otherwise known as the **Milli Theatre**, has the feel of a long-established institution. Set before a pretty fountain that came with the reconstruction of 2008, and a statue of the 16th-century poet Fizuli himself, this venerable establishment was founded in 1873 and has staged Shakespeare and all the classic works of Azeri drama.

Prominent embassies – American, Russian, Turkish – surround one of Baku's most curious sights, the sculpture of **Richard Sorge**, in the park of the same name.

Teze Bazaar

SIGHTS

Baku railway station.

Azerbaijan National Drama Theatre.
See p77.

SIGHTS

Baku's main **railway station** is an architectural sight in itself. Not only is this a major traffic hub, where two metro stations – 28 May and Jafar Jabbarli – and two metro lines meet, the large open square here will see the opening of Baku's second major shopping mall.

Heading north-east from the station, you'll come to the areas of **Narimanov** and **Ganjlik**, site of **Baku Zoo** (*see p146*) and the **national football stadium** (*see p149*).

Baku railway station

Jafar Jabbarli Square (012 499 5488). Metro 28 May/Jafar Jabbarli. **Map** p220 D3.
Baku's railway station was planned from 1880, when the City Council decided to build a 'first-class passenger' station at the same time as the Tbilisi-Baku line was being built. The site chosen was then on the fringes of the city's residential area. It is thought that the station was designed by the same architect behind similar ones on the Trans-Siberian line; however, it has its own motifs with eastern touches, similar to ones on Azeri carpets, plus ample use of tiling and stucco. There were waiting rooms for first-class passengers only, a telegraph office and plenty of room for luggage. When it opened in early 1884, the newspapers used the term 'imperial' with abandon. The Tsar himself arrived with his family in 1888. Around the station, the great roads of north-eastern central Baku were built, linking it to downtown and the Black City. The Soviets rebuilt the station in 1926. The building, although underused, remains worthy of a look around, ornate and high-ceilinged. From here, there are night sleepers to Tiblisi, and trains set off for the 60-hour trek to Moscow three times a week. There are also night services to other main towns in Azerbaijan.

The Eyes of the Spy

Super-spy Richard Sorge worked for Moscow against Nazism.

As if in keeping with his reputation and achievements, the sculpture of super-spy Richard Sorge in the park named after him, in the embassy district of Nasimi, gives you the impression that he's observing you, even now, nearly 70 years after his death. A curved slab of concrete dotted with fake bullet holes depicts a narrow cross-section of Sorge's facial features, as far up as the furrows on his forehead and as far down as just before tip of his nose. At the centre of the likeness are hollow, piercing eyes that glow faintly and eerily in the dark. No other detail is given – and perhaps none is needed.

An ethnic German Communist born in Baku, Sorge travelled the world during the rise of Nazism in the 1930s and 1940s, posing as a journalist under the name of Ramsay. Working for Moscow, he lived in Germany, England, China and, finally, Japan. A serious drinker who had many lovers, Sorge formed a spy ring in Tokyo that enabled him to warn Stalin of the impending attack on Pearl Harbor and the exact launch date of Operation Barbarossa, Hitler's invasion of Russia – information that Stalin famously chose to ignore. He kept the Kremlin constantly informed on Japan's designs on Russia.

His bravery cost him his life: he was hanged in Sugamo Prison in Tokyo in November 1944, along with his informant Hostumi Ozaki. One of his Japanese lovers, Hanako Ishii, regularly visited his grave in Tokyo until she died in 2000. Acknowledged by many experts – Kim Philby, Ian Fleming, Tom Clancy – as the greatest spy of all time, Sorge has been the subject of many posthumous books and films.

SIGHTS

The Flag of God

'The linesman says no!'

With greying hair and a brush moustache, Tofik Bakhramov would seem an unlikely addition to England's football hall of fame. Yet this Baku-born official played a significant part in the greatest triumph of the nation's sporting history: the winning of the World Cup in 1966. Staged at Wembley Stadium against a German side instructed to be on their best behaviour some 20 years after the war, the match became the most dramatic of World Cup finals.

The game, on a knife edge at 2-2, turned on a single moment in the 101st minute. Official film shows linesman Bakhramov running level with play as the ball is crossed into the German penalty box. English striker Geoff Hurst turns and shoots, the ball bouncing off the crossbar then... either on the line or over it, depending on whose view you take. The English claim a goal – Hurst's fellow striker Roger Hunt could have ended half a century of controversy by simply poking in the rebound – while the Germans wave in frantic motions of negation. Swiss referee Dienst rushes to Bakhramov for

clarification. 'No, the linesman says no!' exclaims the BBC commentator. Bakhramov is seen to nod emphatically to Dienst – who then points to the centre spot. 3-2. Bakhramov, for years referred to as 'Russian' even though he was an Azeri from the Soviet Union, later wrote that he thought the ball was over the line before it hit the goal line, coming back from under the net.

The English went on to win the World Cup for the first and only time, and Bakhramov officiated for many years afterwards. He died in Baku in 1993 at the age of 67. A decade or so later, with the England team in Baku for a qualifying match, the national stadium was renamed after Bakhramov in a high-level ceremony featuring Hurst himself. England fans laid flowers on his grave and went to the game in the red shirts of 1966 bearing his name.

Outside the stadium stands a statue of Bakhramov in a classic pose, perhaps using the very gold whistle that Queen Elizabeth II granted him in appreciation after the match, if not the controversy, was over.

Sahil & East Baku

Upmarket hotels and restaurants, and Baku's best contemporary art.

While Fountains Square is most definitely the heart of town, the area around Sahil metro station – the only one in the modern city centre – feels busy and business-like. Equidistant between the main square and the waterfront, this area is where you'll find the main tourist office, the main post office and important places such as the **Landmark Building**, a complex of upscale restaurants, bars and a hotel. The arrival of two five-star hotels nearby, either side of Government House, should also signal more openings in the not too distant future.

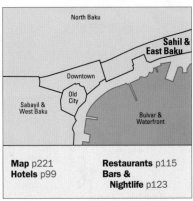

Map p221	**Restaurants** p115
Hotels p99	**Bars &**
	Nightlife p123

Further east, the major streets of Nizami and, parallel to it, Uzeyir Hajibeyov, lead to an ugly tangle of rail lines, a road bridge and one of Baku's most noteworthy attractions: the **Museum of Contemporary Art** (*see p82* **The Best of Azeri Art**). Again, the area around here should change dramatically with the opening of another landmark, the **Port Baku Towers** (*see p74*), a commercial and administrative complex attached to the harbour nearby.

SIGHTS

Around Sahil, the one-way traffic is busy and the surrounding roadworks arecurrently significant – there's a price to pay for all this renovation and erection of new hotels. Look around, though, and much of the cityscape is classically Tsarist-era, thrown up when the railway station (*see p79*) just to the north-east warranted the opening of major roads around it. Bul-Bul prospekt, for example, was named after one of Baku's best-loved singers, Murtuza Rza Mammadov, whose nickname stems from the Azeri word for 'nightingale'. Mammadov had chosen it for his stage name back in his early days in Shusha, before he moved up to Baku and the State Conservatory. The flat where he lived from 1937 until his death in 1961 is now the **Bul-Bul Memorial Museum**.

As you approach Government House, passing the city's main tourist office and post office, you'll notice a number of basement businesses with people queuing outside holding manila files and official documents. This is the hub for notaries and translation agencies – on fine days, there may be a couple of people on the street bashing out text on an old typewriter.

East of Government House, the traffic peters out as you come to a quiet stretch of east Baku. Here you'll find Baku's best modern attraction: the **Museum of Contemporary Art** (*see p82*).

Bul-Bul Memorial Museum

Bul-Bul prospekt 15 (493 5697). Metro Sahil. **Open** 10am-6pm Mon-Sat. **Admission** AZN2. **No credit cards. Map** p222 J2.
A classical singer, a teacher and a musicologist, Bul-Bul was as as well-versed in opera (appearing at La Scala) as he was in the traditional instruments of his homeland. This lovely little museum, set in the apartment where he lived for 25 years, shows the range of his activities and influence. Three rooms are filled with old gramophone records, pedagogical papers, manuscripts, and various letters and telegrams from major personalities from across the Soviet Union.

★ Museum of Contemporary Art

Yusuf Safarov Street 5 (012 490 8404, www. mim.az). All buses to Yusuf Safarov. **Open** 11am-6pm Tue-Sun. **Admission** AZN5; AZN2 students; free children. **No credit cards. Map** p220 E3. *See p82* **The Best of Azeri Art.**

The Best of Azeri Art

The Museum of Contemporary Art: home of modern Azeri painting and sculpture.

Of all the high-profile projects to have changed the face of Baku in the last five years – towers in the shape of flames, a museum building designed in the form of a rolled-up rug – this is the most impressive.

Launched under the personal initiative of Azerbaijan's First Lady, Mehriban Aliyeva, Baku's Museum of Contemporary Art consists of 900 works of fine art, graphics and sculpture covering the period 1943 to 2009. Its concept, as well the museum's impressive design, can be accredited to Baku-based artist Altay Sadigzadeh, whose work made waves at the Azerbaijan Pavilion of the 2011 Venice Biennale.

Two storeys of stark white, connected by a see-through lift, feature the finest work to emerge from Azerbaijan, or from Azeri artists, over the last seven decades. Paintings, the main focus, are given room to breath as you wander through interlinked spaces that appear to present no limitations or awkward angles. Perspective is paramount. The paintings are also clearly labelled in Azeri and English, with the year of their creation and artist's birthdates

alongside. The museum has an excellent café (*see p115*), a decent bookshop and can provide a knowledgeable and useful guide to show you round in English for an extra AZN5.

Before you even start your tour, though, there are sculptures to peruse outside, fabulously intricate and thought-provoking pieces such as Sadigzadeh's *Observer of the Stars* (2010) and Fazil Najafov's *Games of the Time* (2008), in which a stick figure appears to be pleading to passing traffic while possessing features from Ancient Egypt.

The ground floor is full – but not crowded – with noteworthy paintings, starting with 1968-born Niyat Najafov's almost child-like *Airplane* and *Balloon*, both from 2009. More abstract but no less contemporary are larger works by the older Ali Ibadullayev, such as *Delight* and *Triptych*. Sadigzadeh injects humour into the creative process with his *The Artist, The Model*, while his *Secret Conversations* is more politically charged. Upstairs, his *21st Century* shows two evidently trolleyed well-to-do citizens clinking cocktail glasses. Comfortable, low-backed, black-and-white sofa chairs allow you to recline and admire.

Between the paintings are striking sculptures such as Natik Aliyev's wide-hipped *Egyptian Woman*, Fazil Najafov's soaring *Stages of Life* and *Abduction* (1994) by Makhmud Rustamov, in which a long-legged, horn-breasted woman in an iron mask is whisked away by a multi-horned beast.

Downstairs also features a well-stocked bookstore, with editions in Azeri, Russian and English, along with the Metropolis Gallery, where items are for sale (prices averaging around AZN3,000-AZN4,000). There's also a TV area where art-related shows are screened, usually in Russian.

Upstairs on the first floor, more space can be given to individual paintings. Mirnadir Zeynali's languid *Sharaf Kahnim Drinking Water* contrasts nicely with the constant blur of street traffic immediately behind outside, while Tofik Javadov's *The Oilmen – 50 Years of the 20th Century* literally stops you in your tracks. Framed by an ample backdrop of white space, his painting shows the resigned features of workers, caps set against the fierce wind, squeezed into a truck with the refinery at their backs. Javadov was active as a painter in the 1950s, and much of the first floor is given over to more illustrative art from deep in the Soviet era. If anything, much of it is more immediately moving. Examples include Elchin Aslanov's *Torgovaya Street* from 1947 and two completely exquisite line drawings by Jabbar Gasimov, *Oil Wells* from 1952 and *Baku Boulevard* from 1957, featuring a young mum and infant, a Sputnik-era pram, and a timeless seafront. Look out also for Huseyn Aliyev's *Baku City* from 1967, and the Caspian scenes of Nadir Gasimov, who died in 2000.

The overall effect on the first-time visitor is satisfying – you feel that you've really been to Baku and seen how it looks, and perhaps begun to understand what makes it tick. You also appreciate, given the dates of many of these works, that Baku's art scene is thriving, up-to-the-minute, and well worth further investigation.

Round off your visit with a quality coffee, snack and cake at the tastefully arty café on the first floor.

Museum of Contemporary Art.

SIGHTS

The smart way of giving

Give the perfect getaway

Browse the full range of gift boxes from Time Out
timeout.com/smartbox

Consume

Three Graces. *See p105*.

Hotels

A wealth of new five-stars in a business-focused city.

In the space of 20 years, the hotel stock in Baku has been transformed from a hangover of the Soviet days to something in keeping with an oil-boom metropolis in the 21st century. Late 2011/ early 2012 sees the opening of a Hilton, a Marriott, a Kempinski and a Four Seasons, all within a few months of each other. What the city still lacks, though, is a solid number of genuine, good-value two- and three-star hotels. Most hotels are geared to the business traveller on expenses, so establishments that would struggle to gain three stars in Spain or France are here categorised as four-star thanks to 24-hour room service and chintzy touches to the decor.

BUSINESS, BOUTIQUE AND BEYOND

The first wave of western-style hotels came in the mid 1990s with the Hyatt, whose success not only changed the face of business accommodation in the city but also created an upscale hub of hospitality and dining around it. Then came the boutique boom, which centred around the recently closed Metropol and its similarly defunct but popular Taboo restaurant, and the 2009 arrival of the Landmark nearby, another nexus of high-end accommodation and gastronomy in east-central Baku near Government House. The opening of the Hilton and the Marriott in the same locality, with their quality culinary and spa options, not to mention the Sahil restaurant complex (*see p110* **From London With Love**), should move the focus away from what has come to be known as the Hyatt area towards the Sahil/Bulvar area.

Meanwhile, the Old City is awash with small-scale hotels of around a dozen rooms, many offering similar services; some are able to take advantage of their location to provide a rooftop view for their diners and drinkers. Older or disabled visitors should be aware that not all places are equipped with lifts. Access around the cobbled streets may also be tricky, given the amount of renovation work going

on and relative difficulty in arriving by car. But, for the able bodied, panoramic Caspian Sea views make all the hassle worthwhile.

VISAS AND SERVICES

Before you choose where to stay, a few guidelines may be helpful. At present, few westerners are going to sleep anywhere in Baku without going through a draconian visa process. Ensure you have that fully under way before you commit to booking anywhere. Obviously, those having their travel arranged by their employers need not worry, but those who will be staying in Baku for a longer period should be aware that they'll find few attractive flats in the city centre or Old City for less than $2,500 a month, while many hotels will be happy to quote a monthly rate.

Practically every hotel charging at least AZN120 for a double will provide free parking (except for those in the Old City), Wi-Fi, room service and help with airport transfers and booking excursions. Air-conditioning, essential in summer, is also generally a given. Many places offer laundry and dry cleaning. Service is generally good, and most receptionists will speak a modicum of English. Standards of hygiene and cleanliness are high.

RATES AND RULES

The rates given in this chapter are the quoted rack rates for a double room and, where relevant, a single one. They include breakfast. There are also significant charges for paying by credit card, plus a nominal local tax.

> ❶ Red numbers given in this chapter correspond to the location of each bar as marked on the street maps.
> *See p58, pp220-223.*

CONSUME

There is no real low or high season in Baku, although some hotels charge slightly more in the autumn. The most significant event is the Caspian Oil & Gas Show (*see p143*), held over a week in early June, which pushes up prices and limits hotel availability almost everywhere for the first ten days of the month. Book way in advance and expect to pay a significant premium for a decent room.

DOWNTOWN
Moderate

Austin
Nizami Street 58 (598 0812, www.austinhotel.az). Metro Sahil. **Rates** AZN200-AZN210. **Rooms** 31. **Map** p222 H2 ❶
For a smart, comfortable Downtown hotel, you probably can't do better than this non-chain establishment with a variety of room types. Set on the upper floors of a handsome townhouse, the Austin strains to provide four-star attractions within its relatively narrow confines, but most guests would agree that the level of relaxation possible amid the soft colours and furnishings of their rooms more than makes up for the lack of the kind of facilities they might find at an international chain. The narrow price difference between a 'standard double' and 'executive suite' makes the more spacious option a no-brainer. A modest sauna complements a slightly larger gym.
Gym. Internet (free, wireless). Restaurant. Room service.

Azcot
Husi Hajiyev Street 7, Lane 1 (492 5477, 497 2507, www.azcothotel.com). Metro Nizami. **Rates** AZN110-AZN140. **Rooms** 41. **Map** p222 G3 ❷
Certainly one of Baku's better mid-range (in fact, practically budget) options, the Azcot is a modestly class act. Set in a lovely turn-of-the-century mansion, its 40-plus aesthetically pleasing rooms feature parquet floors, oriental vases and refined art, lush furnishings and handy conveniences such as a mini bar, fridge, tea- and coffee-making facilities. Staff are also happy to book flights, arrange airport transfers and sort out your laundry. Recommended.
Internet (free). Parking (free). Room service.

Balion
Tarlan Aliyarbeyov Street 12 (418 4329, www.balionhotel.com). All buses to Fountains Square. **Rates** from AZN130. **Rooms** 21. **Map** p222 H3 ❸
Location is the key here. What the Balion lacks in style, it makes up for in convenience. A short walk from the main square, it is also right in the middle of the city's bar hub. The 24-hour room service appeals to the many oil-industry employees who stay here, as does the use of a fridge, iron and coffee-making facilities in each of the spacious bedrooms. Wi-Fi throughout is another boon.
Internet (free, wireless). Parking (free). Room service.

Boutique Palace Hotel Baku
A Aliyev Street 9 (492 2288, www.boutique-palace.com). All buses to Fountains Square. **Rates** AZN220-AZN240. **Rooms** 11. **Map** p223 G4 ❹
Ticking both the boutique and business-friendly boxes, this fin-de-siècle establishment is riding the wave of another oil boom a century later. Here, your 200-plus manats isn't paying for a pool or prime dining, but location and design touches. Built into the Old City wall, with easy access to Baku's historic treasures and modern-day amenities, this three-storey building was completely revamped after Azeri independence with a riot of decorative energy. In a fit of nationalist pride, each room has been named and themed after an Azeri hero (the Shamsaddin Eldeniz Suite, Shah Ismayil Suite,

CONSUME

THE BEST HOTELS

For a quiet pint in authentic surroundings
Red Lion Inn. *See p89.*

To shoot pool in a 17th-century cellar.
Meridian. *See p89.*

For Caspian views from the bar and restaurant
Sultan Inn. *See p94.*

For striking architecture
Flame Towers Fairmont Baku. *See p95.*

For decor that's a tribute to Frank Lloyd Wright
Hotel Hale Kai. *See p89.*

For sports
Hyatt Regency Baku & Park Hyatt. See p96 and p98.

Best spa
Excelsior Hotel Baku. *See p99.*

Javad Khan Suite, and so on), with sophisticated western standards of decor and furnishing. Note the ornate ceilings throughout.

Bar. Internet (free). Parking (free). Restaurant. Room service.

★ Hale Kai

Mirza Ibrahimov Street 18 (596 5056, www.hotelhalekai.com). All buses to Fountains Square. **Rates** AZN130-AZN230. **Rooms** 23. **Map** p222 G2 ⑤

'Welcome to the world of Frank Lloyd Wright' says the website of this hotel, an architectural paean – inside and out – to the American legend. The hotel is suites-only – standard, junior and executive – and their indigenous artwork, hand-made stained glass and carpets, and parquet or stone floors combine successfully with touches redolent of Frank Lloyd Wright. Add in heated bathroom floors, orthopaedic mattresses and kitchenettes, American management and staff eager to assist with all kinds of bookings and arrangements on your behalf, and you have a very strong argument for a visitor to choose somewhere ambitious and original over anything the chains can offer in this price range.

Bar. Business Centre. Internet (free, lobby only). Parking. Room service.

Radisson Blu Plaza

Nizami Street 69 (498 2402, www.radisson.com). All buses to Fountains Square. **Rates** from AZN220 double. **Rooms** 40. **Map** p222 G2 ⑥

Renovated to incorporate a high-end restaurant and café provided by the Azza group (*see p101*), this remnant from Baku's first wave of quality international hotels in the 1990s has had to raise its game to keep up with the newer competition. Set at the top of the ISR Plaza, one of the city's first tower blocks, beside Fountains Square, the Radisson has 40 spacious rooms, each with a sweeping view of the Caspian Sea or the Baku rooftops. Attractions include an indoor pool, sauna and gym, as well as car rental and transfers. Note that not all lifts from the ISR lobby go as far as the upper floors – you may have to wait a while.

Bar. Business Centre. Gym. Internet (free, wireless). Parking (free). Pool. Restaurant. Room service. Spa.

Budget

Red Lion Inn Hotel

Yusuf Mammadaliyev Street 7 (493 0354, www. redlion.az). All buses to Fountains Square. **Rates** from AZN85. **Rooms** 11. **Map** p222 H3 ⑦

Price- and location-wise, this is the ideal spot for a visitor of modest requirements who wishes to relax after a hard day's work. Set above one of the quieter pubs in this bar hub, the Red Lion provides king-size beds in all of its 11 comfortable rooms. Each room also features a large-screen TV with a DVD player and a selection of films, tea and coffee, and free Wi-Fi.

Deluxe rooms also have balconies with city views, but the word you're looking for here is 'homely'.

Bar. Internet (free, wireless).

OLD CITY

Expensive

Meridian

A Zeynalli Street 39 (497 0808, www.meridian hotel.az). Metro Icheri Sheher. **Rates** AZN280. **Rooms** 15. **Map** pp58 N5 ⑧

Something of a landmark hotel, this – hence its hefty rates and solid reputation. The Meridian has been a notch above since it opened in 2003, its façade in Middle Eastern appearance – a familiar part of the cityscape. Back then, much attention was paid to the chic appearance of the 15 guest rooms, slightly minimalist in feel, which still offer a lesson in interior design to some of the Meridian's brasher nearby competitors. Notable other attractions include the City View restaurant, its floor-to-ceiling windows facing out on to the Old City, and the pool table set in the 17th-century cavernous basement. Guests pay extra for the sauna.

Bar. Internet. Parking. Restaurant. Room service.

Moderate

Atropat

Magomayev Street 11-13 (497 8950, www.atropat hotel.com). Metro Icheri Sheher. **Rates** AZN200. **Rooms** 30. **Map** p58 N3 ⑨

The Atropat set high standards for mid-range accommodation when it opened in 2008 and is still a good choice in the Old City. It's hard to find fault with the facilities and services here, especially the rooftop bar, but whoever designed the 30 guest rooms needs a lesson in colour coordination. Everything seems to clash with the carpets and stripy wallpaper, which is a shame as the rooms are a decent size. Aware of the fact that there's now a lot of nearby competition in this price bracket, the Atropat lays on as many services as it can from the friendly reception area, including travel booking, transfers and tour guides. Sadly, Wi-Fi is only provided downstairs rather than every room.

Bar. Business Centre. Concierge. Gym. Restaurants (2). Room service.

CONSUME

The Fab Five

A flurry of five-stars arrives in Baku.

A cluster of luxury hotels will put the Azeri capital on a high-end international footing by the start of 2012.

At a meeting of cabinet ministers in January 2011, President Ilham Aliyev announced in his closing speech that the coming Year of Tourism would produce 'large and remarkable results', given the fact that five five-star hotels would be opening towards the end of it.

The names of the hotels involved would grace any major capital: Four Seasons, Kempinski, Hilton, Marriott and Fairmont. Of these, the most architecturally impressive is the **Fairmont** (*see p95*), which occupies the second of three 200-metre plus (650-foot) towers fashioned in the shape of flames, national symbol of Azerbaijan.

Four Seasons Hotel Baku.

Constructing such a complex building amid the notorious high winds of Baku has proved problematic since the project was launched by the Azeri-Turkish concern DIA Holding in October 2007, and various opening dates – December 2010, April 2011 – have come and gone. The latest estimate for when this 305-room curiosity will open is the first quarter of 2012. The other two towers (*see p69* **The Famous Flames**) will be given over to residential and business use. Note that the complex stands opposite the National Assembly, lending the location extra gravitas.

Equally anticipated is the opening of the **Four Seasons Hotel Baku** (*see below*) in early 2012. With a portfolio including the Gresham Palace in Budapest and the London at Park Lane, this Canadian company has come a long way since building their first hotel in the red-light district of Toronto in the 1960s. Also responsible for the recent and impressive overhaul of the Savoy in London, and the Marriott in Baku, UK architects ReardonSmith were hired to provide a *fin-de-siècle* touch to the façade, which has a classical French look redolent of the mansions of the Oil Boom era. Note that the Hadjinski Mansion (*see p71*) is nearby.

The same design team also worked on the Marriott, or, rather, the **Absheron**

Baleva

Sabir Street 12 (437 2115, www.balevahotel.com). Metro Icheri Sheher. **Rates** AZN100. **Rooms** 12. **Map** p58 N3 ⑩

Set back from a pleasant plaza off one of the main thoroughfares of the Old City, the Baleva is another good option for those wishing to stay within Baku's historic heart. Each of the dozen rooms comes with Wi-Fi, air-conditioning, a minibar and kitchenette, the latter handy for those visitors taking advantage of the AZN2,100 deal for monthly stays. A roof terrace with sea views, a bar with pool table and a full English breakfast provide further encouragement to choose the Baleva over its rivals. A recent change of management may see improvements to the slightly tired look of the guest rooms from late 2011 onwards.
Bar. Internet (free, wireless). Room service.

Boyuk Gala

Mirza Mansur Street 68 (437 2582). Metro Icheri Sheher. **Rates** from AZN120. **Rooms** 15. **Map** p58 M5 ⑪

There's little wrong with this neat, 15-room guesthouse in the heart of the Old City. All the rooms have balconies, some with sea views, and guests can also take advantage of the bar and pool table. Decor is a little funkier than at most establishments in a similar price range, and the service tends to be more personable.
Bar. Internet (free, wireless). Room service.

Buta

Gasr Street 16 (492 3475, www.butahotel.com). Metro Icheri Sheher. **Rates** from AZN100. **Rooms** 9. **Map** p58 M4 ⑫

The Buta is a small guesthouse at the lower end of the market in the Old City. Rooms come in three types: single, double and studio, the latter an ideal choice for two visitors here on a business trip. Decor and furnishings exude an indigenous, ethnic atmosphere, with traditional Azeri art and artefacts dotted around the lobby and public areas. Airport transfers and city excursions can be arranged.
Internet (free). Parking (free). Room service.

CONSUME

Fairmont.

JW Marriott Hotel & Residences (*see p96*), occupying a prominent spot near Government House where the former Absheron Hotel accommodated many a delegate in Soviet times. This mixed-use development will host high-spending hotel guests over four floors, with apartments, offices and retail outlets over the other 16.

Facing it, and vying for a similar clientele, is the new **Hilton Baku** (*see p96*), with 300-plus guest rooms. Making best use of its seafront location, the new Hilton features a rooftop bar, terrace restaurant and Caspian-facing balconies. With the **Landmark** (*see p99*) also within easy reach, the opening of the Marriott and

the Hilton creates a high-end business and leisure hub around the otherwise very Soviet-looking Government House.

The final big player is Kempinski, with its new property stuck out at Badamdar, a little-known area behind Sabayil and Martyr's Hill. With plenty of room to breathe up there, the **Kempinski Hotel Badamdar, Baku** (*see p95*) is part of a large residential and commercial complex. A short taxi ride from destinations such as the **Chinar** (*see p109*) restaurant and new **Carpet Museum**, the Kempinski should have no problems attracting business travellers to its 250 rooms and suites, Aqua Park Café and luxury spa.

CONSUME

Four Seasons Hotel Baku
Neftchilar prospekt 77-79 (404 2424, www.four seasons.com). Metro Icheri Sheher. **Rooms** 171. **Map** p58 N6 ⑬
Set beside the Old City with waterfront views, the five-star Four Seasons combines the belle époque style of the nearby oil-boom mansions with contemporary amenities such as a penthouse spa and atrium-roofed pool. Most of the 170-plus guest rooms (incorporating nearly 30 luxury suites) feature a balcony overlooking the Caspian or the Old City. Set to open in early 2012. *Photo p97; see also above* **The Fab Five**.

Giz Galasi
Mirza Mansur Street 34 (497 1785, www. gizgalasi.com). Metro Icheri Sheher. **Rates** AZN120. **Rooms** 16. **Map** p58 L5 ⑭
This somewhat modest-looking establishment in the heart of the Old City offers a handful of features rarely found at other hotels in this price range. The small swimming pool is a welcome attraction, as are

the gym and sauna. The restaurant has panoramic sea views from its lofty position four floors up. The guest rooms (15 doubles, one single) are comfortable enough, without breaking new ground design-wise. *Gym. Internet (free). Parking (free). Pool. Restaurant. Room service.*

Horizon
Mirza Mansur Street 62 (492 6786, www.the horizonhotel.biz). Metro Icheri Sheher. **Rates** from AZN120. **Rooms** 12. **Map** p58 M5 ⑮
In business for the best part of a decade, the Horizon is somewhat bizarre, but in a perfectly pleasant sense. First, its pledge: 'If you want to take pleasure in each instant of your life, the Horizon Hotel is at your service.' Secondly, in order to deliver on it, it has decided to name its dozen rooms (spacious, light and tasteful) after golf courses in the British Isles – although golf doesn't seem to be a decorative theme anywhere else. If anything, these eccentricities seem to add to the Horizon's charm, giving it a little more character than the

several other ten-a-penny venues within ten minutes' walk. A half-decent restaurant also helps.
Bar. Internet (free). Restaurant. Room service.

Icheri Sheher
Mamedyarov Street 1/34 (492 5315, 418 9998, www.icheri-sheher.az). Metro Icheri Sheher.
Rates AZN170. **Rooms** 8. **Map** p58 L4
Named after the Old City itself, the Icheri Sheher charges some AZN50 above the going rate for hotels in this neighbourhood, thanks to its imposing and impressive exterior, and tastefully decorated rooms and public areas. The eight rooms (six doubles, two singles) come in two categories, the 'improved' ones featuring heated bathroom floors in addition to the standard Wi-Fi, mini fridges and LCD TVs. One notable feature is the bar on the upper floor, allowing for memorable views over an early-evening drink.
Bar. Internet (free, wireless). Room service.

Kichik Gala Boutique Hotel
Kichik Gala Street 98 (437 1950, 050 548 1122 mobile, www.kichikgalahotel.com). Metro Icheri Sheher. **Rates** AZN100. **Rooms** 13.
Map p58 M2 ⑰
Not boutique but not bad either, the Kichik Gala does an acceptable job of providing reasonable comfort in the AZN100 price range, while also offering the usual 24-hour room service, Wi-Fi, laundry, dry cleaning and airport transfers. Rooms are large enough and done out in light colours. The noon check-in time may also be handy, given the 2pm check-in found almost everywhere else.
Internet (free). Room service.

Museum Inn
G Mahammad Street 3 (497 0722, 497 1522, www.museuminn.az). Metro Icheri Sheher.
Rates from AZN180. **Rooms** 8. **Map** p58 O3 ⑱
Considering the difference in price – just some AZN20 more expensive that one of the three regular doubles – it's worth booking the deluxe upper room of this unusual and attractive anomaly of a hotel, set opposite the Sultan Inn and above a medieval dervish's house. As well as a Jacuzzi, your extra manats get you a beautiful private balcony, peace, privacy and a panoramic view. The other seven rooms aren't shabby either, though they come in a variety of shapes and sizes (and some are small), but the communal vine-strewn terrace where breakfast and other meals may be taken more than makes up for any sense of claustrophobia. Air-conditioning, free Wi-Fi, tea and coffee are provided throughout. Note that the website doesn't begin to do the hotel justice.
Bar. Internet (free). Restaurant. Room service.

Old City Inn
Dalan 10, Kichik Gala Street 16 (497 4369, 497 1448, www.oldcityinn.com). Metro Icheri Sheher.
Rates AZN100. **Rooms** 15. **Map** p58 M3 ⑲

Noah's Ark. *See p95.*

CONSUME

Hilton Baku. *See p96.*

One of the more popular options in the Old City, with pushbikes parked by the lobby a semi-permanent feature, the Old City Inn garners much of its trade from its role as the Business and Tourism School for the Western University, with links to Holland, Edinburgh and Dublin. The 15 rooms are a bit of a mish-mash in terms of size, shape and style, most with grand old fireplaces, others with fabulous views. The roof café is certainly a major feature, though it's a steep climb and there's no lift. All in all, given Baku's equally steep hotel rates, this is a well-priced and attractive establishment in which staff offer guests genuine care and attention.
Bar. Internet (free). Room service.

Old Gates
Kichik Gala Street 8/1 (497 8723, 050 550 3939 mobile, www.oldgateshotel.az). Metro Icheri Sheher. **Rates** from AZN100. **Rooms** 11. **Map** p58 N2 ⑳

This is another example of an establishment in which the extra AZN20 laid out for the 'penthouse' suite is probably worth it – providing you like plenty of space. Other guestrooms are by no means poky, but are hardly cluttered with furniture. The Old

Gates caters to many business customers from the former Soviet Union, hence the conference facilities and Russian-language website (one click brings you to an English version). There are also three bars; the one with a lovely sea view doubles up as a restaurant. Bathrobes are a nice touch.
Bars (3). Business Centre. Internet (free). Parking (free). Restaurant. Room service.

Sultan Inn
Boyuk Gala Street 20 (437 2305, www.sultan inn.com). Metro Icheri Sheher. **Rates** from AZN230. **Rooms** 11. **Map** p58 O3 ㉑

Baku's stand-out boutique hotel also enjoys a stand-out location, close to the Maiden's Tower and with bar and restaurant terraces on its upper floors with great views. All 11 rooms, done out in tasteful shades of brown, come equipped with a stately fireplace and are lent a further sense of grandeur with a split-level layout in both the standard and superior categories, the difference between the two being space and AZN20. In winter, you can gaze at a roaring fire from the comfort of your sizeable bed. The Nuans hospitality group ensures that standards are high at the two restaurants and bar; the

CONSUME

Terrace Garden and Open Space are destinations in their own right, partly thanks to perhaps the finest view from a bar stool or dining table in all Baku – expansive and sea-facing. Inside, the House of Sultans also offers quality Azeri and international cuisine, continuing the historic design theme with contemporary touches.

Bar. Concierge. Internet (free). Parking (free). Restaurants (2). Room service.

▶ *For reviews of the Terrace Garden and Open Space, see p109 and p121.*

Budget

Azeri Guest House

Asef Zeynalli Street 39 (497 0228). Metro Icheri Sheher. **Rates** *from AZN80.* **Rooms** *11.* **Map** *p58 N5* ㉒

The main feature at this standard B&B in the Old City is the kitchenettes provided in each of the 11 rooms, allowing guests modeshome- cooking facilities. Room service, laundry service and free Wi-Fi, are other perks, as is free parking. Peaceful, historic surroundings are, of course, a given in the Old City.

Concierge. Internet (free, wireless). Parking (free). Room service.

Noah's Ark

Ilyas Efendiyev Street, off 10th Gala Ln (437 3996, 437 3886, 497 0982, www.noahsark-hotel.com). Metro Icheri Sheher. **Rates** *AZN82-AZN92.* **Rooms** *8.* **Map** *p58 M3* ㉓

What is remarkable about this hotel is not only the price, perhaps the cheapest in the Old City, but the standard of service and services. The rates given above are for a room only – an extra three manats will get you breakfast (plus tea, coffee and Wi-Fi), an extra 13 manats buys lunch, and extra 50-odd buys dinner as well. There's also some kind of 'all-inclusive' package that includes a computer and

fax machine. All guests have the friendly receptionist at their beck and call for 24 hours a day (not to mention room service), as well as access to the Ark Club rooftop restaurant and bar (sadly there's no lift). The smaller rooms are, well, pretty small, but it's surprising how many guests here are repeat visitors or here by recommendation. The grocery store and cashpoint downstairs provide extra convenience. *Photos p93.*

Bar. Internet (free). Parking (AZN1). Restaurant. Room service.

SABAYIL & WEST BAKU

Expensive

Flame Towers Fairmont Baku

Martyr's Hill (www.fairmont.com). All buses to Martyr's Hill. **Rooms** *305.* **Map** *p221 B6* ㉔

The most dramatic of the big five hotel openings, now scheduled for 2012, the Flame Towers Fairmont is also the most complex. It's of a triumvirate of buildings on the top of Martyr's Hill that are fashioned, quite incredibly, in the shape of rising flames. *See also p90* **The Fab Five.**

▶ *For more about Flame Towers, see p69.*

Kempinski Hotel Badamdar, Baku

Mikayil Mushfig Street 23 (538 9090, www.kempinski.com). **Rates** *AZN154-AZN250.* **Rooms** *283.* **Map** *p221 A5* ㉕

One of the big five openings of late 2011, the Kempinski is a part of a huge complex named after the previously underused area of town above Sabayil and Martyr's Hill: Badamdar. In addition to rooms and suites, the five-star hotel has a spa area, offices, private residences and a commercial centre. *See p90* **The Fab Five.**

Bar. Business centre. Gym. Internet. Restaurants. Room service. Spa.

Park Inn by Radisson. *See p96.*

CONSUME

BULVAR & WATERFRONT
Expensive

Absheron JW Marriott Hotel & Residences
Azadlig Square (www.marriott.com). Metro Sahil. **Rooms** 243. **Map** p221 D4 ㉖
Right on Azadlig Square by Government House, close to the Hilton and set to open in early 2012, the Marriott fills the space where the landmark Absheron Hotel used to be, with 243 rooms, a luxury spa, pool and a huge amount of meeting space. *See p90* **The Fab Five**.

Hilton Baku
Azadlig prospekt 1 (464 5000, www.hilton.com). Metro Sahil. **Rates** from AZN225. **Rooms** 309. **Map** p221 D4 ㉗
Dominating the waterfront by Government House, the Hilton, which opened in late 2011, takes full advantage of its waterfront location. The rooftop bar, terrace restaurant and pricier of the 309 rooms all enjoy Caspian views. A spa, gym and business facilities maintain Hilton's usual international standards. *See p90* **The Fab Five**. *Photo p94.*
Bar. Business centre. Gym. Internet. Restaurants. Room service. Spa.

Moderate

Park Inn by Radisson
Azadlig prospekt 1 (490 6000, www.park inn.com). Metro Sahil. **Rates** from AZN195. **Rooms** 248. **Map** p221 D4 ㉘
Park Inns are Radisson's funky, urban brand, whose logo, rooms and public areas feature striking, primary colours and whose smart staff are trained under the mantra 'Yes, I can!' That said, this great monolith set on the seafront near the Museum Centre feels like most other chains accommodating visiting groups of business travellers – the half-dozen meeting rooms allowing such visitors the facility of never having to leave the hotel at all. To that end, all said meeting rooms feature an element of natural light, and the Glory restaurant, Victor's bar and the eleven bar/club/sushi restaurant keep guests fed, watered and entertained to international standard. There is also a gym, cashpoint and currency exchange on-site. Around half the rooms are blessed with a view of the Bulvar and Caspian (the others look out over Baku's traffic-swamped city centre). All have been renovated relatively recently and all have been given at least the illusion of individuality with Park Inn's signature bright colours, even down to the cups guests can use to make a tea or coffee. Wi-Fi, 24-hour room service and spacious work desks are also a given. Having said that, with the late 2011/early 2012 opening of the Hilton and Marriott on the seafront nearby, the Park Inn is going to have to raise its game in order to keep its occupancy rates healthy. *Photos p95.*

INSIDE TRACK CHEAP SLEEPS

Such are the draconian visa regulations imposed by Azerbaijan, that casual travellers are thin on the ground these days, and Baku suffers from a dearth of decent hostels – the hostels that do exist tend to cater to Turkish truck drivers and small-time traders. Cheaper hotels with shared bathroom facilities include **Hotel Araz** (Yusif Safarov 30) and **Hotel Velotrek** (Tbilisi prospekt 3007, 012 431 5187) – but even then you can expect to pay at least AZN20-AZN30 per person.

Bar. Business centre. Gym. Internet (free). Parking (free). Restaurants (2). Room service.
▶ *For a review of eleven, see p122.*

Sea Port
Neftchilar prospekt 58 (493 6071, www.seaport.az). All buses to Bulvar. **Rates** AZN145. **Rooms** 14. **Map** p221 D4 ㉙
Part of the gleaming new(ish) harbour building on the edge of Baku city centre, the Sea Port provides 14 rooms (singles and doubles) of relative comfort but little charm or character. If staying at the harbour is a priority and you're not short of cash, then it may be worth laying out an extra AZN15 for the reasonably impressive suite. Until this eastern end of Baku's seafront is fully developed (note the nearby Park Plaza business and commercial complex, set to open in 2012), and until Baku's harbour can service regular, scheduled passenger traffic to and from other Caspian destinations, the Sea Port Hotel will continue to exude a somewhat ghostly atmosphere. On the positive side, its sea-view terrace café and restaurant (*see p113*), without winning any prizes, has a setting that makes it a destination in itself.
Bar. Internet (free). Parking (free). Restaurant.

NORTH BAKU
Expensive

Park Hyatt
Izmir Street 1033 (490 1234, www.hyatt.com). All buses to the Bakikhanov roundabout. **Rates** from AZN240. **Rooms** 248. **Map** p220 B2 ㉚
Neighbour and sister to the Hyatt Regency (*see p98*) around the corner, the Park Hyatt shares the same top-of-the-range attractions: three pools, tennis and squash courts, and spa. Space is the key here: the Park, Club King and Club Twin Rooms are generously sized, and some rooms have balconies; suites range from large to mansion-like. The better suites are seriously luxurious, featuring saunas, baths with spa jets, art by notable Azeri artists and handmade carpets. But guests in the standard rooms can

still soak in baths of black granite, with bathroom fittings in easy-on-the-eye shades of brown. Live music is laid on at the ground-floor bar, the Park Lounge. Another plus is the fact that all of the hotel didn't officially open until 2010, so it still feels new and fresh – the Park Hyatt should give the high-end newcomers a run for their money for a good while to come.

Bar. Business Centre. Concierge. Disabled-adapted rooms. Gym. Internet (free). Parking (free). Pool. Restaurants (3). Room service. Spa.

Qafqaz Point

Kazimzade Street 118 (510 878, http://qafqaz pointhotel.com). Metro Elmlar Akademiyasi. **Rates** from AZN240. **Rooms** 74. **Map** p220 A3 ㉛

This lesser-known hotel in the top price bracket, part of the first Azerbaijani hotel chain, offers a range of attractive features, not the least of which is the very appearance of its exterior, slightly off-kilter and set at unusual angles. Inside, 74 rooms (44 standard, 26 superior and four suites) are comfortable and spacious, modern in look, with high-speed Wi-Fi to boot. Many enjoy striking city views, as does the Panorama restaurant at the top of the building.

Bar. Business Centre. Gym. Internet (free). Parking (free). Pool. Restaurants (2). Room service. Spa.

Moderate

Ambassador

Samed Vurgun Street 934 (449 4930-3, www.hotelambassador.az). **Rates** AZN180. **Rooms** 58. **Map** p220 B1 ㉜

With the scheduled opening of five spanking new hotels in the same category by late 2011/early 2012, all of serious international pedigree, this somewhat staid and functional five-star business hotel is going to be left out on a limb. A location just north of the Azerbaijan Medical University amid nondescript streets hardly helps either. There's little to fault the rooms, all spacious and furnished to modern tastes, and equipped with a sofa as well as a Jacuzzi in the equally spacious bathrooms. A gym and pool also help push the Ambassador's case but the other public areas – most notably the Colonnade restaurant where breakfast is taken, the Volume lobby bar, the Patiserie Karamelka and the 6-th Avenue Roof Bar – barely deliver on the 'typical European ambience' promise as mentioned in the brochure. Perhaps the management, local C-Group Hotels of which this is the flagship, should begin to veer away from bland attempts to ape anything 'typically European', and instead aim for something of local personality and character.

Bar. Business Centre. Gym. Internet (free). Parking (free). Pool. Restaurants (2). Room service.

Chirag Plaza

Tbilisi prospekt 49C (499 7200, 050 313 8550 mobile, www.chiragplaza.az). All buses to the Bakikhanov roundabout. **Rates** from AZN182. **Rooms** 42. **Map** p220 A1 ㉝

Newly opened in Baku's hub of business hotels, this swish, 42-room establishment was built by a German concern and is expected to rely on Germany for 30% of its custom. Not yet fully operational at the time of writing – a lobby bar and rooftop restaurant are expected to open in early 2012 – the Chirag

Four Seasons Hotel Baku. *See p91.*

CONSUME

CONSUME

Chirag Plaza. *See p97.*

is already looking spruce, with stylish Spanish furniture in each of the spacious brown and white rooms. Bathrooms are equally roomy, with nice big bathtubs and rain showers. The only downside is the views of Baku, more attractive in the historic scenes mounted in the corridors than out of some of the guestroom windows.

Bar. Business Centre. Concierge. Disabled-adapted rooms (2). Internet (free). Parking (free). Restaurant. Room service.

Grand Hotel Europe

Tbilisi prospekt 1025-30 (490 7090, www. grand-europe.com). All buses to the Bakikhanov roundabout. **Rates** AZN165-AZN200. **Rooms** 96. **Map** p220 A2 ③④

In the days before there were Hiltons and Marriotts going up in Baku, this showy upscale business hotel was the bee's knees in showy upscale business hotels. Now it's looking very dated indeed, its Capone's nightclub a sorry remnant of the get-rich-quick era in the years following Azeri independence. Guest rooms display a similar gaudy appearance, all chintz, although all are inarguably spacious, some with distant views to to sea. Nothing wrong with the Olympus Health Club & Spa, either, with its Technogym equipment and cardio machines. All in all, though, a dinosaur from an ever more distant era, and in need of an overhaul.

Bar. Business Centre. Gym. Internet (free). Parking (free). Restaurant. Room service.

Hyatt Regency Baku

A Bakikhanov Street 1 (496 1234, www.hyatt.com). All buses to the Bakikhanov roundabout. **Rates** from AZN210. **Rooms** 182. **Map** p220 B2 ③⑤

When Hyatt transformed the former Hotel Nakhchivan of Soviet lore in the mid 1990s, it not only brought Baku its first proper western business hotel, but gave this locality, around the Bakikhanov round-about north of the city centre, a de facto expat name: the Hyatt area. The fact that the complex now features the Park Hyatt around the corner (*see p96*) only confuses first-time visitors. So what does today's business visitor get for his 200 manats? Well, more than most hotels can provide the active guest, that's for sure. Tennis courts, squash courts, aerobics, table tennis, a spa and three pools for a start. Rooms, categorised as 'queen', 'twin' and 'deluxe queen', feature goose-down pillows, marble baths, a minibar and high-speed internet. Of the three bars, you'll find quality cocktails at the Beluga and a proper pint at the Britannia, both open in the evening only. Carnivores will be hard pushed to find a better steak in town than at the Grill. Of all the other amenities and services, perhaps a babysitter and a florist are the most useful.
Bars (3). Business Centre. Concierge. Disabled-adapted rooms. Gym. Internet (free). Parking (free). Pool. Restaurants (3). Room service. Spa.

SAHIL & EAST BAKU

Expensive

Excelsior Hotel Baku
Heydar Aliyev prospekt 2 (496 8000, www.excelsior hotelbaku.az). Metro Nariman Narimanov. **Rates** from AZN250. **Rooms** 61. **Map** p220 E2 ③⑥
The Excelsior is where Baku meets Las Vegas – they could even have filmed the closing scene from *Oceans Eleven* outside it. Dripping with opulence and unsurprisingly popular with visiting Russians, the Excelsior contains 61 rooms that range in size from the generous to the gigantic (the 300sq m Imperial Suite). Amenities and services are equally luxurious, starting with the Aura Wellness Center, so far the finest hotel spa in Baku. Aromatherapy, reiki, hot-stone therapies and sea-salt massages feature among the treatments, as well as classes in belly dancing, yoga, pilates and aerobics. Along with the spa, there's also a beauty salon, sauna, tennis court, squash courts and state-of-the-art gym. A 24m heated indoor pool complements an almost equally large outdoor one with a sunbathing terrace and poolside bar, one of six bar-restaurants on-site. The only downside, apart from the cost, is the distance from the city centre – but you're close to the main road for the airport, only a 20-minute limousine drive away.
Bar. Business Centre. Gym. Internet (free). Parking (free). Pool. Restaurants (6). Room service. Spa.

Moderate

12 Inn Bulvar
Uzeyir Hajibeyov Street 27 (498 1203, 498 1205, www.12inn.az). Metro Sahil or 28 May. **Rates** from AZN170. **Rooms** 21. **Map** p221 D4 ③⑦

A lot of paint has been used in this somewhat unusual, mid-range hotel in the city centre, and not all of it wisely. A look at the names of each of the 12 standard rooms gives you a clue as to how they might look: Cherry; Aquamarine; Lemon; Kiwi, and Lilac. Braver visitors may also wish to risk Safari, Delight or Oriental. Somehow, this allows the 12 Inn to call itself 'boutique'. On the plus side, all rooms come with a plasma-screen TV, internet and a minibar. Another main feature is the 24 Café, so named after its non-stop operating hours, offering cocktails, cigars, breakfasts until 11am and *biznis* lunches. It's all a bit bizarre but at least original, and very much against the grain of Baku's often-staid hotel stock in this price bracket.
Bar. Internet. Parking (free). Restaurant. Room service.

Hotel Respublika
Khagani Street 24 (598 1048, www.hotel respublika.com). Metro Sahil. **Rates** from AZN200. **Rooms** 27. **Map** p221 D4 ③⑧
One line in the introductory blurb on the website should tell you all you need to know about the Hotel Respublika: 'All rooms are suite and presidential, that is the reason of presence of the visitors only of appropriate level.' The Respublika, we may construe, is a suitably palatial establishment for high-ranking officials, diplomats and businessmen. Set in one of those stately mansions that makes you appreciate the kind of money that was made here a century or more ago, the Respublika accommodates its guests in the style to which they are accustomed, from the sizeable baths to service provisions such as 'personal security'.
Bar. Business centre. Internet (free). Parking (free). Pool. Restaurants. Room service.

Landmark Hotel
Nizami Street 90A (465 2000, www.the landmarkhotel.az). Metro Sahil. **Rates** from AZN200. **Rooms** 64. **Map** p221 D4 ③⑨
Landmark by name, landmark by nature, this high-rise dominating east-central Baku makes full use of its splendid location. Its Sky Bar provides wonderful sea views, but the two-floor health club – high-tech gym, 28m pool, sauna and steam bath – also enjoy panoramic vistas thanks to floor-to-ceiling windows overlooking the Caspian. The 64 rooms, too, are flooded with natural light and either face out to sea or across the city. Within, luxury comes in the form of Egyptian cotton bed linen, king-sized beds and 32-inch flatscreen TVs. Spacious bathrooms feature heated floors and towel rails, rain showers and fluffy robes. In operation since 2009, the Landmark still feels new and eager to please – perhaps more so now with so much keen competition coming on board.
Bar. Business centre. Concierge. Disabled-adapted room. Gym. Internet (free). Parking (free). Pool. Restaurants (5). Room service. Spa.
► *For a review of the Sky Bar, see p123.*

CONSUME

Restaurants & Cafés

Plenty of good restaurants – as long as you can swallow the bill.

Eating out in Baku is prohibitively expensive and, perhaps worse, rather hit-or-miss. Financial burdens can be eased by the fact that nearly everywhere puts on an affordable daytime *biznes lanch* of two or three courses, but the capricious nature of the local restaurant trade – most notably where service is concerned – might be harder to swallow if you're paying AZN30 for a main course and just as much for wine.

Wine, in fact, is a regular point of complaint of many expat diners, tired of paying Mayfair hotel tariffs for a bottle of distinctly average plonk. There are good Azeri wines (*see p39*) but only a few establishments that know how to advise on selecting them properly. Sadly, the one proper wine bar to operate in the Old City, Ibrus, closed in 2011. Baku most certainly needs another.

CONSUME

THE RESTAURANTS

Azeri cuisine can be very good with the right chef, right meat and right *mangal* grill or *sadj* skillet. Accompanying vegetables – aubergines, tomatoes, potatoes – can also be a delight. (For more, *see 34-39* **Food & Drink**.) Throw in the right atmosphere, ideally a lively night in one of the converted caravanserai establishments in the Old City, and you will have a memorable experience indeed. The best such location is the **Mugham Club** (*see p109*). Outside the Old City, **Sultan's** (*see p105*) or **Penjere** (*see p115*) are probably your best options.

For international cuisine, the ambitious and all-conquering Azerbaijani Hospitality Group has cornered the market in Asian food in fashionable surroundings – **Zakura** (*see p107*) and, above all, **Chinar** (*see p111*), pack out with high-spending expats every night. The group's next venture, **Sahil** (*see p113*), opening around the time this guide is published, should prove interesting as it is slated to feature contemporary Azeri cuisine, a first.

There are surprisingly few Indian restaurants, perhaps because landmark bar **Adam's** (*see p118*), now in a new location by Fountains Square, has long been known for

---

❶ Blue numbers given here correspond to the location of each restaurant as marked on the street maps. *See p58, pp220-223.*

---

offering exemplary curries at affordable prices. A number of other expat faux pubs have followed suit. Expat Americans tend to favour the burgers in the **Sunset Café** (*see p105*).

There are a number of above-average Italian establishments, most notably **Scalini's** (*see p115*) and **L'Oliva** (*see p104*), but Baku has yet to witness the opening of a top-quality French or Spanish restaurant. Of the regional Caucasian and Russian spots, only the **Georgia Café** (*see p109*) in the Old City stands out.

As most cafés also function as restaurants, we've included both in this chapter – venues such as **Ali & Nino** (*see below*), **Mirvari** (*see p113*) and **Café Mozart** (*see p102*) are more known as being places for tea and cakes or snacks, but offer hot dishes too.

DOWNTOWN

★ Ali & Nino

Z Taghiyev Street 16-18 (493 1530). All buses to Fountains Square. **Open** 10am-11pm daily. **Main courses** €€. **Map** p222 H3 **❶**
International

In the same family as the recommended chain of book-shops of the same name, itself named after the well-known love story of an Azerbaijani youth who falls in love with a Georgian princess, Ali & Nino sits oppo-site the chain's most central branch, just off the main square. Tastefully and artistically themed, its main room at street level is long, light and narrow, the kind of room Ali, Nino and their fictitious contemporaries

might have spent time in, with a wind-up gramophone, old lampshades and family portraits from the Tsarist era. Note the mounted copies of seminal satirical periodical *Molla Nasreddin*. A clock is set to 5.15, fateful hour of Ali's death. There's a lovely detailed mural depicting scenes from the book, with the wedding as centrepiece. Service here starts with breakfast, continental or English with bacon, then the kitchen sta;ys open into the evening, providing pastas (fusilli with aubergine and chicken, farfalle with chicken liver), salads (duck and orange), and mains such as salmon in orange and coriander sauce, and trout in parsley and wine. Drinks-wise, there's Illy coffee, smoothies and themed cocktails (an Ali & Nino consists of Martini, cassis and Malibu; a Springtime in Baku is Absolut, Malibu and juices). Everything is priced affordably for Baku, and there's a mezzanine for reading about the romance – or fomenting it.
▶ *For a review of the bookshop, see p127.*

Azza Fyujin
Radisson Blu Hotel, 17th floor, ISR Plaza, Nizami Street 69 (498 2402, www.azza.az). All buses to Fountains Square. **Open** noon-11pm daily. **Main courses** €€€€. **Map** p222 G/H2 ❷ **Fusion**
Expanding from a chain of café-bakeries, Azza now runs three panoramic venues at the Radisson Blu, including this 17th-floor Asian fusion restaurant. If you can cast your eyes away from the jaw-dropping view of Baku and the Caspian Sea, you may wish to consider a menu that combines the flavours of China and elsewhere in the Far East. Dishes of crispy duck, duck with apricot and cream sauce or jumbo prawns in wine sauce will set you back the best part of AZN30, unless you go for the sushi option – the house nigiri with beluga is complemented by crab, squid, and maki or uramaki. The business lunch is affordable and unadventurous, with standard favourites self-served from a central buffet station.

Prices

To provide some kind of indication on meal prices, for each restaurant we give a code in euro symbols. As the prices of main courses can vary so wildly, even on the same menu, these are only rough guidelines:
€ Budget
€€ Moderate
€€€ Expensive
€€€€ Luxury
Not that these codes are for dining à la carte – most venues also offer a discount business lunch.

Beyrut
Z Taghiyev Street 19 (598 0665). All buses to Fountains Square. **Open** 11am-midnight daily. **Main courses** €€. **Map** p222 H3 ❸ **Lebanese**
This restaurant deserves to be better known. Unfortunately, the decor is rather tired, but the atmosphere is welcoming and the food good. As the name suggests, the cuisine is Lebanese and provides an interesting change from the mostly Azeri/Turkish places in the area. The menu is comprehensive, the salads fresh, exciting and innovative. The main courses, if you can manage one, are both satisfying and substantial.

★ Café City
Islam Seferli Street 1 (598 8686, www.caspian coast.com). All buses to Fountains Square. **Open** 11am-midnight Mon-Thur; 11am-2am Fri, Sat; noon-midnight Sun. **Main courses** €€. **Map** p222 G3 ❹ **Café**
One of the best choices on the main square, the recently opened and very popular Café City offers

Ali & Nino.

CONSUME

shade and sunshine, a view of the fountains and plentiful, fairly priced cuisine. Don't be put off by the pages of colourful photographs that make up the extensive menu – you can order the kebabs (lamb, beef or *khan*; plum sauce extra), steak or salmon happy in the knowledge that dishes are well cooked, carefully presented and served (eventually) with a smile. At AZN8, the daily-changing business lunch (noon-3.30pm) is a veritable bargain: soup, salad and a hot dish with rice or pasta, plus juice or water. Standard cocktails are in the AZN6 range, coming into their own when this late-opening spot turns more bar-like after dark. If it's too windy, there's plenty of room inside, in the stark white, contemporary interior.

Café Mozart

Ali-Zadeh Street 2 (493 1911). All buses to Fountains Square. **Open** 8am-2am daily. **Main courses** €€€. **No credit cards.** Map p223 H4 ❺ Café

'Since 1992' boasts the bright orange menu cover, and the garish colour theme continues through to the decor. Like the Klimt reproductions lamely expressing the notion of Vienna, the Mozart feels old and past it, much like its staff, slow and forgetful even by Baku standards. Yet such is the prominence of its location, right behind the Azerbaijan cinema, with one enclosed terrace adjoining an open one, that the Mozart remains one of Baku's most popular meeting places. The menu promises steak camembert, pan-fried lamb and fried duck, though you may be better opting for something simpler and cheaper, perhaps an aubergine pizza or tuna salad. Breakfast (AZN12) consists of a boiled egg, cheese and olives but, morning or night, most customers are content with a fresh juice or milkshake. A kitschy 1960s pop soundtrack adds a touch of fun.

Dalida

3rd Floor, Nargiz Trade Centre, Rasul Rza Street 340 (496 8861, www.dalida.az). All buses to Fountains Square. **Open** 11am-2am daily. **Main courses** €€€. Map p222 G3 ❻ International

Perched on the roof of Nargiz Mall, overlooking bustling Fountains Square, Dalida's expansive, shady roof terrace makes it the ideal place for a spot of people-watching. Drinks are reasonably priced and there is a decent selection of cocktails, although they can be a little on the weak side, so don't be afraid to ask for another splash of liquor. The food menu is vast with a variety of international dishes available, including pasta, pizza, steaks and burgers. Baku is not flush with decent outdoor spots, so the roof terrace fills up fast during the summer months with a mix of locals and expats.

Dragon

Samed Vurgun Street 25 (493 2112, www. dragon-dining.az). Metro Sahil. **Open** noon-3pm, 6-11pm daily. **Main courses** €€€. Map p222 J1 ❸❻ Fusion

Watch out, or you'll walk right past this one. Just up from City Mart, Dragon has a plethora of cocktails and unusual combinations of Asian fusion food, with a particular focus on seafood – options include scallop tempura, lobster, tuna with black beans, wasabi prawns and crab, although our favourite is definitely the nasi goreng. Owned by the same people behind the Zakura sushi restaurant further downtown, Dragon is tucked away and worth the extra few minutes' walk from the centre. Home or office delivery is also available.

Favvara

Fountains Square (050 215 4568 mobile). All buses to Fountains Square. **Open** 10am-midnight daily. **Main courses** €€. Map p222 G3 ❼ Café

CONSUME

Dalida.

Reading the Menu

What's what in Azeri food and drink.

chörek generic bread.
tandir bread from a tandir oven.
lavash flatbread.
yag butter
pendir cheese
khama cream
gatig yoghurt
bal honey
chay tea
gähva, kofe coffee
südlü gähva
coffee with milk
yumurta eggs
gaiganag, omlet omelette
su water
süd milk
duz salt
istiot pepper
gänd sugar
yag oil
sirkä vinegar
dondurma ice-cream
khämir yemäyi pasta
pitsa pizza
düyü rice
salat salad

MEAT
guzu mutton
mal äti beef
toyug chicken
bildirchin quail
balig fish
forel trout
kolbasa pork sausage
kebab kebab

FRUIT AND VEGETABLES
kartof potato
pomidor tomato
badimjan aubergine

istiot pepper
shü-ud dill
tarxun tarragon
soghan spring onions
sarimsagh garlic leaves
reyhan purple basil
kir salat wild rocket
khiyar cucumbers
turp radish
nar pomegranate
khurma persimmon
heyva quince
müräbbä preserved fruit or jam
goz nut
alma apple
üzüm grape
lumu lemon
yemish melon
portaghal orange
shaftali peach
gavali plum
alcha sour plum
chiyäläk strawberry
böyürtkän wild strawberry
tut mulberry
garpiz watermelon

DRINKS
pive beer
chakhir wine
girmizi red
guru dry
agh white
gazli sparkling
shampan champagne
mineral su mineral water
arag vodka
viski whisky
brendi, konyak brandy
buz ice
meyvä suyu, sok fruit juice

**CUTLERY, CROCKERY
& MISCELLANEOUS**
bichaq knife
chängäl fork
gashig spoon
boshgab plate
shüshä bottle
stäkan glass
banka can
älsilän napkin
dish üchün chöp toothpick
külgabi ashtray
hesab the bill

CONSUME

This new spot, under the same managerial umbrella as the Three Graces, benefits from a Fountains Square location but suffers from the lack of a terrace. It feels more like a café than a restaurant – everything is a little too new and white, with Russian pop videos blaring far too loudly in one corner – but there's little wrong with the food or the prices. For AZN10, the business lunch (noon-4pm) is prefaced by complimentary appetisers of olives, spreads and fresh breads, before a tasty daily-changing soup arrives. The mains choice of pasta, burgers or pizza won't break new ground gastronomically but all are well prepared. Greek-style grilled lamb, oven-baked pike perch and beef medallions in a creamy mushroom sauce are highlights on the à la carte menu. Mention must be made of the desserts, each enticingly displayed on a plate with the name of the restaurant squiggled in chocolate around it, ideal for taking with you and sitting by the fountain.

▶ *For a review of the Three Graces, see p107.*

Sultan's.

Flavour

Zarifa Aliyeva Street 12 (498 1030, www. flavour.az). All buses to Fountains Square or metro Sahil. **Open** 11am-2am daily. **Main courses €€€. Map** p223 J4 ❽ **Azerbaijani/ Turkish**

With its own London phone box outside, an impressively wide entrance and Armani located just next door, Flavour has a pretty glam feel to it – and Baku's privileged classes will feel very much at home among the ornate, classical decor, complete with gold statues. The predominantly Azeri and Turkish cuisine, with a Russian influence, is on the expensive side. Live classical music and a private room complete the package as a place for special occasions.

Inkino

Nizami Street 63 (596 0304, www.inkino grandcafe.com). Metro Sahil. **Open** 11am-11pm Mon-Fri; noon-midnight Sat, Sun. **Main courses €€€. Map** p222 G3 ❾ **Italian**

Hidden away on a back street, the recently opened Inkino is an as yet relatively unknown Italian restaurant just a block from Fountains Square. Inside it is light, modern and quirky, with a well-stocked bar and inviting sofas. The pizzas are slightly disappointing but the pasta dishes are much better, although portions are on the small side. Attentive Italian maître d' Giraudo Fabrizio is happy to cater to different food needs, while the waiters are friendly. And where else in Baku can you find the daily business lunch option posted on Facebook? A mini cinema is available for sports/Eurovision screenings.

★ L'Oliva

Z Taghiyev Street 14 (493 0954). All buses to Fountains Square. **Open** noon-10.30pm daily. **Main courses €€€. Map** p222 H3 ❿ **Italian/ Japanese**

This venue just off Fountains Square has two restaurants and a cocktail bar. The cosy bistro-style Green Olive restaurant serves excellent, reasonably priced Italian food, coupled with a warm ambience and pleasantly rustic charm. The varied menu features soups, pastas, pizzas and salads to start, followed by the likes of salmon, steaks and quail. The wines list is impressive and reasonably priced. There's an excellent business lunch deal during the week, including a platter of sushi and a soft drink for AZN10. Downstairs, the Red Olive (open 6pm-2am) is a complete contrast. This cocktail bar-cum-Japanese restaurant has plush furniture and a sophisticated atmosphere – dark red sofas and soft lighting create a quiet haven after an energetic day. The bartender knows his cocktails and willingly accommodates personal tastes. The oriental food menu is intriguing, though not cheap.

Paul's Steak House & Rock Bar

Zagarpalan/Rafibayli streets (050 502 5507 mobile). All buses to Fountains Square.

CONSUME

Paul's Steak House & Rock Bar.

Open noon-late Mon-Sat. **Main courses** €€. **Map** p222 F3 **Steak**

Paul's may not be in an easy location for the visitor, nestled as it is in a quiet backwater behind Azerbaijan prospekt opposite the MUM department store, but it's worth seeking out if you're craving a good steak. And the steak is very good, rivalled only by the potato salad. Sausage and chips is another tasty option. Equally attractive is the surprisingly green beer garden, which provides a cool, shady place to enjoy a beer in a desert city during summer. In winter, the mostly foreign clientele pack into the small chalet-style restaurant. Rock music plays continuously but quietly in the background. Apart from its notable hospitality, Paul's wins out as an offbeat, quirky find among the more conventional Baku eateries – an in-the-know spot with a reliable contact for authentic caviar.

Ravioli

Rasul Rza Street 31 (495 4510). All buses to Fountains Square. **Open** noon-11pm daily. **Main courses** €€. **Map** p222 H2 Italian/Asian

Who would have thought it would be possible to mix Italian and Asian successfully and avoid creating a tacky muddle? Renovated at the beginning of 2011, Ravioli seems to have managed the feat, although many don't yet know about its new incarnation. While indulging in a spot of people-watching on Rasul Rza, feast on tasty European salads, pastas and pizzas, Chinese dumplings and spring rolls, or Japanese noodles. The prosciutto is particularly good here. Prices are reasonable and the location is hard to beat.

Sultan's

Khagani Street 10 (598 0555). All buses to Fountains Square. **Open** noon-midnight daily. **Main courses** €€. **Map** p222 J2/3 **Azeri**

With an open-plan grill for cooking kebabs along one wall and bread ovens along another, this airy, friendly restaurant produces mouthwatering dishes and also provides ample people-watching potential. Order a selection of wonderful meze dishes by pointing at the trolley, but be aware: they are accompanied by hot, puffy bread straight from the oven, which is delicious but invites serious over-indulgence. Follow this with a kebab from the main menu – liver kebab threaded with lamb-tail fat is particularly good and a well-known local delicacy. Drinks are reasonably priced and the meal is always finished with *chay*, which does not appear on the bill. The service is especially good.

★ Sunset Café

Rasul-Zadeh Street (492 2292). All buses to Fountains Square. **Open** noon-11pm Mon-Sat; noon-10.30pm Sun. **Main courses** €€. **Map** p223 G4 **American**

Every expat's favourite, this oasis of Americana sits behind an unassuming façade by the Azerbaijan cinema. Current chef Ryan Kerr learned his chops at the James Beard House in New York, Italy and Barcelona, before arriving here to up standards and add authenticity to the mainly Tex-Mex offering. Sourcing ingredients as best he can – even converting part of his flat into a herb garden – Kerr uses prime, Brazilian meat in his steaks and burgers (available in classic, alpine Swiss and smokehouse varieties). There are also hot dogs and chilli, salads (spicy Thai, roquefort steak) and sandwiches (including the sunset club of roast chicken, bacon and philly). A side of raw fries (thinly sliced potatoes fried from raw) is the classic option in all cases. Kids are taken care of with their own menu (AZN6.50) and family-friendly weekend brunches, when they run amok with crayons around the somewhat cramped interior, which is decked out in old Schlitz beer ads, *Casablanca*-rama and guess-the-title film posters in

CONSUME

CONSUME

Seto at **Landmark**. *See p116.*

Russian. Wine, as everywhere in Baku, is unfeasibly expensive – stick to the beer or tasty cocktails.

Three Graces
Molokan Square (598 2172). All buses to Fountains Square. **Open** 10am-midnight daily. **Main courses** €€€. **Map** p222 J3 ⑭ **Azeri**
This architecturally stunning glass structure in the cool shade of Molokan Square is situated next to a picturesque fountain containing a sculpture of the eponymous ladies surrounded by stalagmites. Sitting upstairs in this Italian restaurant in the evening, gazing out at the illuminated scene, is a romantic and sophisticated experience. There is a large non-smoking section, but choose the smoking area for maximum ambience. Avoid dishes that are likely to be from tinned ingredients, such as the asparagus and artichoke starters, but otherwise the food is authentic and well presented. The local Azeri wines are reasonably priced and very quaffable, especially the shiraz. Downstairs, there is a sushi bar that is popular in the evenings, and a café that serves pastries during the day. *Photo p109.*

★ Zakura
Ali-Zadeh Street 9 (498 1818, www. zakura.az). All buses to Fountains Square. **Open** noon-3pm, 6pm-2am daily. **Main courses** €€€. **Map** p223 H4 ⑮ **Sushi**
This first link in Baku's rapidly expanding Chinar chain, Zakura was head and shoulders above the competition when it opened in 2009. Modelling itself on a high-end *izakaya* – but really more of an upscale sushi bar – Zakura brought London standards to bear when the management had Blue Sky Hospitality take care of its classy design and train its staff. Kenneth Lim of Nobu London fame created a menu featuring house-style sashimi with sea bass, king crab or beef; sushi rolls of salmon skin, foie gras or eel and cucumber; and hot mains such as the popular steamed black cod with spicy red bean miso. You'll pay around AZN15 for the mains or AZN10 for the Zakura-style sashimi and sushi rolls. Eat in the stylish restaurant or make up a quick snack in a bento box. *Photo p108.*
▶ *For sister restaurant Chinar, see p111.*

OLD CITY

ART Garden
Asef Zeynalli Street 22 (050 669 1331, www.artgroup.az). Metro Icheri Sheher. **Open** 11am-midnight daily. **Main courses** €€. **No credit cards. Map** p58 N4 ⑯ **Azeri**
ART Garden is the most overtly modern of the handful of atmospheric, historic caravanserais that have been converted into restaurants in the Old City. Laid out in traditional fashion, the venue comprises a large, round central courtyard surrounded by alcoved dining spaces, each with a flatscreen TV, self-controlled air-conditioning and notable examples of modern art – hence the name. It belongs to the same group that

THE BEST RESTAURANTS
For burgers and fries **Sunset Café**. *See p105.*
For pan-Asian treats **Chinar**. *See p111.*
For stellar kebabs **Sultan's**. *See p105.*
For kiln-baked bread **Tandir**. *See p109.*
For rustic charm and superb pasta **L'Oliva**. *See p104.*
For a Caspian view on the side **Terrace Garden**. *See p111.*

runs the ART Salon, Azerbaijan's first and biggest post-Soviet private gallery. The Azeri menu features a range of kebabs – liver, beef, entrails – as well as stewed sturgeon and lamb. If these don't sound appealing, then it's worth investigating the salads (pomegranate, beef tongue, brinza cheese and sweet peppers) and soups (ideally *dushbara* with minced lamb and pasta). Caviar (black AZN50, red AZN25) is another starter option. Sheesha pipes (AZN25-AZN50) come in apple, grapefruit and pineapple varieties, and cocktails (AZN10) include the house 'Secret' which seems to feature copious amounts of vodka.

Café Caramel
Boyuk Gala Street 21 (598 0573). Metro Icheri Sheher. **Open** 10am-11pm daily. **Main courses** €€€. **Map** p58 N3 ⑰ **International**
This recently opened branch of the ever-popular mini-chain is a welcome addition to the Old City. Café Caramel is a major haunt of Baku's 'ladies who lunch' – a modern, bright, bustling restaurant that also offers sumptuous cakes and good coffee. Situated opposite the police station, it has a small outdoor area opposite a carpet shop, so you can sit with a coffee and admire the local handicrafts. It is also a haven for foreign visitors, as the menu is in English and the waiters are more fluent than usual. Business lunches from AZN7 (soup and salad) are particularly good value. It is also a good venue for brunch at weekends.
Other locations Ali-Zadeh Street 7 (012 498 9353).

★ Caravanserai
Gala Street 11 (492 6668). Metro Icheri Sheher. **Open** 11am-11pm daily. **Main courses** €€. **Map** p58 03 ⑱ **Azeri**
The courtyard of this wonderfully atmospheric 14th-century caravanserai has a central fountain and recesses in the walls for private dining. The

CONSUME

CONSUME

Zakura. *See p107.*

tables are set with crisp, white linen and the walls are decorated with colourful textiles and ceramics. Opposite is an overflow restaurant that caters for weddings and other large groups. Unfortunately, though, the spectacular setting and willing waiters do not make up for the slightly disappointing food. *Photo p112.*

Chocolate
Boyuk Gala Street 21 (492 3526). Metro Icheri Sheher. **Open** noon-midnight daily. **Main courses** €€. **Map** p58 N3 ⑲ **International**
The most restaurant-like of this local chain of cafés, Chocolate offers a full menu of steaks, fish, soups and salads, and is a tastefully decorated spot with a slightly French feel. The Gallic ambience is chivvied along by a *chanson* or two in the background.

INSIDE TRACK QUICK CHANGE

Few cities see as many venues opening and closing as quickly as Baku. The high duties and taxes levied on restaurateurs and the goods they have to import take their toll on the byzantine logistics of running an eaterie in the Azeri capital. Another factor is the spending power of expat customers, and the number of expat workers coming to Baku, both of which have fallen since the economic downturn. At the same time, a significant amount of money is still flowing into the city – four five-star hotels opened in a three-month period towards the end of 2011, meaning new restaurants being unveiled on an almost weekly basis.

Starters include the likes of salmon terrine with broccoli and bell peppers, and fried mushrooms with mascarpone and rosemary, while among the substantial mains are fillet of sea bass, grilled sturgeon and Holland steak with white sauce. There are also traditional kebabs, pizzas and pastas. Chocolate also functions as a café, and many people simply come here to indulge in a cherry puff pastry, cinnamon bun, Black Forest mocha coffee, crème brûlée latte, cinnamon hot chocolate or Amaretto coffee with whipped cream. Alcohol is served, most notably in cocktails such as an absinthe blow (absinthe, Bacardi and grenadine) or a snow (Bailey's, Malibu, ice-cream and milk). Try to reserve a table in the lovely, curtained-off private area, with its glazed illustration of the Old City. Note also the intricate line drawings of Dubai by the main door.

Filharmonia Café
Filharmonia Park (055 359 0099, 055 200 7172 both mobiles). Metro Icheri Sheher. **Open** 11am-11pm daily. **Main courses** €. **No credit cards**. **Map** p58 L4 ⑳ **Ice-cream parlour**
The pretty Philharmonia Café can be found in the park of the same name, located just beside the spectacular pyramid of glass that forms the Old City metro station. It serves good coffee and delicious cakes, but the main reason to visit is to sample the ice-cream, which is arguably the best in the capital, and certainly a tempting indulgence after a stroll under the beating Baku sun. Flavours alternate regularly, but favourites include the likes of caramel, white chocolate, cherry and pistachio. Sit at one of the white wrought-iron tables on the pleasant outdoor terrace and enjoy the view of the warm, sandy-coloured medieval battlements to one side, and the trees near the Philharmonia to the other. The light interior, with its glass walls and high ceilings, feels very Italian.

Georgia Café
A Zeynalli Street 16A (492 3610). Metro Icheri Sheher. **Open** 10am-1am daily. **Main courses** €€. **No credit cards.** **Map** pM5 ㉑ **Georgian**

Don't allow the decor to dissuade you from trying this restaurant. It is a real gem, serving authentic Georgian food, and is a great place for breakfast or lunch. Try the *mengreli* or *khachapuri* (cheese pies) or, even better, the *ajaruli* (a large loaf with a raw egg and butter on top, which cooks in the hot bread). Follow the excellent soups and salads with *khingali* (spicy meat dumplings). The beer isn't expensive either.

★ Mugham Club
Rzayeva Street 9 (492 4085). Metro Icheri Sheher. **Open** 5pm-midnight daily. **Main courses** €€€. **Map** pp58 O4 ㉒ **Azeri**

If you only eat out once in Baku, this is the place to come. This ancient and hugely picturesque two-storey caravanserai gives the visitor a taste of good local food and an insight into the traditional local musical culture of *mugham*, performed in song and dance. The centrepiece of the courtyard, which is open in summer, is a fountain with two large fig trees alongside. The trees are bedecked with fairy lights, and there are tables beneath. You can also sit in one of the atmospheric alcoves decorated with colourful carpets and ancient graffiti. The Azeri music and dancing only add to the magic of the evening. While this restaurant is not cheap, the food is good, the service is attentive and helpful, and it is one of the few places where local culture can be experienced. In addition, the upper storey comprises handicraft shops for the tourist, which are definitely worth visiting. Carpets and camel-hair pashminas are good value, but accept a cup of tea and bargain hard. After dinner, a walk through the Old City provides a wonderfully quiet contrast to the noise and bustle of modern Baku.

★ Old City
Mammadov Street 24 (492 0555). Metro Icheri Sheher. **Open** 11am-midnight daily. **Main courses** €€. **Map** p58 N5 ㉓ **Azeri**

Old City is the place for foodies interested in really good local cuisine. It's hard to miss, thanks to the large hardwood cut-out of a chef inviting you down the steps into the beautiful restaurant; the real chef within is world-class. Shah Hussein, or Kerimov Shah-Hüseyn, has won many awards and his food is mouthwateringly good. The menu is comprehensive and some of the Azeri dishes may seem daunting to neophytes, but the waiters are helpful, even though their English is limited. If in doubt, just try a selection of the smaller dishes on offer. The ambience is almost as tasty as the food, the low vaulted ceilings, with traditional wall-hangings and metalware creating a uniquely Azeri atmosphere.

★ Tandir
Boyuk Gala Street (417 2216, 050 760 2216 mobile). Metro Icheri Sheher. **Open** 9am-8pm daily. **Main courses** €. **No credit cards.** **Map** pp58 O3 ㉔ **Azeri**

Perhaps the most authentic and atmospheric spot in the Old City, Tandir is named after the clay oven that fills half the space of this simple wooden hut. The other half comprises four wooden tables, where locals and tourists devour the delicious naan-type bread baked on the inside of the beehive-like kiln; you can watch your breakfast being made and savour the smells at the same time. There's not much of a menu – in fact, there is no menu – but the Russian-speaking manager will have a tray of cheese and jams, a large pot of tea and a basket of bread out to you in no time. It's a popular place to bring visiting VIPs – note the photo of Gérard Depardieu. Loaves of bread can be bought to take away for AZN1.

Three Graces. *See p107.*

CONSUME

From London With Love

New three-in-one restaurant complex Sahil joins a small stable of stylish venues.

Chinar.

The Azerbaijan Hospitality Group is the fastest-growing and most ambitious restaurant team in Baku today. Starting out with the Japanese *izakaya* **Zakura** (*see p107*) in 2009, the AHG set the tone by bringing in London's Blue Sky Hospitality to train staff and improve the decor.

Blue Sky's creative director Henry Chebaane oversaw the development of **Chinar** (*see p111*), Baku's top destination restaurant, serving pan-Asian cuisine, with what is perhaps the city's best cocktail bar, the **Dragon Lounge** (*see p124*) upstairs. Next in line is **Sahil** (*see p113*), the AHG's most ambitious project so far, a three restaurant complex that will house Baku's

first contemporary Azeri restaurant, plus quality Italian and Latin-American eateries, sitting right on the Caspian seafront.

According to Chebaane, 'If we had tried this five years ago, it would have been too early. Now we're spot on in terms of emerging trends, locally and internationally.

'We started working in Baku with a small, 50-seater project called Zakura, a Japanese bistro in collaboration with an ex-Nobu chef. Its success gave our client the confidence to develop a 1,500sq m restaurant-club-bar lounge, Chinar, which opened in 2010. This has been simply phenomenal, with more than 20,000 followers on Facebook and several investors from Asia asking us if we could do something similar for them.'

Chinar was not just fusion cuisine with a duck oven – it became the hangout for everyone in Baku, a destination for film stars and those involved in the oil industry. And by retaining the same name and location as a much-loved Baku landmark, the Chinar teahouse, it kept the local community onside rather than isolating it. Attention to detail is all at Chinar – even the chopstick holders are shaped like a small branch of the indigenous chinar tree of the type that still lines the pretty front terrace. The same kind of attention to detail is now being invested in Sahil, due to open in late 2011 or early 2012.

Says Chebaane: 'As with Chinar and Zakura before, Sahil will unlock untapped commercial potential. Azeri people are very congenial, they enjoy going out. They are also sophisticated and understand quality... In all our international restaurant projects we endeavour to engage culturally with local consumers with a narrative-rich concept that involves history, architecture, lighting, technology, cuisine, graphics, music and much more.'

The developers see Sahil as a natural progression for the city, matching the fast development of its centre, particularly its grand waterside boulevard, where a lot of construction work for upmarket shops and hotels is under way.

Sahil will be different in that it won't be one restaurant but three. 'Sahil will deliver its promise on three floors, each with its own kitchen, restaurant, bar and outdoor terrace overlooking the Caspian. It will be a cosmopolitan, experiential venue that could not be easily replicated in other world capitals.'

And what next? For Chebaane, aware of the fact that four five-star hotels will open in town just as Sahil is being unveiled, the sky's the limit. 'We are pleased to be involved in the development of the restaurants for two of the top hotels opening soon. We believe that this will be a positive boost to the regional economy and to social development, and will foster higher expectations and requirements for the quality of goods and services in the region. Let's keep in mind that Baku has been and is again developing as an important regional hub between Moscow, Istanbul, the Middle East and Asia. That's a lot of potential visitors.'

★ Terrace Garden

Sultan Inn Hotel, Boyuk Gala Street 20 (437 2305, www.sultaninn.com). Metro Icheri Sheher. **Open** noon-midnight daily. **Main courses** €€€. **Map** p58 O3 ㉕ **Azeri/international**

Of all Baku's luxury dining options with a view, the Terrace Garden, occupying the third storey of the boutique Sultan Inn Hotel, surely wins out with its spectacular sea-facing vista. An entire sweep of the Caspian lies before you, plus, of course, the rooftops of the Old City all around. Start with a full-bodied lentil soup, then move on to a Sultan's Inn salad with quail's egg, chicken and roast beef, before attacking the lamb chops or pepper steak. Leave room for the apple baklava for dessert. Mains range from AZN15-AZN30. So, given the setting and the (excellent) service, the two-course business lunch is a steal at AZN15, with a complimentary appetiser to boot. The pristine, uniformed waiters are a little stiff, but loosen up as a most enjoyable meal progresses.

SABAYIL & WEST BAKU

★ Chinar

Shovket Alakbarova Street 1 (492 0888, www. chinar-dining.az). All buses to Funikulyor. **Open** 10am-late. **Main courses** €€€. **Map** p221 B6 ㉖ **Asian**

Chinar is destination dining at its best – it's where Catherine Deneuve is taken when she's in town. Occupying the former teahouse of the same name that thrived in Soviet times, the contemporary Chinar is not just a pan-Asian restaurant with an expansive front terrace and location close to the waterfront: this is an upscale hangout with two adjoining bars, a tea station and a DJ booth. It also looks great, designed by London's Blue Sky Hospitality, which also trained the staff in the open-plan kitchen and out on the floor. Expat regulars from the oil industry swear by the crispy duck, and the stand-out dish of black cod in spicy miso. Also highly recommended are the scallop tempura with flying fish roe, pan-seared *wagyu* beef with burdock, and the lobster salad. Everything else is wok-fried, pan-seared or honey-roasted – you'll be hard pushed to find a duffer. Upstairs, cocktail drinkers in the Dragon Lounge may choose between the main restaurant menu and a select sushi one. This being the prime spot in all Baku, and given the standard of cuisine, prices for main courses could have been set at twice what they are – instead you'll be forking out around AZN20, and AZN8 for sushi bites. ▶ *For more on the story behind Chinar and other restaurants, see left* **From London with Love.**

Telegulle

Baku TV Tower, Abbas-Gulu Abbas Zadeh Street (537 0808, 070 770 7070 mobile). All buses to Sabayil. **Open** noon-midnight daily. **Main courses** €€. **No credit cards. Map** p221 B6 ㉗ **Azeri**

Baku's Televizya tower can be seen from almost anywhere in town, and is lit with changing colours at

CONSUME

INSIDE TRACK MENU MATTERS

All but the cheapest restaurants in Baku usually display menus in Azeri, Russian and some kind of English. Translations tend to be bizarre and quirky rather than laugh-out-loud howlers – note the category 'farinaceous foods' in the **ART Garden** (*see p107*) in the Old City, for example. Also be aware that an extensive menu by no means indicates that all these dishes are available – ask your waiter.

night. Built in 1996, the rotating restaurant on the 29th floor has the best views in town but is surprisingly under-used. Most of the food is Azeri (kebabs and the like). Read the English menu carefully as there are wide variations in price (caviar is AZN40), and the staff speak very little English, so understanding the difference between items (particularly salads) can be difficult. Service is slow, but at least it gives you time to soak up the sublime views.

Khazar

Below Bibi Heybat mosque. Turn left beyond the mosque and follow the small road; restaurant is on the right (050 584 8884 mobile). All buses to Bibi Heybat mosque. **Open** 9am-11pm daily. **Main courses** €€. **No credit cards.** **Map** p221 B7 ㉘ **Fish**
For the more adventurous visitor, a trip south out of town to the famous Bibi Heybat mosque, followed by a further trek down the road to this restaurant, is a great way to experience local Azeri culture at its most authentic. Sit outside under the trees with a beer

watching people bathing and relaxing. Then enjoy a starter of salads, local cheese, pickles and olives, followed by fish, steamed, grilled or roasted – the trout is particularly good. No English is spoken but the universal language of 'point and smile', a little patience and a willingness to accept whatever you get makes dining here a memorable occasion. Another bonus is the price – less than AZN20 per person. *Photo p113.*

BULVAR & WATERFRONT

Fillet House

Neftchilar prospekt 145 (598 0573, 012 222 2770). All buses to Bulvar. **Open** noon-11pm daily. **Main courses** €€€€. **Map** p221 E4 ㉙ **Grill**
This establishment, next door to Pub 145, prides itself on its fillet steaks and fish, and has a Scandinavian theme. The steaks are well cooked and presented on a wooden platter with vegetables and sauces, but are a little overpriced at AZN30. Service is perfunctory and the dark interior doesn't help.

Kitchenette

4th floor, Park Bulvar, Neftchilar Prospekt (598 0573, www.kitchenette.com.tr). All buses to Bulvar. **Open** 10am-1am daily. **Main courses** €€€. **Map** p221 D5 ㉚ **International**
Part of a brasserie-themed Turkish chain widespread across the homeland, Kitchenette Baku enjoys a prime location overlooking the Caspian from an upper floor of the Park Bulvar shopping mall. With a harlequin-tiled floor and French gastronomic vocabulary emblazoned over its tables, Kitchenette maintains a Parisian touch in its menu: breakfast is *'petit déjeuner'*, comprising fresh pastries from the pâtisserie in a corner by the door; daily specials are *'plats du jour'*; and the thin-sliced steak

CONSUME

Caravanserai. *See p107.*

Khazar.

CONSUME

with fries (AZN19) takes the moniker Café de Paris. Cakes are another speciality; try the dark chocolate and blackberry, chestnut and chocolate or pistachio. The rest of the menu is mostly Azeri/Turkish, with the likes of seabass salad (AZN24) and fish kebab (AZN23). Mention must also be made of the range of coffees (chocolate mint, frozen latte macchiato), the rarer Efes beers Gusta and fruity Mariachi, and the four-choice kids' menu (AZN7-AZN8).

★ Mirvari

Neftchilar Prospekt (no phone). All buses to the Bulvar. **Open** 10am-10pm daily. **Main courses** €€. **No credit cards. Map** p223 J4 **③** Café
A Baku institution, the 'Pearl' has been serving refreshments and lighter dishes to promenading locals since Soviet times. There are many cafés lining the Caspian seafront, but only one has been fashioned in the shape of a pearl. Mirvari, in fact, comprises three areas: the raised pearl building itself, where meals are served, and two adjoining terraces. A dovecote stands in the middle and an old local in statue form welcomes you in, but these accoutrements matter little to locals, who've been meeting up here for decades. Cakes, ice-cream, chocolates and preserved fruit, as well as endless cups of tea, are the order of the day. When you get to place that order is another matter – service is so slow you could probably row to Turkmenistan and back before anyone deigns to attend your table. But once the drinks arrive, you'll be here watching the waves for an hour or two. *Photo p114.*

★ Sahil

Neftchilar Prospekt. All buses to Bulvar. **Open** opening late 2011/early 2012, hours to be decided. **Main courses** €€. **Map** p221 D5 **②** Azeri/Latin American/Italian
Set beside the Park Bulvar mall, this major undertaking is the latest by the Azerbaijan Hospitality Group, also responsible for Zakura and Chinar. This is the most important and ambitious culinary venture that Baku has seen in a very long while. It's not just the location – there aren't any proper restaurants on the waterfront apart from in the mall itself – or the pedigree ('Another Legend Reborn' ran the text around the hoarding when this was a building site), but what is being proposed for this multi-floored establishment. As well as a decent Italian on the ground floor – quality pizzas, pastas and proper ice-creams for promenade-strolling families – there will be Baku's first Latin American spot and, most importantly, a restaurant where contemporary Azeri cuisine will be the main feature. This pioneering part of the operation remains the most attractive and, at the time of writing, elusive to pin down in terms of chef and menu. Suffice to say, it should be well worth investigating when the doors open, around the time this guide is published. ▶ *For more on the Sahil development, see p110* **From London with Love**.

Sea Port Hotel

Neftchilar Prospekt 58 (498 1013, www.seaport.az). All buses to Bulvar. **Open** 10am-10pm daily. **Main courses** €€€. **No credit cards. Map** p221 D4 **③** Azeri
This hotel restaurant in the main harbour building is a generally empty and spacious spot (with terrace) to watch the sea over a simple, standard main dish or pot of tea with preserved fruit (AZN6). The menu is dominated by fish or meat kebabs, 15 in all, along with more adventurous *saj* dishes of chicken (AZN15), beef (AZN18) or fish (AZN24). You can also play safe by choosing a cheaper pasta or go the whole hog with a plate of *monastir* beef (AZN12) or steak with mushroom sauce (AZN14). Draught beers include Efes and Edelweiss wheat.

★ Zeytun

Park Bulvar, 4th floor, Neftchilar Prospekt (598 7420). All buses to Bulvar. **Open** 10am-1am daily. **Main courses** €€€. **Map** p221 D5 **③** International
While the third floor of Baku's main mall, the Park Bulvar, is filled with family-friendly sit-down or takeaway joints, the fourth features two restaurants

Mirvari. *See p113.*

of note: Kitchenette (*see p112*) and the more upscale Zeytun. Like Kitchenette, 'Olive' enjoys a sea view, the waves of the Caspian creating a glimmering effect in the glass panes of the front terrace. Fish, in particular sturgeon, is a main feature of the extensive international menu, making an appearance as a soup with sea bass and pike-perch or pan-fried in olive oil. Meats are prepared over a charcoal grill, namely lamb kebabs, rib-eye steaks, plus other delights such as oven-baked marinated leg of lamb. Main courses will set you back around AZN30, while the notable cocktails (frozen strawberry margarita, mixed berry mojito) are around AZN10-AZN12 each. A pianist entertains most evenings in the tastefully furnished main room. *Photo p115.*

NORTH BAKU

Baku Roasting Company
corner of Matbuat Prospekt/Shahriyar Street (537 1794). All buses to Yasamal. **Open** 9am-9pm daily. **Main courses** €. **Map** p220 A3 ❸❺ **Café**

INSIDE TRACK BIZNES LANCH

Almost every restaurant in Baku, from budget to luxury, offers a discount meal during the day – the ubiquitous '*biznes lanch*'. This usually consists of two or three courses at one or two set prices, perhaps with another category for two persons. The day's offer will be displayed on a board outside, along with the period of time that it is available – often noon to 3pm, sometimes until 4pm or even 5pm. All-in deals for AZN6-AZN10 are the norm, but high-end spots can charge AZN15. Complimentary bread and spreads are generally thrown in, plus a soft drink and maybe coffee.

This café near Baku State University is a cool, quiet sanctuary amid the noise and bustle of the city, and serves the best coffee and cakes in Baku. It roasts its own beans, which can be bought on the premises whole or ground, alongside mugs, cafetières and T-shirts. Students frequent the premises, creating a lively atmosphere, and there's plenty of reading material around, such as second-hand books and newspapers. The café regularly hosts exhibitions of photography, arts and handicrafts.
Other location Alasker Alakbarov Street 12 (012 510 9876).

Finestra
Nakhchivani Street 14 (436 7854). All buses to Yasamal. **Open** 11am-11pm daily. **Main courses** €€€. **Map** p220 B3 ❸❼ **International**
This restaurant in an out-of-the-way location is unmistakable thanks to the fairy lights adorning the entrance. Finestra purports to be Italian but the menu also includes sushi, Mexican food and local dishes. The food is slightly disappointing – a result, perhaps, of trying to be all things to all men – but the staff are keen to please.

Grill
Hyatt Regency Hotel, Bakikhanov Street 1 (496 1234, www.baku.regencyhyatt.com). All buses to Hyatt Regency. **Open** noon-3pm, 6.30-11pm daily. **Main courses** €€€. **Map** p220 B2 ❸❽ **Grill**
Such was the significance of the opening of this hotel at the major Bakikhanov roundabout, that it gave its name, unofficially, to the otherwise nondescript zone around it: Hyatt Area. And the restaurant within doesn't disappoint. Wilsdon Design Associates, responsible for London's Royal Garden Palace, Andaz London and the Churchill, have created something truly chic and striking. Surrounded by hues of brown, sweeps of natural light and glass pillars, well-trained staff deliver top-grade

American beef, New Zealand lamb and stupendous kebabs to a well-heeled clientele. Although this is no place for vegetarians, fish-eaters haven't been forgotten, with seafood stews and skewers too. You'll also find salads, but that's not really what you're here for – you're at the Grill, after all.

Mado
Inshaatchilar Prospekt 33 (497 5544). Metro Elmlar Akademiyasi. **Open** noon-midnight daily. **Main courses** €€€. **Map** p220 A3 ❸
Japanese
If miso soup is the best test of quality of a Japanese restaurant, then Mado reaches a high standard. The sushi menu is comprehensive, yet easily accessible. The sashimi is fresh and well presented, and the tempura batter is light and delicious. There is a four-course business lunch on weekdays for AZN15. The decor is typically Japanese – calming and minimalist – and service is attentive without being overwhelming. Although this restaurant is not in the traditional tourist area, it's definitely worth a detour.

★ Penjere
Abdullah Shaig Street 245 (510 3700). All buses to Yasamal. **Open** noon-11pm daily. **Main courses** €€€. **Map** p220 A3 ❹ Azeri
If you're going to eat anywhere Azeri, this may well be the best choice. Part of the group that includes Mado and Finestra – which, according to the PR blurb, are 'windows' on to Japan and Italy – here you 'open your window to old Country of Fire'. Fortunately, Penjere is far better than its marketing

Zeytun. *See p113.*

might suggest. Highlights on the menu include delicious meat and fish *shashliks* prepared in a brazier, and hearty *govurma* stews. Dishes are gorgeously conceived and served in a neat pine-lined space – there's a garden area for the warmer months too. A full range of Azeri and Georgian wines are available, at prices that the generally suit-and-tie clad clientele don't baulk at.

Scalini's
Bakikhanov Street 2 (598 2850). All buses to Hyatt Regency. **Open** noon-2.30pm, 7-11pm Mon-Sat; noon-10.30pm Sun. **Main courses** €€€€. **Map** p220 B2 ❷ Italian
Once known as the best Italian restaurant in Baku, Scalini's has since been equalled, if not surpassed, by other establishments that offer better ambience and value. And while the food remains very good here, the clientele, which seems to be made up mostly of businessmen on fat expense accounts, has done the place no favours. It retains a certain reputation, though, particularly among certain sections of the expat community.

SAHIL & EAST BAKU

Art Café Expression
1st floor, Museum of Modern Art, Safarov Street 5 (490 8404). Metro Khatai. **Open** 11am-9pm Tue-Sun. **Admission** AZN5. **Main courses** €. **No credit cards. Map** p220 E3 ❸ International
Located inside the excellent Museum of Modern Art, the Art Café Expression is easily the best museum café in Baku. It consists of a small, dark room decked out with original local art – sadly none of it for sale – and a terrace overlooking the ground floor of the museum. On offer are superior sandwiches (grilled black Angus beefburger with coleslaw and fries; tortilla with smoked salmon and herb mayonnaise); excellent soups (chicken with coconut milk and lemongrass; tomato with pesto drizzle); and fine salads (grilled chicken with orange salsa, sesame seeds and fettuccine). Desserts such as Black Forest cake and apple crumble are pretty decent too, while cocktails and mocktails are artily themed. It's almost worth paying the AZN5 museum admission just to sample the coffee here – strong, delicious and in flavours as varied as tropical moccha (AZN4.50), with coconut, cherry, chocolate syrup, espresso and milk. All in all, a thoroughly commendable venue and manned by young, English-speaking staff too.

Galereya
Nizami Street 117 (498 9191). Metro 28 May. **Open** 1pm-midnight daily. **Main courses** €€€. **No credit cards. Map** p220 D3 ❹ Azeri/International
Attached to the Konti Bar with its separate entrance round the corner, Galereya may not appeal at first – particularly if there are a couple of serious bouncer

CONSUME

CONSUME

types in the lobby, which can happen. But persevere as this is basically a friendly if slightly weird cellar restaurant – weird enough to be interesting, anyway, as you don't quite know what's going on. When the food arrives, it's actually pretty decent. Dishes include the likes of steak in whisky sauce (AZN15), salmon in strawberry sauce (AZN9) and sturgeon (AZN15), all chosen from a menu shaped like a beer mug. All kinds of vodkas are sold by the bottle, and are left chilled by your table.

▶ *For Konti Bar, in the same building, see p122.*

Landmark
Nizami Street 90A (465 2000, www.the landmarkhotel.az). Metro 28 May. **Open** *19th Floor Bar & Lounge 7am-2am daily. 20th Floor Bar & Lounge/Caspian Lounge & Terrace 7am-midnight daily. 90A, La Bodega Old Mill, Seto noon-11pm daily. Shin Shin 7am-11pm daily.* **Main courses** €€€. **Map** p221 D4 ⑮ International

Dining options are varied at the Landmark hotel and business complex on Nizami, behind the palace-like Dom Soviet government building – but most function for the business crowd, providing chic fine dining and options for functions and celebrations. Around the courtyard on the lower levels, and primarily serving the lunchtime crowd in the surrounding offices, Restaurant 90A, the Old Mill Café and La Bodega all offer acceptable food in a pretty sterile environment. But take the lift up to the 19th to 21st floors and your dining experience is enhanced by wonderful city views.

The Sky Bar & Lounge on the 19th floor is a cocktail bar dealing mainly in pre-dinner or post-function drinks, with piano music. Sharing the same spectacular city vistas and minimalist decor, the Japanese Seto and Chinese Shin Shin restaurants on the next two floors above (accessed via the stairs from the 19th floor), offer sushi and Asian fusion food in spacious surroundings. On the 20th floor, the Caspian Lounge & Terrace is a standard

upscale bar-restaurant with a great balcony area. Ideal for summertime drinks, it has memorable views of the Caspian – but beware of the strong winds. *Photo p106.*

Mamounia Lounge
Uzeyir Hajibeyov Street 51 (493 8800). Metro Sahil. **Open** *12.30pm-1am Mon-Thur; 2pm-1am Fri, Sat.* **Main courses** €€€. **Map** p221 D4 ⑯ International

This is the restaurant for the wealthy young Baku set. The stylish interior is modern, simple and dark, with a well-stocked bar and substantial disco area. The comfortable outdoor terrace is set far enough back from the main road for the experience to be enjoyable and the food is very good. The menu is mainly European, but there's also sushi and local dishes on offer. The cocktail list is interesting and not too pricey. Mamounia is busy during the week, particularly at lunchtimes. Weekends are quieter, but busy late at night.

★ Sumakh
Khojali Street 20/22 (480 2121, www.sumakh.az). Metro Khatai. **Open** *11am-midnight daily.* **Main courses** €€€. **Map** p220 E3 ⑰ Azeri

Situated away from the tourist areas, but within walking distance of the Museum of Modern Art and the new Port Baku complex, this establishment offers local Azeri cuisine cooked with great sophistication. It is modern, airy and beautifully decorated, and the carpets illuminated on the walls are stunning. The service is impeccable – attentive but not intrusive. However, it is the food that is the star here and a well-structured menu makes it accessible to the non-Azeri speaker. Try a plate of *lavanghi* (delicious tiny dumplings with a variety of fillings) to start with, accompanied by a couple of salads, including the wonderful *mangal* salad of roasted aubergine. Follow this with a *saj* – a dish of roasted meats and vegetables – and finish with one of the many *plov* on offer. There is an interesting wine list featuring mostly local wines at competitive prices.

Waggon Paris Bistro Boutique & Café Brasserie
Rashid Behbudov Street 15 (493 6445). Metro 28 May or Sahil. **Open** *10pm-midnight daily.* **Main courses** €€€. **Map** p222 K1 ⑱ French/International

Opened in the spring of 2011, the Waggon Paris Bistro is a test concept for the company: in a first anywhere in the worldwide chain, they have combined a boutique clothes shop and an arthouse café. While the dolls hanging from the chandelier are a bit unnerving, and the boutique seems to only sell clothes sized for mannequins, the food is excellent. Grilled dishes are a strength, so it's a good option for meat-eaters, but there's also a decent choice for vegetarians, and all food and drinks are elaborately presented and prepared.

INSIDE TRACK IN GOOD TIME

While Baku has seen a boom in international restaurants in the last five years, many of these have not produced a significant improvement in terms of service. Local waiters, occasionally slow to the point of making you wonder if you might actually have become invisible, are seemingly expert in ignoring the would-be diner, particularly if you're on your own. This is partly cultural – Azeris like to eat out in groups as a communal experience, and the speed at which dishes arrive at the table is less important than the collective atmosphere around it.

Bars & Nightlife

Pints and pool make for a winning combination.

In this chapter we focus on places where people go out to drink, listen to DJs and dance. In terms of category, some of the venues reviewed in Restaurants & Cafés (*see pp100-116*) are good places to enjoy a drink as well as to eat, but the primary function of the establishments featured in this chapter is clear. You won't be served alcohol everywhere in Baku – tea is the national drink in this majority Muslim country– but at all these venues you should at least find beer, perhaps absurdly expensive wine and, in certain cases, a cocktail. Beer is almost universally Turkish Efes or local Xirdalan. Occasionally there may be Russian Baltika, but this is rarely available on draught.

DRINKING IN BAKU

Opening times for bars tend to be around noon. Closing times are flexible, usually when the last guest leaves. Thursday and Friday nights are busy in the small bar hubs near Fountains Square, but gone are the days when downtown Baku made merry all through the week. The drop in expat workers coming to Azerbaijan, and their spending power, means that foreigner-friendly destinations such as **Adam's** (*see below*) now attract a far higher number of young Azeris. They drink less and stay in one place longer. They're not only attracted by Efes, but also by a game of pool; nearly every downtown bar has a pool table – an essential feature – and the local pub league is taken very seriously indeed. One thing you may not find much of, though, is women. Bars are very much male domains.

It has been suggested in certain circles that Baku's nightlife is more buzzing than in many other cities. This is palpable nonsense. The city has a small handful of half-decent discos for fashionable young Azeris to enjoy their new-found wealth, and loads of karaoke bars. Big-name international DJs are rare visitors. In fact, since byzantine visa regulations were

imposed in 2010, any kind of international musician has been a rarity. In terms of live music beyond cover bands in pubs, you might catch a sympathetic rock/alt-rock combo in the **Corner Bar** (*see p118*), but classic 200-capacity bar back rooms simply don't exist. Live music means jazz (*see p146*).

PUBS & BARS

Downtown

★ 808
Off Z Taghiyev Street (050 310 1709, 051 886 6808 both mobiles). All buses to Fountains Square. **Open** 5pm-last guest daily. **No credit cards.** **Map** p222 H3 ❶
This is a lovely little bar, set down a narrow, nameless street off Z Taghiyev. It's close to the city's main bar hub, but as it's pretty much exclusively Russian-speaking, it's mercifully free of beery Brits. It consists of two small spaces, the front one almost entirely filled by a pool table that's the focus of all attention. Irina behind the bar also makes sure to play a few decent tunes through the evening, and has the good grace to chill the beer glasses before pouring. If you speak a little Russian and enjoy shooting pool, you won't want to leave.

Adam's
Hajiyev Street 7 (497 1507). All buses to Fountains Square. **Open** noon-midnight Mon-Thur, Sun; 11am-last guest Fri, Sat. **No credit cards. Map** p222 G3 ❷

Finnegan's.

CONSUME

In June 2011, it took a seismic shift for Adam's to relocate from its long-established spot in the bar hub of Ali-Zadeh. But here it is, right on Fountains Square, with more spacious premises and an outdoor area to boot. Absolutely everyone knows Adam's, a home from home run by a lovely couple from Mumbai. It combines the familiarity of the village pub with the communal passion of a sports bar, coupled with the flavours of a thoroughly decent curry house. The new premises are even large enough to provide a no-smoking room, and a full English buffet breakfast is served here on Sundays. Although every Brit expat has supped here, these days Adam's is attracting more and

---

THE BEST PLACES

For own-brewed ale
The Brewery. See p120.

For cool cocktails
Dragon Lounge. See p124.

For rooftop views
Open Space. See p121.

For drinking in the atmosphere
Otto. See p119.

For a snack with your beer
Pub 145. See p122.

For kitsch decor
USSR Bar. See p120.

---

more young Azeris: friendly, tracksuited locals happy to shoot pool and swap mobile ring tones.

Corner Bar

Corner of Tolstoy/Rasul Rza streets (494 8955, www.thecornerbaku.com). All buses to Fountains Square. **Open** 6pm-4am daily. **No credit cards.** **Map** p222 H2 ❸

Occupying a corner of the other, shadier bar hub in the city centre where Tolstoy meets Rasul Rza, this sympathetic little spot is the closest Baku gets to the kind of homely watering hole you'd be happy to find in any town in the UK or Europe. Friendly and pub-like – other places spend a fortune on faux decor and miss the point entirely – the Corner comprises two rooms. The back one is dedicated to pool, the front one to live acts who set up in a cramped space by the front door, allowing punters to prop up the bar and watch proceedings. The music is generally rock, grunge rock, heavy rock or garage rock, executed by charmingly enthusiastic young locals whose mates heckle them at close quarters. Look out for the 33 beer sign – although the beer's Efes.

Finnegan's

A Ali-Zadeh Street 8 (498 6564). All buses to Fountains Square. **Open** 11am-2am daily. **No credit cards.** **Map** p223 H4 ❹

Baku's prime Irish bar sits in the city's most prominent bar hub where Ali-Zadeh meets Tarlan Aliyarbeyov, also home to Otto's, Shakespeare and the ghost of Adam's. Fitted out like any other Irish pub in the world, Finnegan's exudes a homely character, encouraged by the low-level bar counter that fills the centre of the main room and lends a round table logistic to social interaction. There's Guinness, of course – note the trademark toucan standing to attention by his own pint – as well as pub grub available until 2am. Pub acts (country & western, R&B) perform on Wednesdays and Saturdays; most other nights there's TV sports of some kind.

Old Forester

S Vurgun Street 23 (050 250 0996 mobile). Metro Sahil. **Open** 11am-11pm Mon-Thur, Sun; 11am-1pm Fri, Sat. **Map** p222 J1 ⑤

Although it's decked out like an English pub, the Old Forester has a squeaky clean, polished feel. Dotted around the place, flatscreen TVs keep sports fans enthralled without annoying other drinkers. Service is good and the drinks reasonably priced, with a good selection of spirits, beers, wine and cocktails. The usual global selection of dishes arrives with a generous complimentary basket of bread and olives.

★ Otto

Tarlan Aliyarbeyov Street 3 (98 6979). All buses to Fountains Square. **Open** 11am-last guest daily. **Map** p223 H4 ⑥

Now the only real bar in the city centre's main bar hub, Otto's is a corner spot of light wood and bright Efes advertising occupying Baku's busiest junction for strolling pub crawlers. It comprises a well-run, dog-leg bar counter surrounded by plenty of space for chairs and tables, the echoes of pub natter bouncing off the bare brick walls. The beer tap fashioned in the shape of a saxophone is a nice touch and the swing doors leading to the toilets lend a suitable saloon feel to proceedings.

Phoenix Bar

Yusif Mammadaliyev Street 10 (050 541 6957, 050 369 4668, both mobiles). All buses to Fountains Square. **Open** 4pm-last guest Mon-Fri; noon-last guest Sat, Sun. **No credit cards.** **Map** p222 H4 ⑦

Another haunt on the downtown pub-crawl route, the Phoenix is larger than most of its nearby competitors. All the action takes place in one bar room at street level, half of it occupied by a pool table. The

Phoenix also attracts expat punters with its happy hours (5-8pm), two-for-ones on Sundays, Guinness at under AZN5 a pint and decent selection of whiskies. The kitchen produces hot and cold dishes until 11pm.

Tequila

Nizami Street 73 (050 354 3852 mobile). All buses to Fountains Square. **Open** 11am-midnight daily. **No credit cards.** **Map** p222 H2 ⑧

Set on a pretty square with a fountain at its centre, Tequila is a friendly anomaly. Although it does stock José Cuervo and Olmeca, and can be relied on to play regular rocking tunes over the speakers, Tequila has quite wonderfully and shamelessly attempted to cash in on the closure of the Caledonia pub nearby by offering such delights as mince and tatties, and bangers and mash, chalked up on a board outside to lure in the unwary Scot. There are no pints of heavy, though, only the standard Efes and Xirdalan poured and served beneath an old Budweiser beer ad. There's also a pool table in the front space awaiting all comers.

Tortuga

Tarlan Aliyarbeyov Street 9 (050 405 0778 mobile). All buses to Fountains Square. **Open** noon-last guest daily. **No credit cards.** **Map** p222 H4 ⑨

No, this is not Hamburg and this isn't a St Pauli bar – the signature skull-and-crossbones flag of the cult football club relates to the pirate theme here, otherwise accentuated by images of Johnny Depp in Jack Sparrow garb and sundry maritime knick-knacks. Tortuga is Azeri-run, with a significant young, local clientele who gather around the bar to flirt with the

Otto.

CONSUME

Tortuga. *See p119.*

CONSUME

friendly waitresses and await their turn on the pool table that fills the intimate main bar room. Items on the menu are kept suitably affordable – house salads at AZN6, ostrich meat at AZN7 and steak at AZN14. Busy during happy hour, Tortuga tends to be the setting-off point for a night's bar crawl of the vicinity.

USSR Bar

Z Taghiyev Street (498 2223). All buses to Fountains Square. **Open** 5pm-last guest daily. **No credit cards. Map** p222 H4 ⑩

Like the state it was named after, this cellar bar has had its day but merits a visit for its curiosity value and eclectic collection of Soviet memorabilia. Among the soldiers' uniforms, rouble notes and portaits of Andropov (what was the Kremlin thinking?) and Brezhnev, you might pick out a montage of the USSR Bar in its heyday, Kodak snaps of red-faced

Brits raising pints to the camera with Russian-looking ladies half their age. The flags of the world on the ceiling include one of Manchester United but the TV is usually given over to reruns of Soviet-era cartoons. Your experience here will inevitably be backdropped by the incidental music from *Nu, Pogodi!* and other long-lost animated classics. Draught beers include Baltika and a strange brew, available in light and dark varieties, called Baki Pilsen. There's a pool table and dartboard.

William Shakespeare

A Ali-Zadeh Street 6 (498 9121). All buses to Fountains Square. **Open** 11am-4am daily. **No credit cards. Map** p223 H4 ⑪

This typical expat pub on the downtown circuit is regularly patronised by beer-bellied Brits, swiftly served by earnest bar staff. This actually feels like a pub, rammed on Friday and Saturday nights when a band belts out rock standards. A full menu includes pepper steak (AZN14), house burgers (AZN6), pork chops in barbecue sauce (AZN9), and various curries. Taking its lead from Adam's (*see p117*), which occupied the building next door for many years, Shakespeare has turned an upstairs floor into a curry house – although it still suffers by comparison.

Old City

The Brewery

Istiglaliyyat Street 27 (012 437 2868). Metro Icheri Sheher. **Open** 11am-midnight daily. **Map** p223 F6 ⑫

Not strictly in the Old City but a short walk from its metro station, the Brewery is, as its business card suggests, 'the Home of Good Beer'. Three varieties of beer – light, dark and medium – are brewed on the premises, a first for Baku. An Austrian firm had the good sense to set up this operation, a dark basement warren of sleek copper vats and piping. Western touches include tours and samplings, and the humorous decorative fixture of separate urinals for each beer. The parent company flies in professionals from Vienna every six months or so to make sure all is running cleanly and smoothly. There's a full, inevitably pricey menu, with extensive beer snacks, but people come here to sup not scoff.

Kishmish

Kichik Gala Street 108 (492 9182, www. kishmish.az). Metro Icheri Sheher. **Open** 2pm-midnight daily. **Map** p58 M2 ⑬

No, it doesn't mean 'mish-mash' but it should do. The Kishmish is a bizarre cornucopia of a bar, both in terms of decor and menu. First, the decor: bringing together exotic elements from the Orient and kitsch international iconography such as the red phone boxes and buses of post-war London, designer and founder Elchin Aliyev has also thrown in German porcelain and Russian samovars, all illuminated by the glow of candlelight and antique lamps. Aliyev selected Absheron stone as his base material, as well

as digging out artefacts from the family archives – his grandmother's diary, sepia portraits – to offer a personal touch. Drinks-wise, this is as much a teahouse as a cocktail bar, with 50 loose-leaf and 100 tea-bag varieties, plus an array of mixed drinks of similarly globetrotting character. Small bites include Iranian halva, dates from Iran and Tunisia, and Turkish delight. Flavours of Mürabba jams include rose petal, mulberry and sweet cherry. By the way, the name means 'raisin'.

★ Open Space

Sultan Inn Hotel, Boyuk Gala Street 20 (437 2308, www.sultaninn.com). Metro Icheri Sheher. **Open** *June-Sept* 11am-midnight daily. Closed Oct-May. **Map** p58 O3 ⑭

This gem of a bar is perched on a hill in the Old City overlooking the Maiden's Tower. It's part of the Sultan Inn boutique hotel, and it serves a largely international clientele. The fact that it's open-air gives it a distinct advantage over other panoramic bars in the city, which are generally encased in glass. On hot afternoons, an ice-cold Efes is the order of the day, while warm summer evenings lend themselves to intimate romance by candlelight.

Sing Your Heart Out

Karaoke rules on Baku's bar scene.

Karaoke is an essential part of Baku nightlife. Every place in the city seems to offer a chance for visitors to shine or humiliate themselves in song, but pride of place must go to the **Pride Lounge** (Natavan 1, 012 493 5308, www.pride.az), which has 20,000 songs on its list, by far the biggest selection. The list is on the website, and many regulars make their choices before they head out. In the unlikely event that they don't have what you want, you can request a track via an online form. More bashful visitors can choose a spot downstairs where the sofas are divided by slinky string curtains into separate areas, each with their own karaoke screen.

Exhibitionists prefer to head to the **Famous Lounge** (Hasan Mejidov 11, 012 436 8018, www.famous.az), where they can take to the stage and play out their childhood pop-star fantasies. Champagne is the drink of choice, and those less worried about protecting their vocal cords can choose from 18 flavours of sheesha pipe.

If you'd rather dabble than dedicate a whole evening to battling for the microphone, head for **Dion de Musique** (Vidadi 89, 012 596 2214), which offers a karaoke bar-cum-lounge club experience. Warbling takes place from the comfort of your seating area, with screens dotted around the bar. This means you have to be considerate of your fellow divas, but the atmosphere is laid-back. And if you tire of singing, there's a club room for dancing.

If, on the other hand, you prefer to keep your crooning largely between friends, **Voices** (B Seferoglu 174, 012 498 7797) offers private booths where you can limit your audience to your most loyal fans. And for die-hard pub-lovers, the **Half Way Inn** (28 May 6, 012 598 0905) is a low-key boozer where you can belt out till last orders to an intimate audience in the separate smaller bar adjoining the main one.

CONSUME

Sky Bar & Lounge.

Bulvar & Waterfront

Eleven

*11th floor, Park Inn Hotel, Azadlig Prospekt 1
(490 6000, www.eleven.az). Metro Sahil.* **Open**
1am-1pm Tue-Sun. **Map** p221 D4 ⓫

Drinking options at this recently opened hotel bar-restaurant include fine whisky (Chivas Regal 25-year-old, Lagavulin 16-year-old, Japanese Yamakazi), vodka (Absolut in almost all flavours), tequila (Olmeca Tezón Blanco or Tezón Reposado), and an extensive cocktail menu. Mixed drinks, which cost around AZN10, include standards such as daiquiris, manhattans and martinis. Japanese in theme, eleven also offers a full range of sushi combinations, prepared before your very eyes by capable chefs. Dinner and drinks come with a wonderful Caspian view, and fashionable customers mingle amid the contemporary decor. Eleven also hosts DJ parties and special nights for big football fixtures and one-off events such as Eurovision.

INSIDE TRACK YOUR BREAK

Nearly every bar in Baku has a pool table. As well as providing easy entertainment, pool is taken seriously in key bars around the city. The Baku Pool League involves some two dozen teams who play in games of singles and doubles – some bars put out two teams. Breaking is decided on the toss of a coin, and players nominate where they should pot the black. Teams are typically comprised of enthusiastic young Azeris and cheery older Brits, with at least one woman in many teams. A 3,000-word set of rules is available for players to abide by.

Pub 145

*Neftchilar Prospekt 145 (493 2898). All buses
to Bulvar.* **Open** noon-midnight daily. **Map**
p221 E4 ⓰

Think Russian hunting lodge and you get an idea of the ambience at this bar-restaurant. Colourful rugs and animal skins on the floor contrast with the peasant wooden furniture of the *dacha*. Note also the necklaces of smoked fish decorating the walls. Set away from the main tourist area and used by locals, this friendly tavern provides draught beer at prices cheaper than most, perhaps accompanied by a plate of fried stringy cheese. For those customers with bigger appetites, smoked fish and sausage are the main focus of a basic, good-value menu with fair attempts at English translations. The welcoming staff also speak adequate service English.

North Baku

Tri Bochki

*Dilara Aliyeva Street 251 (418 0240, 498
0812, 050 578 5226 mobile). Metro 28
May.* **Open** 24hrs daily. **No credit cards.** **Map**
pp220 D3 ⓱

An unusual find this, but one you might appreciate if you're coming in to or going out of Baku by train, due to its location. The 'Three Barrels' is a 24-hour pub with a decent but affordable menu and the welcome draught beer options of Paulaner, Krusovice and Efes. Elvis, Homer Simpson and the black-and-white stripes of Juventus all get a decorative look-in, while the bar food complements copious consumption of ale: smoked sausages, chicken wings and fish 'specially smoked for beer', most notably mackerel. The choice runs up to pepper steaks and *shato brian*, but you're really here to raise a toast to your arrival or departure.

Sahil & East Baku

Konti Bar

Nizami Street 117 (498 9191). Metro 28 May.
Open 1pm-midnight daily. **No credit cards.**
Map p220 D4 ⑱
Attached to the lesser-known Galereya restaurant (*see p115*) near the Landmark hotel, this spot swiftly gained popularity thanks to its key gimmick – punters pour their own beer. All the action takes place in a dark room – part-beer hall, part-hunting lodge – which can feel ghostly when empty but provides bags of fun if there are crowds of you. The Konti shares its tankard-shaped menu with the Galeriya, but don't expect all the items to be available. *Photo p124.*

München

Nizami Street 125 (493 7600). Metro 28 May.
Open 1pm-midnight daily. **No credit cards.**
Map p220 D4 ⑲
This rather splendid new(ish) bar near the Landmark building brings a bit of Bavaria to Baku. Decked out in bare, dark wood and the blue and white colours of Bayern, München feels almost church-like in its reverence for beer. Schnitzel, sausages and potato salads are served to accompany the decent range – draught Paulaner, Zipfer and Heineken complement the ubiquitous Xirdalan, Efes and Baltika. Flatscreen TVs await football action.

Sky Bar & Lounge

Landmark Building, Nizami Street 90A (465 2000, www.thelandmarkhotel.az). Metro 28 May. **Open** 9pm-2am daily. **Map** p221 D4 ⑳
Many swear by the 17th-floor Sky Bar as *the* place for cocktails in Baku, although choices are somewhat unadventurous and the decor is so inappropriate it

hurts. But the Caspian view is amazing, and the long island iced tea, manhattan and sex on the beach (all AZN12) are decent enough, when they arrive. Selena Vickovic was the Serbian artist responsible for the mutilated teddy bears and images of sundry bloodied body parts that provide the decorative backdrop as expats unwind, jazz piano tinkling in a corner somewhere. There are also standard bottled beers and wine, although prices are sky-high: AZN75 for a chablis premier cru, AZN105 for a rioja gran reserva. Thin toasted sandwiches join salads, pastries, ice-cream and fruit platters on the menu.

CONSUME

Dragon Lounge. See p124.

CLUBS

150 Bar & Grill

Izmir Street 9, North Baku (537 0516). Metro 20 Yanvar. **Open** noon-1am daily. **Map** p220 A2.
Located in the same complex in the edge-of-town congress quarter as the Opera Lounge (*see right*), this sophisticated, mellow late-night hangout comprises a lounge bar and restaurant. Decorated in plush neutral tones, 150 has a chilled-out atmosphere, augmented at weekends when the resident DJ spins ambient house and jazz. A relaxing spot for evening cocktails, 150 also has an extensive international food menu. In summer, the concertina windows are pushed back, making it convivial for early dinner with sundowners.

★ Dragon Lounge

Chinar, Shovket Alakbarova Street 1, Sabayil & West Baku (492 0888, www.chinar-dining.az). All buses to Funikulyor. **Open** 6pm-last guest. **Map** p221 B6.
The upstairs cocktail bar of the Chinar restaurant takes its name from the statue at the centre of the roundabout opposite, a dramatic depiction of the Azeri equivalent of St George and the Dragon. No less dramatic are some of the drinks at this evening-only establishment, staff delivering flaming beverages into a traditional *armudi* cup, offsetting the slight burnt flavour with a grapefruit zest. This is a proper cocktail bar, where a complimentary bowl of spicy dried peas comes with your drink as you relax in comfortable leather seats. Customers may choose from the sushi selection up here or dishes from the Chinar restaurant downstairs. A distinctly clubby atmosphere takes over when the DJ mans the decks above the main door, dry ice and all.

Hezz Club

Nazim Hikmet Street 27 (510 6600, 050 240 6600 mobile). Metro Elmlar Akademiyasi. **Open**

INSIDE TRACK GOING SOFT

One of the more bizarre aspects of ordering drinks in Baku is particularly noticeable in summer. With the temperature sweltering outside – it's a desert city, after all – you stagger into the nearest bar and ask for a Coke. The waiter will then ask if you'd like it cold or at room temperature. While your brain does somersaults trying to figure out who in their right mind would ever drink Coke at room temperature at any time of the year, you should simply and politely suggest 'Cold, please', and have him bring you one.

10pm-late Fri, Sat. **Admission** AZN30-AZN50. **Map** p220 A3.
The Hezz is the name to drop in Baku at the moment. In Yasamal, north-west of Elmlar Akademiyasi metro station, this upmarket club and restaurant is done out in minimalist decor – not unlike the studio of some cool TV station. As is the trend among upmarket clubs and bars in Baku these days, the cuisine is Japanese. An extremely wealthy clientele often hire out the whole club for celebrations, so do phone ahead to check it's open. The club hosts quality international DJs – Fedde Le Grand was a recent visitor. You won't be surprised to learn that, in line with the capital's other fashionable venues, prices are high.

Living Room

Z Taghiyev Street 17 (493 8725, www.living room.az). All buses to Fountains Square. **Open** 9pm-6am daily. **Map** p222 H3.
This underrated all-night bar-club, attracting a complete cross-section of (mainly) locals, is just a few minutes' walk from Fountains Square. With tasteful decor, sympathetic staff, half-decent music most of the time and bearable drinks prices, the Living Room is a wel-

Konti Bar. *See p123.*

Metkarting.

come alternative to the overpriced and over-the-top clubs spread out across the city. Food is of the pan-Asian variety, and you can happily spend an evening shooting pool, supping beer and nibbling onion bhajis.

Metkarting
Aliyar Aliyev Street 1993, North Baku (564 3332, 050 250 5200 mobile). Metro Bakmil. **Open** 7pm-late daily.

Situated in Narimanov, north of the city centre, this disco is a Baku landmark. Combining go-karts and clubbing, Metkarting comprises a mini race circuit with a bar-club alongside, attracting locals to dress up and dance beneath the mirror balls. Reasonably well-known DJs plying their trade around the former Soviet Union usually make a good fist of providing mainstream, danceable sounds, while outside the sun loungers come into their own after May. All in all, Metkarting is fun, inclusive and affordable – three elusive terms as far as most local nightlife is concerned.

Opera Lounge
Izmir Street 9, Sabayil & West Baku (418 0660, www.operalounge.az). Metro 20 Yanvar. **Open** noon-1am Mon-Thur; noon-2am Fri, Sat; 3pm-1am Sun. **Map** p220 A2.

Set beside the Grand Hotel Europe, near the International Business Center, this stylish, contemporary bar, restaurant and club attracts a well-heeled clientele. Predominantly local visitors sip cocktails in intimate booths, occasionally gazing at the flatscreen TV dedicated to each seating area. During the day and early evening, Opera Lounge operates more as a restaurant – food leans towards pan-Asian, with sushi and noodle dishes among the offerings. All standard spirits are available, along with a limited wine selec-

tion. Classic cocktails are priced the same as the standard long drinks – note the favoured Opera Mojito, a fruity variation on the norm. Hookahs are on offer in a variety of flavours. At weekends, when reservations are recommended, DJs play house music to a crowd of young, glamorous regulars.

World Fashion Club
Uzeyir Hajibeyov Street 33-35, Sahil & East Baku (050 433 3306-8 mobile). Metro Sahil. **Open** 10pm-5am Fri, Sat. **Admission** AZN20-AZN40. **Map** p221 D4.

Set behind Government House, this is the kind of high-spending club that can be great fun if somebody else is paying. The minimum spend for a table for four is AZN200 – about £150 or $230 – and for that you'd think the service would be a little swifter and more polite. The DJing is acceptable, and ladies' nights seem to be all the rage. Other than this, the World Fashion Club doesn't seem to attract that many westerners to join the inner circle of cash-flashing local businessmen who seem to gather here.

INSIDE TRACK
GIRLS NOT ALLOWED

A quiet unaccompanied drink in Baku as a lone female can be uncomfortable. It is not uncommon in drinking spots of all kinds to find that the only other women present are of the working variety. Also, despite the prevalence of smoking in Azerbaijan, it is frowned upon for women to smoke and they are generally not seen doing so in public.

Shops & Services

Big-name brands and beautiful carpets.

First-time visitors might stroll along the pedestrianised commercial strip of Nizami and down the Bulvar, gawp at the windows of Gucci, Versace and Dolce & Gabbana, and gain the initial impression that Baku is a shopper's paradise on an equal footing with Moscow or any capital in the West. But don't be fooled – the town centre contains only one proper supermarket worth the name, and offers little to hint at the creative forces at work within the city itself. There are far too few places in Baku to find pieces by indigenous clothes designers or artisans.

CONSUME

SHOPPING IN THE CITY

The unfortunate fact is that little here entices the curiosity of the hardened traveller, with few of the dusty bric-a-brac shops you'd find across the Balkans or in hubs of the former Soviet, Persian or Ottoman empires. Baku has virtually no second-hand bookshops, for example, and not much in the way of unusual knick-knacks or souvenirs. It has no bazaars – not of the kind that makes Istanbul such a wonderful proposition. This must also be one of the few capitals in the Eurovision zone where you can't pick up a postcard without paying for some kitschy boxed-up collection, a remnant of Soviet days.

The colourful exception to this tale of tack and globalised brands is the carpet trade (*see p138* **Cutting a Rug**). Every other shop around the Old City seems to sell what many westerners think of as Persian carpets (in fact, many carpets in modern-day Iran were actually created by Azeri hands). With a revolutionary new museum dedicated to this rich aspect of local culture being unveiled in early 2012 (*see p76*), carpets merit investigation.

Most of the carpet stores around the Old City also deal in women's silk scarves, or *kelagayi*, Astrakhan hats and other decorative accessories that make attractive gifts.

OPENING TIMES AND PRICES

Few businesses in Baku open before 10am, so don't rush out thinking you might snag a bargain. Sales, in fact, are few and far between, and the price of a pair of jeans – or, in fact, pretty much anything – is up to a third more expensive than you would find in London or most Western capitals. On the plus side, stores stay open late, until 9pm or 10pm in summer.

Note that many of the local stores still operate a system whereby you have to pay for something at the cash desk (and therefore asking for/describing it) before taking your receipt to the assistant who actually hands over the goods. Credit cards are widely accepted at international stores, but rarely at local shops.

INSIDE TRACK BARGAINING

It's inevitable. You're drawn into a boutique in the Old City by the accented patter of the shop owner ('My friend, just look'), and before you know it you're having tea and talking about the price of carpets. Just as the price you start at will appear to you as pleasingly cheap, the one your counterpart is bargaining with will be too high. Before you know it, you're bargaining, the age-old ritual of trade in this part of the world. As you seem to be reaching some kind of middle ground on a fair fee, you might even throw a curveball by attempting to leave, but your trader is wise to such ruses and comes back with a seemingly unbeatable offer. You accept, shake hands (making sure to make eye contact) and walk out with what you think is a bargain – at what is probably the price your salesman had in mind when you walked in. Both parties satisfied, said trader walks back out and begins his pitch once more: 'My friend, just look.'

General

DEPARTMENT STORES

Debenhams
1st & 2nd Floors, Park Bulvar, Neftchilar prospekt (598 7131/2/3). All buses to Bulvar. **Open** 10am-10pm daily. **Map** p221 D4.
Dominating the ground floor and first floor of the modern Park Bulvar mall, this UK department store brings a touch of home to pining expats. Fashion, footwear and sundry accessories are all available – although there's little in the way of homewares. *Photo p128.*

★ MUM
Azerbaijan prospekt (944 390). All buses to city centre. **Open** 10.30am-7pm daily. **No credit cards. Map** p223 H4.
Opposite the Ministry of Internal Affairs, this is Baku's equivalent of Moscow's GUM, just on a much smaller scale. 'Moom' looks exactly like the Soviet-era department store it is, opened the same year that Yuri Gagarin flew into space – 1961. As much a tourist sight as a shopping experience, MUM offers three floors of frilly wedding dresses, made-to-measure suits, cheap watches and jewellery, along with practical items such as three-pin plug adaptors. Mass-produced crafts and souvenirs are also available. Always crowded, but worth visiting for the spectacle.

MALLS

Until the planned 2012 opening of a new mall near the 28 May metro station and a selection of upscale outlets at the Port Baku Towers development (*see p74*), the main mall in the city is the **Park Bulvar** on the seafront. First-time visitors should bear in mind that Azeri floor numbers start at level 1 (ground floor), followed by level 2 (first floor), and so on.

★ Park Bulvar
Neftchilar prospekt (598 8080, www.park bulvar.az). All buses to Bulvar. **Open** *Shops* 10am-10pm daily. *Restaurants & entertainment* 10am-1am daily. **Map** p221 D4.
Opened in 2010, this is Baku's first (and so far) only modern shopping mall. Its location on the seafront means its key eateries (Zeytun, Kitchenette) have fabulous Caspian views. The swish complex also contains Baku's only real supermarket, Citi Mart, and features branches of Debenhams, Benetton, Oasis and L'Occitane, along with the six-screen Park Cinema, Bohm Planetarium, a bowling alley and kids' play zone.

Pasaj
Corner of Rasul-Zadeh Street & Ali-Zadeh prospekt (no phone). All buses to city centre. **Open** 10.30am-9pm daily. **Map** p222 H3.
The Passage Arcade was conceived in the classic western style of the day in 1898 by Azeri oil baron

Park Bulvar.

Debenhams. *See p127.*

CONSUME

Taghiyev. It was a beautiful structure then and, after a recent renovation, remains a pleasure to walk through. It is lined with outlets such as Benetton, Passport and Naf-Naf.

Khagani Ticaret Merkezi

Corner of Khagani & Rasul Rza Streets (349 1969). All buses to city centre. **Open** 10.30am-7pm daily. **No credit cards. Map** p222 H3.
Khagani is full of shops selling cheap wristwatches, little animals made of cut-glass and cheap fashion. Its one saving grace, apart from its central location, is the souvenir shop of Soviet junk on the third floor.

MARKETS

You shouldn't come to Baku expecting the attractive, tourist-friendly bazaars of Istanbul or other cities in the region. The city has just one main food market, a produce market and a catch-all chaos of a place, the **Teze Bazaar**. *See p132* **Where the Stalls Have No Name.**

Specialist

BOOKS & MAGAZINES

English-language

★ Ali & Nino

Zeynalabdin Taghiyev Street 19 (493 0412, www.alinino.az). All buses to city centre. **Open** 10am-9pm daily. **Map** p222 H3.

A real success story, this, born out of a gap in the market for contemporary books in English, Azeri and Russian. Ismail Imanov and Nigar Köçarli are the driving force behind the chain, which takes its name from a popular local novel. They made a success of two Downtown stores, opening a literary café opposite one of them, before unveiling a branch inside the entrance of the Park Bulvar mall and, in 2011, a modest store in the Old City. Thanks to good contacts with UK publishers, new books arrive regularly, and what cannot be displayed through pressure of space can be ordered on the (so far) Azeri-only website.
Other locations Nizami Street 91 (493 9368); Park Bulvar, ground floor (598 7156).
▶ *For Ali & Nino café, see p100.*

Chiraq

Istiglaliyyat Street 47 (492 3289). Metro Icheri Sheher. **Open** 10am-7pm daily. **No credit cards. Map** p58 M2.
This long-established bookshop stocks a limited number of English-language titles, mainly guidebooks and presentation albums. It's a short walk from Fountain Square or, if you're coming across town, a climb up Istiglaliyyat from Icheri Sheher metro station.

General

Book House of the Administration Department of the President of the Republic of Azerbaijan

Fountains Square (no phone). All buses to city centre. **Open** 10am-7pm daily. **No credit cards. Map** p222 G3.

You might be able to tell from its snazzy name that this bookshop is Soviet-era. Right on Fountain Square, it stocks a whole range of books in Russian and Azeri, along with a small selection of English-language tourist guides and albums relating to Azerbaijan. Annoyingly, it's also still run on Soviet lines, so everything is under glass and you have to ask the shuffling old manager to take out and hand over whatever you're interested in – you can't just browse. There's a comfortable adjoining space selling art, and stationery on offer too.

Used & antiquarian

Kitab Magazasi Elman
Gulla Street 10, Old City (492 6290, 050 377 0960 mobile). Metro Icheri Sheher. **Open** 10am-2pm, 3-6pm Tue-Sun. **No credit cards. Map** p58 O4.
Facing the Maiden's Tower, this old-style bookshop was actually opened in 1997, but the old gent who runs it looks like he's been working here since 1897. There's not too much in English, but Russian speakers can feast their eyes on lovely old hardback copies of Pushkin, Tolstoy and others. It's also a good source for city maps at a knockdown AZN3 a pop.

CHILDREN

Armani Junior
Neftchilar prospekt 91 (437 2702, www.armani junior.com). All buses to Bulvar. **Open** 10am-9pm daily. **Map** p223 H5.
All the latest Italian fashions for babies, juniors and teens, right on Baku's shop-window boulevard.

Baby Dior
Neftchilar prospekt 131 (498 0660, www.dior.com). All buses to Bulvar. **Open** 10am-9pm daily. **Map** p222 K3.
The latest seasonal fashions for chic kids and toddlers about town, all the way from Paris.

Mothercare
Rasul Zadeh Street 8, off Fountain Square (498 0052). All buses to city centre. **Open** 10am-9pm daily. **Map** p223 G4.
The most central of the four Baku branches of this familiar British retailer, with clothes, toys and handy items for expectant parents, babies and kids up to eight years old.
Other locations Azerbaijan prospekt 42 (596 0553); Nariman Narimanov prospekt 125 (447 4440); Huseyn Javid Street 81 (448 0902).

ELECTRONICS & PHOTOGRAPHY

Baku Electronics
28 May Street 12 (493 2853, www.baku electronics.az). Metro 28 May. **Open** 10am-7pm daily. **Map** p220 D3.

This is the most conveniently located branch of this extensive chain, which stocks all kinds of goods, from washing machines and vacuum cleaners to iPhones and laptops.
Other locations throughout the city.

Bang & Olufsen
28 May Street 12 (498 0333, www.bang-olufsen.com). Metro 28 May. **Open** 10am-7pm daily. **Map** p220 D3.
International traders Italdizain brought the Danish audio giant to Azerbaijan, selling high-end music and sound systems, and other electrical finery, to Baku's big spenders.

MG Center
Azadlig prospekt 14 (437 2253, www.mgstore.az). Metro 28 May. **Open** 10am-8pm daily. **Map** p222 J2.
The biggest branch of this chain of stores specialises in photographic and video equipment, and appliances of all sizes. There's also a home delivery service available. Another outlet (*see p140*) specialises in musical instruments.

FASHION

There are too many international outlets now trading in Baku to list them all – a stroll down the Bulvar or Nizami will reveal a host of familiar global brands. The following are some of the biggest names.

Ali & Nino.

Tom Ford.

CONSUME

Boss

Rasul Rza Street 6 (498 8787, www.emporio armani.com). All buses to city centre. **Open** 10am-8pm daily. **Map** p222 H3.

Hugo Boss's high-end menswear from Metzingen, Germany has a city-centre window to show off its striking cuts and styles.

Burberry

Neftchilar prospekt 121 (498 9656, www. burberry.com). All buses to Bulvar. **Open** 9.30am-8pm daily. **Map** p223 J4.

It's checks, mate, all the way from Basingstoke to Baku: blue-chip British menswear, womenswear, shoes and accessories.

Céline

Neftchilar prospekt 105 (437 3935, www. celine.com). All buses to Bulvar. **Open** 10am-8pm daily. **Map** p223 H4.

Céline has a range of luxury Gallic togs, clogs and bags from the House of LVMH, with new looks by the season.

Dior

Neftchilar prospekt 105 (437 6202, www.dior. com). All buses to Bulvar. **Open** 10am-8pm daily. **Map** p223 H4.

This must be one of the most handsomely located branches in Dior's global empire, overlooking the Caspian Sea with Baku's Old City in the background. The whole Dior universe is here – prêt-à-porter, jewellery, menswear and womenswear.

Dolce & Gabbana

Neftchilar prospekt 117 (493 4082, www.dolce gabbana.com). All buses to Bulvar. **Open** 10am-8pm daily. **Map** p223 J4.

This branch of the Italian luxury fashion house stocks menswear, womenswear, shoes and accessories, including sunglasses.

Emporio Armani

Rasul Rza Street 4 (498 1808, www.emporio armani.com). All buses to city centre. **Open** 9.30am-9pm daily. **Map** p222 H3.

A city-centre rather than seafront location for the Baku outlet of this iconic, ready-to-wear brand, with clothes, shoes and accessories for both sexes.

Ermenegildo Zegna

Neftchilar prospekt 89 (497 8923, 050 520 8046 mobile, www.zegna.com). All buses to Bulvar. **Open** 10am-9pm daily. **Map** p223 H5.

Wonders in wool for men from this century-old Italian fashion house, with footwear and accessories to match the suit or jacket.

Gucci

Neftchilar prospekt 117 (498 0055, 050 245 1115 mobile, www.gucci.com). All buses to Bulvar. **Open** 10am-8pm daily. **Map** p223 J4.

Italy's biggest-selling brand numbers Baku among its 300-odd stores worldwide, giving moneyed Bakuvians the chance to splash the manats on outerwear, underwear, swimwear, shoes, bags and accessories for him, her and their offspring.

boom years and featuring a likeness of General de Gaulle on a plaque commemorating his visit in 1944. Today, you'll find luxury menswear by the designer who revolutionised Gucci.

Versace
Neftchilar prospekt 125A (417 6125). All buses to Bulvar. **Open** 10am-8pm daily. **Map** p223 J4.
This high-profile label made a suitably big splash when it launched in Baku in 2010, offering fashion lines for men and women, plus accessories.

FASHION ACCESSORIES & SERVICES

Cleaning & repairs

Citimart
Level -1, Park Bulvar mall, Neftichilar prospekt (598 7177). All buses to Bulvar. **Open** 10am-11pm daily. **Map** p221 D4.
Located to the left of the main entrance to the city's leading supermarket (*see p127*) is this dry-cleaning outlet offering all the usual services.

Hats

★ Modalar Atelyesi
Beside MUM, Azerbaijan prospekt (055 550 1616 mobile). All buses to city centre. **Open** 10am-8pm daily. **No credit cards. Map** p223 H4.
If you're looking for something a little different to take back from Baku, then a hat made by Ramin should be just the ticket. Ramin's father opened the cave-like shop more than 50 years ago, and today there are loads of different styles available – highly recommended is the traditional *mullah papag*, made from the grey fleece of karakul lambs from Astrakhan.

Jewellery

Bulgari
A Aliyev Street 1 (437 6232, www.bulgari.com). All buses to city centre. **Open** 10am-7.30pm daily. **Map** p223 H5.
Luxury stones and gems from this age-old Italian company, plus watches, fragrances and accessories.

Cartier
28 May Street 2 (493 8929, www.cartier.com). Metro 28 May. **Open** 10am-8pm daily. **Map** p220 D3.
Cartier opened here in 2008 with a ceremony at the Philharmonia. At this somewhat prosaic location – this is hardly Baku's Fifth Avenue – you'll find classic jewellery, timepieces and leather accessories.

Tiffany
A Aliyev Street 1 (437 6252, www.tiffany.com). All buses to city centre. **Open** 10am-7.30pm daily. **Map** p223 H5.

Mango
Bulbul prospekt 21 (498 0598, www.mango.com). Metro Sahil. **Open** 10am-9pm daily. **Map** p222 J1.
Six locations in town for the ever-popular Spanish chain of mainstream womenswear. This one near the corner with Nizami is the most prominent; there's another in the Park Bulvar mall.
Other locations throughout the city.

Paul & Shark
Uzeyir Hajibeyov Street 8 (493 5355, www.paul shark.it). Metro Sahil. **Open** 10am-9pm daily. **Map** p222 J3.
Classic Italian casual gear for men and women, along with striking jackets and strides.

Quiksilver
Z Taghiyev Street 19 (493 9015). All buses to city centre. **Open** 10.30am-9pm Mon-Sat; 11am-9pm Sun. **Map** p222 H3.
This international brand of sporty, casual beach gear from California washed up in Baku in May 2011 and proved an instant hit with young Azeri. Prices for T-shirts, shorts and general summerwear are a notch above what you'd pay in Europe or the US. Staff are friendly and quick to help.

Tom Ford
Neftchilar prospekt 103 (437 3967). All buses to Bulvar. **Open** 10am-8pm daily. **Map** p223 H5.
Of all the locations for a shop in Baku, it doesn't get better than this: the ground floor of the sumptuous Hajinski Mansion, built a century ago during the oil

CONSUME

As part of its worldwide expansion in the last few years, this New York jeweller now hangs out its shingle in a city-centre outlet of the Azeri capital.

Shoes

Bata

Nizami Street 91 (493 5005, www.bata.com). Metro Sahil. **Open** 11am-9pm daily. **Map** p222 J2.

Comfortable, affordable footwear for all the family, thanks to eight generations of cobblers from Zlin in the Czech Republic.

Ecco

Jafar Jabbarli Street 21 (597 0604, www.ecco. com). All buses to Yasamal. **Open** 10am-9pm daily. **Map** p220 B3.

Innovative, casual footwear from Denmark at a slightly out-of-the-way outlet north of the city centre.

Where the Stalls Have No Name

Fruit, vegetables and much more – fresh from the back of a car or van.

The markets in Baku, where local people shop, are utilitarian and lacking in charm. Having said that, they do provide an interesting insight into how people live in Baku, and what they eat and drink; few tourists venture into these crowded, noisy, dusty and chaotic places.

On the up side, they are vibrantly authentic and exciting. The people are friendly and enjoy bargaining, you can find almost anything, and the fresh produce tastes wonderful. In addition to the Central Vegetable Market, there are two other key trading hubs, both of which merit a visit in their own right.

The **Yashil Bazaar**, (or 'Green' Bazaar) on Khatai Prospekt, sells mostly fruit and vegetables, transported from the countryside in the back of whatever vehicle happens to be to hand. An old Lada full to the brim with apples, with only just enough space for the driver, jostles for space with

an ancient lady perched on a motorbike of similar vintage, its panniers full of onions. These mounds of precariously balanced fresh produce are hazards for the unwary, as are the mud and dust underfoot, so stout footwear is essential.

The fruit and vegetables are seasonal. Don't expect the perfect-looking, hot-housed specimens of a typical British or US supermarket. Here they are misshapen, malformed and covered with the very soil they were grown in. And they taste wonderful – lemons come in from Astara in the south, pomegranates from Goychay to the west, apples from Guba in the north, okra and other vegetables from Beylagan, and much, much more. Also worth looking out for are the nuts and dried fruit, both of which are high quality and reasonably priced.

Local saffron is available alongside other dried herbs and spices. Yet it is the smell of fresh herbs that scent the air.

CONSUME

Muya
Istiglaliyyat Street 49 (492 9979, www.muya.com).
Metro Icheri Sheher. **Open** 10am-9.30pm daily.
Map p58 M2.
A Turkish success story, this Avcilar-based
footwear brand was started in 1994 by two child-
hood friends. The comfortable and affordable shoes
are available at this downtown outlet a ten-minute
walk from Fountain Square or a climb from Icheri
Sheher metro station.

Other locations Ahmad Rajabli prospekt 3/27
(465 2880).

FOOD & DRINK
Bakeries

★ **Azza**
Khagani Street 15 (www.azza.az). All buses to city
centre. **Open** 8am-7pm daily. **Map** p222 H3.

Large bunches of parsley, dill, coriander,
tarragon and mint are good value. Less
widely available but generally present in
the market is cheese, which can be tasted
directly from the sheep's skin in which it has
fermented. Also look out for the occasional
trader offering fresh, tiny eggs from quails
and bantam hens. And small chickens
complete with head and feet, but fully
plucked, provide a contrast to the oversized
birds you might find at home. Just before
leaving the Yashil Bazaar, check out the
live fish for sale, wriggling in tubs of water.

By contrast, the **Teze Bazaar**, where
Samed Vurgun meets Asgarova, sells
absolutely everything. Here, the smell is
of fresh red meat from the row of butchers'
stalls. Nearby are fish slabs for washing and
boning unrecognisable species of fish and
seafood, as well as sturgeon. Beware the
stallholder who offers you caviar, as it may
be fake – the real stuff is very expensive.

The many varieties of leaf tea might provide
a nice gift for friends and family.

Leaving behind the rows of dry produce,
you walk through a large area devoted
to electrical supplies, plumbing, lighting,
bathrooms, carpentry, cooking, and more
piping, cables, nuts, screws and bolts than
you could possibly imagine. Meanwhile,
puppies, kittens, rabbits and birds for
sale provide a rather pitiful backdrop.

Although dilapidated, the **Central
Vegetable Market** (*see p134*) is, all in all,
a more civilised and enjoyable affair. As
its name suggests, it is centrally located –
beside the Ministry of Internal Affairs and
accessed through a narrow colonnaded
gate of Greek pillars – and is the place to
head for fresh fruit and vegetables. Set in
a delightfully run-down courtyard, it's a great
spot to spend half an hour bargaining for
nar (pomegranates) and all manner of fresh,
seasonal produce.

CONSUME

This is the closest branch to Fountain Square of this successful chain of pâtisseries, serving delicious cakes and pastries. The Azza group has since expanded into cafés and restaurants, where its signature desserts still feature.

Other locations throughout the city.

★ Brothaus

Nizami Street 78 (498 5959, www.brothaus.az). *Metro Sahil.* **Open** 8am-10pm Mon-Fri; 9am-10pm Sat, Sun. **No credit cards. Map** p222 K2.

Just east of the city centre, this great German-style bakery offers an enticing range of unusual breads: *sonnenblumenkernbrot* with sunflower seeds; *weltmeisterbrot* with poppy and sesame seeds; and the extra crusty, 37% rye *krustenbrot*. There are gooey cakes too – topped with wild berries, raspberries or exotic fruit – as well as a selection for diabetics. Coffee is also served, and there's plenty of space to tuck into one of the home-made sandwiches.

Drinks

★ Wine City

Lermontov Street 76 (437 2886). All buses to city centre. **Open** 10.30am-10pm daily. **Map** p221 B5.

Wine City provides the best choice of labels in Baku, but be warned – it's very expensive. You can get a half-decent French chardonnay or Australian shiraz here, but you will pay through the nose. A bottle of South African Tall Horse, for example, costs AZN22, five times the UK price. Better value might be a dry red from the local Ismayilli winery.

General

Citimart

Level -1, Park Bulvar mall, Neftchilar prospekt (598 7177). All buses to Bulvar. **Open** 10am-midnight daily. **Map** p221 D4.

This is the supermarket that all the expats head to, set in the downstairs, car-park level of the Park Bulvar

Fantasia Bathhouse. *See p136.*

mall. Citimart isn't particularly large, but it stocks a reasonable range of items from across the region. You might even find celery, otherwise as rare as hen's teeth in this town. There's a separate bakery area too.

Other locations Samed Vurgun Street 19 (447 2330).

Kontinental

Nizami Street 68 (493 7541). All buses to city centre. **Open** 9am-9pm daily. **Map** p222 J2.

This supermarket may not have the full range of goods you would normally expect, but it's at least partly targeted towards the expat market. It's the place to come and indulge yourself with wines, cheeses, chocolates and spirits, all at prices you wouldn't dream of paying at home.

Markets

★ Central Vegetable Market

Nigar Rafibeyli Street (no phone). All buses to city centre. **Open** 8am-5pm daily. **No credit cards. Map** p222 F3.

This dilapidated courtyard, hidden by a colonnaded gate, is the place to come for fresh, seasonal produce. *See p132* **Where the Stalls Have No Name**.

Specialist

Patchi

Nizami Street 70 (498 0072/3, www.patchi.com). *Metro Sahil.* **Open** 10am-9pm daily. **Map** p222 J2.

Patchi offers a wonderful array of luxury chocolates from Lebanon, decorated in an imaginative variety of styles and ideal for special occasions.

INSIDE TRACK
DYNAMO, LOKOMOTIV
& SPARTAK

For that perfect gift for the football fan who has everything, the little kiosk beside the double gates of the Old City is a treasure trove of rare Soviet and Eastern European football badges. Sold at a bargain across-the-board price of AZN1, AZN2 or AZN3, depending on an unfathomable system of valuation, they feature the iconic emblems of clubs such as Dynamo, Lokomotiv and Spartak. The friendly guy behind the window will gladly fold out the felt display for you to peruse.

CONSUME

Valonia

Zivarbey Ahmadbeyov Street 2 (596 6881).
All buses to Yasamal. **Open** 10am-8pm daily.
No credit cards. Map p222 G1.

Best described as a chocolate shop, 'Wallonia' (as in Belgium) specialises in pralines and other naughty delights, prepared according to Belgian recipes. Valonia also sells cakes, sundry desserts and does a side business in outside catering.

GIFTS & SOUVENIRS

You may also find a piece suitable for a gift or souvenir at **Antiquary** (*see p140*).

★ Ancestors Footsteps' Art Centre

Boyuk Gala Street 15 (492 3390). Metro Icheri Sheher. **Open** 10am-7pm daily. **No credit cards. Map** p58 N4.

This intriguing little shop in the Old City sells high-quality, handmade souvenirs, and is worth a look if only to watch the owner at work. She weaves small carpets for use as mouse mats, paints pictures of the petroglyphs of Gobustan on hand-dyed silk, and creates spangled containers of varying sizes, from jewellery and make-up boxes to small trunks. She also demonstrates the various techniques of Azeri carpet-making. Look out for the large doll in traditional Azeri dress in the doorway. *See also p138* **Cutting a Rug**.

Sehrli Dakhmajig

Near Maiden Tower, Old City (437 3286,
www.bakufairtrade.com). Metro Icheri Sheher.
Open 10.30am-5pm daily. **No credit cards.**
Map p58 04.

Also called 'Fair Trade Souvenirs', this tiny shop, tucked away down some steps around the corner from the Maiden Tower, is a rare and welcome example of an enterprising outlet for Azeri artisans. The owners buy handmade pottery, painted glass and colourful hand-knitted socks directly from producers across the country. Check out the paintings done in Caspian oil by local artist Mutteqi. Most of the profits go to those who produce the goods.

Souvenir Shop

Khagani Ticaret Merkezi, corner of Khagani &
Rasul Rza Streets (349 1969). All buses to city
centre. **Open** 10.30am-7pm daily. **No credit cards. Map** p222 H3.

Three floors up by lift in the sad, antiquated central shopping centre of Khagani, the prosaically named Souvenir Shop does a fine line in old postcards of Lenin and Kirov, old Communist badges and sundry memorabilia perched among the gaudy dolls in national dress and other knick-knacks.

Yusif Mirza Gallery

Khagani Street 4 (050 347 8543 mobile). All
buses to city centre. **Open** call for details. **No credit cards. Map** p222 H3.

Three minutes' walk from Fountains Square, and tucked away behind Sultan's restaurant, this friendly little gallery is run by the charming Yusif Mirza, whose striking works depict Baku in days gone by. Expect to pay AZN100 for a framed drawing and around AZN250 for an oil painting on canvas. Although it's usually open during normal business hours, it's best to phone ahead so Yusuf can get the kettle on and fill a bowl with sweets to welcome you.

CONSUME

HEALTH & BEAUTY

Shops

Inglot
Rasul Zadeh Street 8, Fountains Square (498 8444, www.inglotcosmetics.com). All buses to city centre. **Open** 10am-9pm daily. **Map** p222 G3.

With its loyal international customer base, Inglot couldn't fail to succeed in Baku. This sought-after cosmetics outlet has one store on the main square and one in the main mall. It offers high-quality cosmetics made from mainly natural materials, and sold at a reasonable price.

Other locations Park Bulvar, Neftchilar prospekt (www.parkbulvar.az).

Spa
Azerbaijan prospekt 4 (497 7207). All buses to city centre. **Open** 10.30am-8pm daily. **Map** p222 G3.

Spa's range of handmade cosmetics, soaps, aromatic oils and bubble baths are not cheap, but they are of excellent quality. This is the place to go for Attirance cosmetics from Latvia, Ashleigh & Burwood premium-quality incense, and all manner of gifts to make you feel good about yourself.

Opticians

Optic Gallery
Aziz Aliyev Street 11 (497 3398, www.optic gallery.az). All buses to city centre. **Open** 10am-8pm Mon-Sat; noon-8pm Sun. **Map** p223 H5.

Located opposite the Azerbaijan Cinema, this is the most central branch of the classy Optic Gallery chain.

INSIDE TRACK STEAM DREAMS

While the **Fantasia** is considered the best hammam in town, the **Taze Bey** (Sheikh Shamil Street 14, www.tazebey.az) dates from the same era and was fully restored to its former glory in 2003. With three types of baths, a pool and a full range of services, all set in beautiful surroundings, the Taze Bey is an attractive proposition – but open to men only. General admission is AZN17, with differing payments for all kinds of treatments, including thrashing with birch twigs (AZN10). In a tradition dating back generations, a groom can also hire a room for his stag night (AZN60). In the Old City, the **Mehellesi**, near Icheri Sheher metro station, is the oldest working hammam in Baku. It serves men and women on different days (women on Mondays and Fridays). Admission and treatments are generally cheaper than at the Fantasia or Taze Bey.

As a complete aside, this purveyor of designer sunglasses occupies part of the building where the writer Lev Nussimbaum lived, believed by some to be the author of cult local novel *Ali and Nino*.

Other locations Azerbaijan prospekt 12 (497 8348); A Radzhivil Street 5 (465 1326); Shuvalan Park, A Ildirim Street 68 (565 8833).

Pharmacies

Aptek
Corner of Azerbaijan prospekt & Ahmad Javad prospekt (596 0712). All buses to city centre. **Open** 24hrs daily. **No credit cards**. **Map** p222 G3.

There are plenty of 24-hour chemists in Baku, where you can buy all manner of pharmaceutical goods and prescription medicines over the counter, but this one stands out: it has a central location, and the helpful manager speaks excellent English.

Other locations throughout the city.

Spas & salons

Baku has three main traditional hammams and one outstanding spa, the **Sabun Nga Thai**. Many of the high-end hotels also offer spa facilities; cream of the crop is the **Excelsior** (*see p99*), with its Aura wellness centre.

★ Fantasia Bathhouse
Chingiz Mustafayev Street 114 (no phone). All buses to city centre. **Open** 10am-8pm daily. **Admission** AZN15 per hr. **No credit cards**. **Map** p222 G2.

If you're going to go to a bathhouse in town, this is the one. Built in 1887 in sumptuous style during the oil boom, Fantasia was Baku's first spa of the modern age, built around a complex of 26 private spaces with one main communal steam room. The waters were, and still are, piped in from the Shollar springs in the Caucasus mountains, while the ornate mouldings, chandeliers, beautifully tiled walls and solid-stone baths have all benefitted from major renovation in recent years. Even the plumbing looks authentic. Little, in fact, feels different to how a relaxing steam and soak would have been in 1887 – apart from the flatscreen TV in the tea room, worth a visit in its own right. Couples can hire a room of their own, otherwise the areas are single-sex. A one-hour session includes a revivifying scrub from expert hands. *Photo p134.*

★ Sabun Nga Thai
Hasanbay Zardabi Street 31-61 (497 0800, 497 0900, www.sabunngaspa.com). All buses to north-west Yasamal. **Open** 10am-8pm daily.

This luxury Thai day spa provides authentic treatments and excellent service. A complex of 16 ornate suites await customers, who are treated by highly skilled professionals trained at the company's academy in Chiang Mai. Exotic body scrubs, beauty treatments, massages and floral baths are among the

Taze Bey.

Cutting a Rug

The wonderful world of Azeri carpets.

One of the real joys of shopping in Baku is visiting the carpet shops. While Persian carpets are renowned in the West, those from Azerbaijan are of an equal standard. In fact, with Azeris making up a significant percentage of the population of present-day Iran, there's a fair chance that a modern Persian carpet will have been made by an Azeri anyway.

As a visitor, you can't fail to notice that carpets are an integral part of the local culture – it's said that every Azeri is born, lives and dies on a carpet. In fact, in 2010 the art of Azerbaijani carpet weaving was included in the UNESCO List of Intangible Cultural Heritage, and in early 2012 a new museum dedicated to the history and art of carpet-making, designed in the shape of a rolled-up rug, is scheduled to open on the Bulvar seafront (*see p76*).

Around the Old City, every vendor is anxious to make a sale, inviting visitors in to 'just look'. This can feel overwhelming at first, but choose a smaller shop in a side alley or down some steps, such as the **Magic Carpet Shop** (Mirza Shafi Street 20, 492 3268), and the experience will be a pleasant one. Accept the cup of tea offered, sit down, relax and allow the carpets to be displayed for you. Most of the sellers speak some English, and they are usually very knowledgeable about their goods.

There's no obligation to buy, even if you have seen 30 carpets. But if you do see something you like, and would like to make a purchase, be prepared to bargain. Carpets make great souvenirs, and the best could be considered as an investment. They vary in quality and size, but one small enough to transport can be bought for around AZN100.

Don't be distracted by the carpets exhibited outside the shops. They simply function as a colourful, if somewhat faded, invitation to enter and offer a preview of what is available.

There are two types of woollen carpet: flat weaves, the most popular being kilims or *sumakhs*; and knotted ones. For the latter, the quality of the carpet largely depends on the number of double knots per square centimetre. The higher the knot count, the better the quality.

Each region of Azerbaijan was traditionally associated with a particular design or motif, though the distinctions have become less clear as makers imitate the designs of

others. The designs are ancient and symbolic, representing the history and culture of each region of origin. Typically, carpets from the Guba and Shirvan areas have geometric patterns such as octagonal shapes alongside animal and bird representations; carpets from Baku have the paisley-shaped *buta* motif associated with Zoroastrians; those from Karabakh have a particularly dominant and large motif that resembles the number two. Nakhchivan, Gazakh and Ganja also have healthy cottage industries making carpets. Lastly, Tabriz carpets, from southern Azerbaijan (but now an area in north-west Iran) have distinctive flower motifs in place of geometric designs. These originate from the so-called golden age of carpet weaving during the 16th and 17th centuries. Most carpet shops in Baku also sell silk carpets, mostly from Sheki, and carpets from other countries such as Iran and Afghanistan. To learn more about the different skills involved in their manufacture, visit the **Ancestors Footsteps' Art Centre** (*see p135*) in the Old City, where the owner demonstrates the different techniques that produce the distinct textures of Azeri carpets as she weaves.

Carpets dyed with natural vegetable material tend to be more highly prized than those that have been chemically dyed. Natural dyes come from sources including pomegranate skin, onions, lemons, grapes and quinces. Saffron, madder flowers, fig leaves and walnuts are also used to produce the soft, subtle, yet intense shades typical of natural dyes. Synthetic dyes, on the other hand, sometimes have a harsh, acidic edge to them. A visit to the **Azer Ilme Carpet Factory** (Shamsi Rahimov Street 2, Nasimi) allows you to view the dyeing room and weaving area where the famous Ardabil Carpet Sheikh Safi, on display at London's Victoria & Albert Museum, is being re-created.

Every carpet larger than one metre square exported from Azerbaijan requires official certification, which carries an additional charge. The carpet seller arranges this, at a cost of around AZN25; you'll need to wait a few days for this to be sorted out. A premium can be paid if you need your carpet within the day. The process is currently carried out at the Carpet Museum (*see p76*), which is moving to new premises in early 2012.

CONSUME

services on offer. To get here, catch a taxi: Hasanbay Zardabi Street is a continuation of the main Matbuat prospekt, which runs to the northern fringes of the city through the western side of Yasamal.

HOUSE & HOME

Antiques

Sadly, authentic antiques shops are pretty thin on the ground in Baku, though you might find a few items in the fin-de-siècle surroundings of the **Pasaj** shopping arcade (*see p127*).

Antiquary
Rasul Rza Street 21 (050 621 6514 mobile). All buses to city centre. **Open** 11am-7pm daily. **Map** p222 H3.
Down a set of stairs on the corner of Rasul Rza and Ali-Zadeh, Antiquary is made up of several small antiques stalls. Here you can buy old ceramics, clocks, glassware and other collectibles. The location, in a bare stone cellar with a vaulted ceiling, lends the place a dungeon-like atmosphere.

General

Idea
Uzeyir Hajibeyov Street 33-35 (498 9660, www. italdizain.az). Metro Sahil. **Open** 10am-8pm Mon-Sat. **Map** p221 D4.
Idea's expansive store opposite Government House is well stocked with Europe's leading home-design styles – kitchen furniture by Lucci & Orlandini, Kube and Snaidero; funky lighting by Italamp, Lucitalia and Lumina; textiles from Nya Nordiska; and candles and chandeliers from Brand van Egmond.

Interiors
28 May Street 5 (493 8363). Metro 28 May. **Open** 10am-8.30pm daily. **Map** p220 D3.
This vast, classy store stocks furniture and accessories by the likes of Barbara Barry, Christopher Guy and Ralph Lauren, with wallpaper and fabrics by de Gournay. Guy himself made a personal appearance at the store's opening ceremony. Consultants are on hand to advise on your choice of design.

MUSIC & ENTERTAINMENT

CDs, records & DVDs

Hong Kong
Rasul Zadeh Street 5 (498 0681). All buses to city centre. **Open** 11.30am-9pm daily. **No credit cards. Map** p222 G3.
No, Hong Kong isn't another Chinese restaurant but an institution among Baku's expat community. For those who want to catch up on all those episodes of *The Sopranos* they've missed or watch the latest movies, Hong Kong has them all – and at AZN2 per

DVD. In case you needed any, Hong Kong also sells handbags and cheap sunglasses.

Musical instruments

MG Musician Academy
Shamsi Badalbeyli Street 98 (437 1149, www. mgstore.az). Metro 28 May. **Open** 10am-8pm daily. **Map** p222 J1.
This is one of two outlets of the MG chain (*see p129*) specialising in musical instruments.
Other locations By Azerbaijan Cinema, A Aliyev Street (497 7028).

SPORTS & FITNESS

United Sport
Bulbul prospekt 16 (493 7588). Metro Sahil. **Open** 10am-9pm daily. **Map** p222 J1.
This is probably the biggest and most well-stocked sports shop in Baku, with Nike, Adidas, Reebok and the rest. All manner of clothes, shoes and equipment line the shelves – chances are that if you can't find it here, then it probably isn't available in Baku.

TICKETS

Theatre & Concert Ticket Office
Opposite Azerbaijan Cinema, Rasul-Zadeh Street (493 3377). All buses to city centre. **Open** 11am-3pm, 4-7pm daily. **No credit cards. Map** p223 G4.
Of the dozen or so kiosks set up at prominent points around the city – each with a byzantine system of opening hours – this one is the most central. You can book tickets for mainstream events at the Opera & Ballet Theatre, Heydar Aliyev Palace, and so on.
Other locations throughout the city.

TRAVELLERS' NEEDS

Alma Store
Neftchilar prospekt 131 (493 2849, 050 766 0030 mobile, www.almastore.az). All buses to Bulvar. **Open** 10am-8pm daily. **Map** p222 K3.
This suitably stark white outlet right on the Bulvar seafront deals with all matters Mac, including sales, repairs and advice.

World Telecom/Azercell
Fountains Square (050 255 5555). All buses to city centre. **Open** 10am-8.30pm daily. **Map** p222 G3.
First-time visitors to Baku are well advised to invest in a local mobile phone service – at present, there is no coverage for Vodafone customers with a foreign account, for example. There are several outlets on Fountain Square where you can buy an Azeri SIM-card, but at World Telecom you can also purchase cheap mobiles and laptops. The employees don't speak much English but are helpful. Look out for the purple sign to the right of the main square as you walk down from the Nizami monument.

Arts & Entertainment

Calendar

Say it with flowers, celebrate Novruz and listen to mugham.

Baku hosts an eclectic range of events across the year. The highlight is Novruz Bayrami, a spring festival celebrated across Iran and much of central Asia, which transforms the Old City into a riot of costume and carnival, and is the one celebration that would be worth timing any visit around. Festivities last for a week, with 20 March as the focus. If you are coming to Baku in early June, bear in mind that all the top hotels will be fully booked for the Caspian Oil & Gas Show, the city's main trade fair. For arts and culture, look out for the Baku Jazz Festival, the Baku International Film Festival and the Hajibayli Music Festival, all of which take place in the autumn.

ARTS & ENTERTAINMENT

WINTER

Martyrs' Day
Across Baku. **Date** 20 Jan.
This national day of mourning marks the killing by Soviet troops of local citizens in 1990. Flowers are taken to Martyrs' Alley (*see p56*) and solemn music plays around the city.
► *For more on Martyrs' Day, see p56 Black January.*

National Theatre Festival
Various venues. **Date** Feb, Oct-Dec.
The showcase event of a ten-year-project instigated by the Azerbaijan Ministry of Culture & Tourism in 2009, the NTF is an annual event launched in two stages in 2010, mainly but not exclusively in Baku and Sumgait. All of Azerbaijan's two-dozen plus theatres are involved, reflecting nearly 140 years of staging drama here. Puppet theatres are also put to good use. A second series of events then takes place from October to December.

International Mugham Festival
International Mugham Centre, Neftchilar prospekt 9, Bulvar & the Waterfront (437 0030, www.mugham.az). All buses to Bulvar/Azneft Square. **Date** Mar. Map p221 B6.
After an opening ceremony at the International Mugham Centre, this celebration of Azerbaijan's most distinctive form of ethnic music takes place over the course of a week at the city's most prestigious venues. Organised around it are symposiums, master classes and a contest for budding mugham performers.
► *For more on mugham see p146 Jazzerbaijan.*

SPRING

★ Novruz Bayrami
Across Baku and Azerbaijan. **Date** Mar.
See p143.

World Forum on Intercultural Dialogue
Gulustan Palace of Baku, Sabayil (www.bakuforum-icd.az). **Date** early Apr, alternate years.
Inaugurated in April 2011, this three-day forum aims to promote cultural diversity and generate cross-cultural dialogue. For the inaugural event, some 500 representatives from 100 countries – ministers of culture and heads of leading international organisations – convened for a series of talks, workshops and initiatives.

Azerbaijan International Travel & Tourism Fair
Expo Centre, Heydar Aliyev prospekt, Surakhani (www.aitf.az). Shuttle bus from metro N Narimanov. **Date** late Apr.
The leading exhibition of its kind in the region, AITF attracted nearly 8,000 visitors in 2011, the majority working of them professionals from the travel trade. One large hall is dedicated to promoting tourism around Azerbaijan, an excellent opportunity to pick up on the latest developments in the hotel and hospitality industry around the country, with stands set out region by region. There are also music performances and sampling of local foods and drinks.

Flower Festival
Various venues. **Date** 10 May.

An official national holiday, this marks the anniversary of the birth of Heydar Aliyev, the president who led Azerbaijan through ten years of post-independence, from war to prosperity. Floral decorations brighten public parks all across Baku.

Caspian Oil & Gas Show

Expo Centre, Heydar Aliyev prospekt, Surakhani (www.caspianoilgas.co.uk). Shuttle bus from metro N Narimanov. **Date** early June.

Approaching its 20th anniversary, this is one of the world's leading showcases and talking shops for the energy industry. Held over four days in early June, the COGS is actually two events in one: the Caspian Oil & Gas Exhibition (incorporating Refining and Petrochemicals) at the Expocentre, and a two-day conference alongside, most recently held at the Hyatt Regency Hotel (*see p98*). Attracting more than 5,000 visitors and nearly 300 exhibitors from 30 countries in 2011, this high-powered shindig ensures that all

Novruz Bayrami

Happy new year!

Novruz Bayrami is the most significant festival in the Azerbaijan calendar and marks the start of the new year according to the old Persian solar calendar. So ancient and important is it that it was designated as part of the Intangible Cultural Heritage of Humanity by UNESCO in 2009. Zoroastrian in origin, this celebration dates back more than 3,000 years and coincides with the spring equinox on 21 March.

The preceding four Tuesdays each have special significance, celebrating the four elements of earth, wind, water and fire, but it is the last Tuesday, Akhir Chershenbe, that is the day of feasts and festivities. Small bonfires are lit in the streets over which children and young men jump for good luck and to have their wishes come true – and to demonstrate their athletic prowess. Anthropologists have linked this ritual to the fire worshipping of the ancient Zoroastrian religion.

Traditionally, homes are spring-cleaned at this time of year and special plates of sprouting wheat and barley, called *semeni* and representing rebirth, can be found everywhere, decorated with ribbon and candles. Food is particularly important and families reconnect over laden tables in much the same way as happens in the West at Christmas. Family members prepare sweet pastries and cakes, replete with nuts and honey. Special rice dishes cooked with milk and raisins are on the menu in restaurants, and huge trays of dried fruits and nuts are exchanged as traditional gifts.

There are festive street performances in the Old City, with traditional music, dance and theatre. Actors dressed as characters from well-known Azerbaijani plays walk around and pose for pictures. And each region of the country erects a stall along the Bulvar and displays its produce and handicrafts.

Public holidays around Novruz are variable, but are usually a week, beginning on 20 March.

ARTS & ENTERTAINMENT

rooms in Baku's top-end hotels are fully booked for the duration, and rates rise accordingly. In 2012, the event takes place between 5 and 8 June.

Baku International Film Festival
Various venues. **Date** Sept.
Rustam Ibragimbekov, who won an Oscar for Best Foreign Film in 1995, is the main organiser of this annual occasion. Categories vary from year to year but have included such unusual ones as Most Humane Message, Brightest Debut and Most Feminine Image. The event is considered the most important of its kind in the Caucasus region.

Hajibayli Music Festival
Muslim Magomayev Azerbaijan State Philharmonia Istiglaliyyat 2, Old City (497 2905). *Metro Icheri Sheher.* **Date** Sept. **Map** p58 L5.
Staged over the last two weeks of September, this festival of classical music features the top orchestras from Azerbaijan and artists from as far and wide as Korea, Russia, the UK and America. The event is named after the Azeri composer and pedagogue from the early 20th century.

★ Baku Jazz Festival
Various venues (http://bjf.az). **Date** Oct.
Inaugurated in 2005, the BJF is Baku's premier annual music festival, whose big-name stars would grace any such event anywhere in the world. Now staged in October, it has featured the likes of Herbie Hancock, Al Jarreau, Joe Zawinul and Billy Cobham. For 2011, this fortnight-long bash saw the appear-ance of Al Di Meola and Keiko Matsui. Venues include the International Mugham Centreand the Heydar Aliyev Palace (for both, *see p148*).

Start International Festival of Student Film
Various venues (http://startfestival.org). **Date** Dec.
The Cinema Centre of Young Cinematographers in Baku that was behind the first Start festival in 2004, establishing awards in five categories: Best Documentary, Best Feature, as well as Best Idea. Entries come from all across the region and beyond, some 60-plus films in all, judged by a panel of directors, script writers and critics.

Rostropovich Classical Music Festival
Various venues. **Date** Dec.
It was in 2006 that the great cellist Mstislav Rostropovich had the notion of establishing a classical music festival in honour of the centenary of the birth of Dmitri Shostakovich. The timing was doubly poignant, in that the Baku-born musician was stricken with cancer and would die a year later. The inaugural Rostropovich Classical Music Festival was duly launched, attracting big-name artists from Moscow and beyond, as well as Baku itself. A press conference at the House-Museum of Leopold & Mstislav Rostropovich announces the upcoming programme.
▶ *Explore the musician's former home at the House-Museum of Leopold & Mstislav Rostropovich, see p54.*

Caspian Oil & Gas Show. *See p143.*

Arts & Entertainment

Keeping the children happy – and the adults too.

The cultural scene in Baku is lively if limited for English-only speakers. Music is the city's strong suit, most notably the indigenous *mugham*, jazz, and the fusion of the two. There is also a laudable tradition in classical music, while the pop and rock scene is dominated by domestic acts or those plying their trade in Russia and elsewhere in the former Soviet Union. The city's **Museum of Contemporary Art** (*see p81*), an outlet second-to-none in the region, reveals that there is a constant flow of work of real quality. Russian (or Azeri) speakers have a number of prestigious venues to choose from as far as local-language film and theatre are concerned, while Baku's bid to host the 2020 Olympic Games should raise the standard of sporting venues, not least the charmingly dilapidated national stadium, named after the most famous linesman in football history.

TICKETS

There are eight booths set up around the city, with opening times clearly posted. The one opposite Government House near Sahil metro station is open 10am-6pm daily, with a lunch break from 1pm to 2pm. On offer are tickets for classical concerts and theatre performances (Azeri- and Russian-language). Cash only.

CHILDREN

The first place to head for on any family day out in Baku is the **Bulvar** at the waterfront (*see pp70-76*). Part promenade, part recreation grounds, part funfair, this stretch of seafront has attractions at every turn. Ranged along the coast are rides (Pirat is popular), dodgem cars and huge transparent balls in which kids can tread through a pool of water. In the warmer months, an open-air fun train (www.funtrain.at, AZN2, AZN1 under-12s) chugs along the Caspian. You can also take a cruise out from a pier near the Harbour Terminal – these are equally affordable and last 30 minutes (*see p73* **Inside Track**).

For refreshments, you'll find large, round orange stalls selling fresh-fruit juices and ice-creams dotted every few minutes along the way. Alternatively, you could go to the **Park Bulvar** mall (*see p127*), where there is a whole floor of food outlets just below the landmark restaurants of Kitchenette and Zeytun, plus the 60-seater **Tusi-Bohm Planetarium** (with few English-language shows) and the five-screen **Park Cinema** (again, few, if any, English-language films). More useful for English speakers, Park Bulvar also has air hockey, a bowling alley (598 7460) on the fourth floor and a **Happy Land** kids' playground (598 7314) on the third floor.

Also on the seafront is the **Children's Puppet Theatre** (Neftchilar prospekt 36, 492 6425, www.kuklateatri.com), whose fin-de-siècle building (this was Baku's first cinema, the 'Fenomen') is worth a look in itself. Again, nearly all shows are in Azeri, with a few Russian-language ones thrown in, but for toddlers the stories would be familiar and, for adults, the standard of puppetry is worth the modest admission fee.

Further afield, the **Baku State Circus** (Samed Vurgun Street 68, 494 9023) hosts top troupes from across the former Soviet Union, in a sadly modern arena built in 1967 that can hold up to 2,000 people. Shows are at the traditional end of the circus genre: expect to see lions jumping through fiery hoops and the like.

Another area worth exploring is a short walk from the Circus, about a kilometre north-east. Here, you'll find two green squares, Richard Sorge and Dzhaparidze, and where they meet, **Koala Park** (Azadlig prospekt 95, 441 6104, www.koalapark.az). It's somewhat pricier than the funfairs on Bulvar, but this park has rides for toddlers (Flight of the Bumblebee, Little Train) and older children (Family Merry Hills). There's also a trampoline, see-saws and so on. On public holidays, there are events with costumed characters.

Nearby, four blocks east of Koala Park, is the **Children's Railway**, which runs every summer from Dada Gorgud station. Rides are cheap (20k for kids) but slow; the little train eventually finds itself at Bahar station 20 minutes later. Trains leave every hour or so from mid morning. Next door, **Baku Zoo**

has been under regular threat of closure due to the cramped conditions the poor animals are kept in. As such, a budget of AZN3 million has been approved for a new and bigger zoo outside Baku in the Absheron peninsula.

Baku will have a new waterpark with the opening of the Kempinski Hotel Badamdar (*see p95*) in early 2012. Free for hotel guests, the **Badamdar Aquapark** will be open to the public at AZN30 for adults, AZN15 6-12s, free under-6s. Note, though, the bizarre opening days of Monday to Thursday only (9am-7pm). The park will feature two pools, a children's pool, water chutes, slides and a whirlpool.

FILM

Cinematography came to Baku very shortly after the Lumière brothers showed the world's first moving film to the public in 1895. A French cameraman named Alexandre Michon made a documentary of everyday life in turn-of-the-century Baku, and other foreign pioneers soon

Jazzerbaijan

Jazz and mugham are made for each other.

Mugham is a unique Azeri musical tradition – included by UNESCO in its compilation of the Intangible Cultural Heritage of Humanity – of which Azeris are justly proud. A two-minute video of a *mugham* performance was included in the 27-track playlist sent out into space on Voyager in 1977 to

Vagif Mustafa-Zadeh.

demonstrate our earth-people's creativity to any passing extraterrestrials.

In essence a classical form of folk story-telling through music, *mugham* is characterised by its adherence to a series of seven modes, or specific scale sets, with ad-hoc musical improvisation around them. It is this improvisation that has led *mugham* to be strongly associated with jazz.

Mugham is generally sung by a single, wailing voice, which leads the improvisation, to the accompaniment of a small band playing some very ancient instruments, many of which are older precursors of more familiar bits of kit. Thus, a *tar* and a *saz* are two forms of lute; a *kamancha* is a kind of fiddle or violin; a *balaban* is a wind instrument with two reeds; and *ghaval*, *davul*, *nagara* and *daf* are all types of drum. Other instruments used include the *garmon*, which is a type of accordion, and a *tutek*, a kind of flute.

Schools of *mugham* are regionally based, with Shusha being acknowledged as the home of the very best school, Karabakh Mugham, while Baku and the Shirvan region are the homes of the two other traditions.

Baku's impressive space-age-looking **International Mugham Centre** (*see p148*) opened its doors in 2008 to showcase the traditional genre. If you're not here for the **International Mugham Festival**

arrived too. The oil industry was a popular subject. Then came the Soviet era, and a state production line of movies for the masses, a studio that later gained the name Azerbaijanfilm. It wasn't until the 1990s that Azeri cinema gained international attention with the Oscar-winning *Burnt by the Sun*, co-created by Rustam Ibrahimbeyov, which focused on life under Stalin. The screenwriter was the driving force behind the setting up of the **Baku International Film Festival** (*see p144*).

For the casual visitor, Baku offers little to watch in terms of English-language film. Movies are either in Azeri, Russian, or dubbed from their original language

PERFORMANCE: MUSIC, DANCE & THEATRE

Baku is home to a number of grand institutions of the arts, dating back to pre-Soviet times, when the city was a flourishing hub of classical music, ballet and opera. Opulent palaces of

high-brow culture and popular entertainment were thrown up in the wake of the oil boom at the turn of the last century, most notably the **Akhundov Opera & Ballet Theatre** on Nizami Street and the **Philharmonia Concert Hall**, originally a casino. The strong tradition in classical music has persisted until today, and Azerbaijan has produced some of the world's most noted exponents in certain fields, including cellist and conductor Mstislav Rostropovich. His former home is preserved as a museum, the **House-Museum of Leopold & Mstislav Rostropovitch** (*see p53*). The nation's greatest singers (Bul Bul, Rashid Behbudov) and composers are celebrated in the city's street names. Composer Uzeyir Hajibayov formed the internationally renowned **Azerbaijan State Symphony Orchestra**, affiliated with the Azerbaijan State Philharmonic Society, which also oversees the **Azerbaijan State Choir**, **Azerbaijan State Chamber Orchestra** and so on, from its base at the Philharmonia Concert Hall.

Mugham performers.

(*see p142*) in the spring, then head to the **Mugham Club** restaurant (*see p108*) for performances every weekend.

In tandem, Azerbaijan has always had a strong tradition of jazz and continues to play host to a succession of the world's greats, including, in recent years, George Benson and Al Jarreau. The most famous Azeri jazz musician was undoubtedly **Vagif Mustafa-Zadeh** (*see p62*), who died in 1979. Mustafa-Zadeh is credited with inventing the

genre of *mugham* jazz, a wholly improvised fusion of the two traditions, based on the same modal forms as traditional *mugham*. Vagif's daughter, Aziza Mustafa Zadeh, lives in Berlin and has taken the fusion to new levels, mixing *mugham*, jazz and opera. At one recent performance in Baku, Mustafa Zadeh showed astonishing vocal dexterity, famously harmonising with the echo of her own voice.

For more on local jazz, see www.jazz.az.

ARTS & ENTERTAINMENT

Philharmonia Concert Hall.

For pop and rock concerts, international names do occasionally pass through, usually playing at the **Heydar Aliyev Palace**, the main venue for mainstream entertainment in the city. There is also a local pop scene, particularly rap, including the four-piece Dayirman, who bring in elements from the traditional a cappella of spoken-word *meykhana* to express passionate, often patriotic, sentiments. The situation in Nagorno-Karabakh is one particular subject they choose to focus on.

Away from local-language rap, Baku is best known for its indigenous *mugham* music and for jazz, and has major festivals that feature each (*see pp142-144*). *Mugham*, and its particular fusion with jazz, is eminently worth investigating (*see p146* **Jazzerbaijan**). As well as the **International Mugham Centre**, a contemporary landmark on the Caspian waterfront, you should also find high-quality performances of the genre at the **Mugham Club** restaurant (*see p108*).

Theatre remains high-brow and almost exclusively performed in Azeri, Russian or, occasionally, Turkish. Russian speakers can enjoy quality performances at the **Russian Drama Theatre**, though the building itself, on Khagani Street, is uninspiring.

Venues

Akhundov Opera & Ballet Theatre
Nizami Street 95, Sahil (493 1651). Metro Sahil. **Map** p222 K2.
Beautifully opulent inside and out, despite two reconstructions in modern times (one after a fire) this grandiose institution was created in 1910 and in its time has hosted all the stars of Russian and Azeri ballet and opera. Classic works by Verdi, Tchaikovsky and Bizet, as well as Uzeyir Hajibayov and Fikrat Amirov, are its stock in trade. The venue is named after Mirza Fatali Akhundov, a kind of 19th-century Molière, who created local-language drama inspired by the European classics, and was heavily involved in literary development throughout the region.

Green Theatre
Istiglaliyyat Street, Sabayil & West Baku (492 4982). Funicular. **Map** p221 B6.
Also known as the Open-Air Theatre, this summer-only venue reopened in 2008 after considerable renovation. Much loved by Baku locals, who remember the halcyon days here in the 1960s, the Green Theatre continues to stage family-friendly concerts and performances: Turkish pop groups, big musicals, that kind of thing. If you don't mind sitting through *Mamma Mia* in Azeri, the atmosphere and location make for a very pleasant evening indeed. You'll find it close to the top funicular station, a shortish, steep walk from the presidential and ministerial buildings where Istiglaliyyat meets Niyazi.

Heydar Aliyev Palace
Bul Bul prospekt 35, North Baku (498 8184, www.ha-saray.az). Metro 28 May. **Map** p220 C3.
Baku's main venue for live performance, usually musicals, dance shows or much-anticipated visits by the biggest names in world jazz. The 2,000-capacity building has gone through a few name changes in its time. Opened in 1972 as the Lenin Palace, this prominent institution occupies most of the square created by Samed Vurgun, Bul Bul, Fizuli and Shamsi Badalbeyli, a few blocks west of Baku railway station.

★ International Mugham Centre
Bulvar (437 0030, www.mugam.az). All buses to Bulvar or Azneft Square. **Map** p221 B6.
Distinctive in its sleek, almost futuristic shape, the International Mugham Centre was created in 2008 as a showcase for this unique Azeri form of music. When illuminated, the building, surrounded by classical pillars, stands out amid a number of landmarks embellishing Baku's impressive waterfront. The venue comes into its own for the International Mugham Festival in March (*see p142*) but there is usually a regular performance agenda throughout the year. Some of the stars you'll see perform are depicted in the Hall of Fame in the foyer. *See p146* **Jazzerbaijan**.

National Academic Theatre
Fizuli Square 1, North Baku (494 4840). All buses to Fizuli Square. **Map** p222 F1.
Founded in 1873, all chandeliers within and fountains without, this formidable institution is where many of the great works of modern-day Azeri drama had their premières – those by Mirza Fatali Akhundov in particular. Local-language Shakespeare, Gogol and Molière are also mainstays. Performances are in Azeri, plus a few in Turkish.

★ Philharmonia Concert Hall

Istiglaliyyat Street 2, Old City (497 2901, www.filarmoniya.az). Metro Icheri Sheher.
Map p58 L5.

If you're going to dedicate one evening of your stay to culture, here is where it should take place. An impressive confection of pastel yellow set in the beautifully landscaped grounds of the former Governor's Garden, the Philharmonia was built in 1910 as the Baku Club, a haven for cigar-smoking and roulette-playing local dignitaries. The architect took his lead from Monte Carlo when he conceived of this riot of German rococo and Italian Renaissance. The Soviets, of course, wanted nothing to do with it, and converted it into a music hall; it became the home of the Baku Philharmonic Society shortly before World War II. Fully renovated, it reopened in 2004. Seven separate national musical bodies, piano trios, orchestras of folk instruments, and more, operate under its wing. The building itself comprises two main arenas sharing the one large stage, the 1,100-capacity Summer Hall and 600-capacity Winter Hall. The Philarmonia also stages open-air shows in the warmer months. As well as hosting performances by the best Azeri ensembles, and noted ones from Russia and elsewhere, the Philharmonia is home to the Hajibayli Music Festival every September.

Russian Drama Theatre

Khagani Street 7, Sahil (493 4048, www.rusdrama-az.com). Metro Sahil.
Map p222 J3.

Russian speakers should not be put off by the most prosaic nature of this Soviet-built edifice – this was once a rather elegant establishment, whose roots date back to 1920. Russian-only productions here – of Chekhov, Gogol and Shakespeare – are of notable quality, and there is a separate programme for children.

Young Spectators Theatre

Nizami Street 72, Sahil (493 8852). Metro Sahil.
Map p222 K2.

A modern building with a glass façade, the Young Spectators Theatre surprisingly dates back as early as 1928. As its name suggests, it stages shows – dance, theatre, musicals – that appeal to a younger audience. Local-language only.

SPORT

Baku is currently bidding to host the 2020 Olympics against five other cities, the decision to be made in 2013. At present, the national stadium, named after famous linesman Tofik Bakhramov (*see p80* **The Flag of God**), is in need of repair, though it manages to host home games of flagship club Neftchi Baku and the Azeri national side. An arena in typical Soviet style, with a grand, classical entrance and a running track, it currently holds 30,000 people, though league attendances are much less than half that.

Set right by Ganjlik metro station, it features strange little outlets around it: a barber's shop, a grocer's, a betting shop, a couple of bars where local fans sip glasses of tea before the game. The Olimp Döner stand between the metro and the stadium will sell you a kebab; a terrapin hut ticket office is right behind it, though staff seem to simply open the gates for league matches. Inside the ground, facilities are basic but the atmosphere is friendly.

For internationals, a little stand for tickets is set up on the ground floor of the **Park Bulvar** mall (*see p127*), to the left as you walk in from the Caspian side.

The venue has been the subject of much debate over its rebuilding – though major decisions are only likely to be made after the Olympic bid decision in 2013.

Fore!

Get going with golf.

To the dismay of many expats, Baku's only golf club, at the Pink Loch on the Absheron peninsula, closed down a few years ago. (Somewhat bizarrely, the Azerbaijan Open still takes place each year – in Dubai.) But now a new facility has opened – and right in the centre of Baku too: **Golfland** (Besti Baghirova Street 2, 436 9337, www.golfland.az, open noon-midnight daily).

An 18-hole stroke play indoor golf area, Golfland is just south-east of the Bakikhanov roundabout, literally walking distance from the Hyatt hotel complex. Its sophisticated golf simulator has a library of 168 courses for the player to choose from and uses revolutionary technology to track the ball accurately through the air, reproducing true ball flight. High-quality 3D images are projected seamlessly to enhance the golfing experience. A well-stocked bar, pleasant restaurant and lounge allow guests to linger and discuss their round. Parking, lockers and a pro shop are also provided.

A day card allowing the use of all the facilities is AZN55, the simulator costs AZN30/hour and lessons are AZN70. There are reductions for children and families, and season tickets are available.

Escapes & Excursions

Nakhchivan.

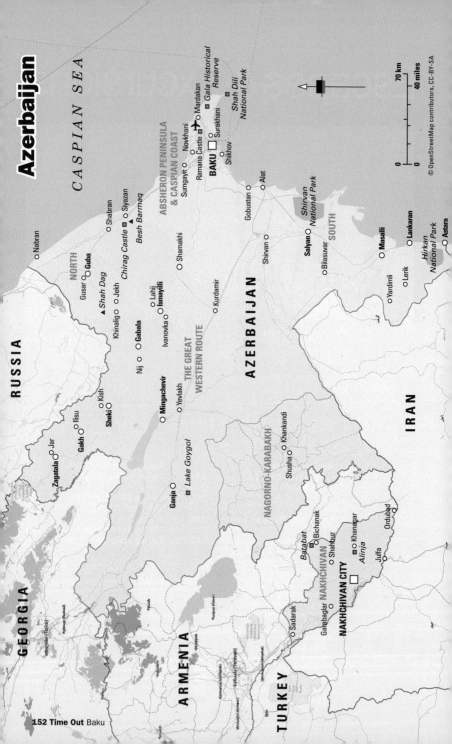

Azerbaijan

CASPIAN SEA

RUSSIA

GEORGIA

ARMENIA

TURKEY

AZERBAIJAN

IRAN

NORTH

ABSHERON PENINSULA & CASPIAN COAST

THE GREAT WESTERN ROUTE

NAGORNO-KARABAKH

SOUTH

Shirvan National Park

Hirkan National Park

Shah Dili National Park

Gala Historical Reserve

Nabran

Shabran

Gusar
Guba

Chirag Castle
Besh Barmaq
Siyazan
Sivazan

Shah Dag

Khinaliq
Jekh
Lahij
Ismayilli
Ivanovka

Nij
Gabala

Shamakhi

Kurdamir

Mardakan
Gala

Novkhani
Surakhani
Ramana Castle
BAKU
Shikhov

Sumgayit

Gobustan

Alat

Shirvan

Salyan
Bilasuvar

Masalli
Lankaran
Astara

Yardimli
Lerik

Kish
Sheki
Ilisu
Gakh
Jar
Zagatala

Ganja
Lake Goygol

Yevlakh
Mingachevir

Khankandi

Shusha

NAGORNO-KARABAKH

Batabat
Bichanak
Khanaqar
Ordubad
Julfa
Alinja
Shahbuz
NAKHCHIVAN CITY
Garabaglar
Sadarak

© OpenStreetMap contributors, CC-BY-SA

70 km
40 miles

152 Time Out Baku

Absheron & the Caspian Coast

Fire-breathing mountains and shocking-pink lakes.

The Absheron peninsula takes its name from the old Persian *ab* ('water') and *shour* ('salty'), and even the most cursory glance past the ubiquitous detritus from the oil and gas industry, across the predominantly flat and barren landscape studded with salt lakes and the odd rocky outcrop, will reveal that this is a place where fresh water is scarce indeed.

Given the paucity of fresh water, the peninsula might seem an odd site for the capital, Baku. In fact, the city is only viable due to the fresh water brought in by canal all the way from the Caucasus mountains. It ends up in the charmingly named Jeyranbatan ('Drowned Gazelle') reservoir, located to the west of the peninsula, between the Soviet-era sprawl of industrial Sumgayit and the township of Khirdalan.

The Absheron peninsula has been inhabited for several thousand years, and its proximity to the sea has made it a magnet for raiders and pirates throughout its history. There remains a network of castles in various states of renovation and/or disrepair across the peninsula, dating for the most part from the Middle Ages.

In this section we take in the beaches, historic sites and salt lakes close to Baku, before heading south to **Gobustan** and north to **Besh Barmaq**.

DAY TRIPS

Some places listed in this section make for obvious combination itineraries. Leaving Baku in the late morning, you can get in a few hours at the **Gala Historical Reserve**, then **Ramana Castle** for sunset and **Yanar Dag** just after dark. If you leave earlier, you can reach the Gala Historical Reserve mid-morning, before heading on to the **Shah Dili National Park**, perhaps visiting Ramana Castle, Yanar Dag and/or the **Ateshgah Fire Temple** on the way back home.

The more ambitious can make an early start from Baku to get to the so-called **Candy Cane Mountains** and Besh Barmaq by mid-morning, then back to **Novkhani beach** for lunch and an afternoon by the seaside, taking in the salt lakes on the way home. Another early start could get you to **Gobustan** mid-morning, before pushing on to the **Shirvan National Park** (*see p194*) or out on to the **Great Western Route** (*see pp160-178*)

or heading back towards Baku for lunch and a dip in the Caspian at **Shikhov beach**.

MARDAKAN, GALA, SURAKHANI & YANAR DAG

The northern coast of the peninsula is sandy and has some reasonable beaches, along with the boomtown of **Mardakan**, which has become something of a weekend playground for Bakuvians keen to escape the heat of the city in the summer months. Mardakan is home to two castles, one round and one square – the former, by far the more impressive, features heavily on local promotional hoardings. The eastern tip of the peninsula, **Shah Dili**, is a national park of interest to birdwatchers but often beset by biting insects and swimming snakes, perhaps escapees from the former antivenom-producing snake farm in the nearby village of Zira. Offshore lie the Oily Rocks, **Neft Dashlari**, site of the world's only town built entirely on stilts in the water. Despite its obvious interest to tourists, it remains only open to visitors if invited by the state oil company, SOCAR.

The road up to **Ramana Castle** winds through some bleak oil townships, where bright, pastel-coloured houses sparkle hopefully among the vast heaps and pools of domestic and oil-industry waste. The fully restored castle may date as far back as the 11th century, depending on your historical source, and lies a few miles to the north of the airport road. There is little else of interest left at Old Ramana, although it has been suggested that its name derives from Romans having been stationed there in the first century. Roman finds have been discovered in the area, and one enterprising legionnaire left even more of a mark at **Gobustan** (*see p159* **Rock of Ages**). The castle is usually locked, but the key is held by a family who live opposite the main gate – they may ask for a small donation to open it up. It is one of the most visually impressive fortresses on the peninsula, offering wonderfully bleak views across the oily wasteland, especially from its battlements at sunset.

More recent settlements in the area include some of the most devoutly Muslim towns in Azerbaijan, including **Nardaran**, with its vast, newly renovated mosque complex – verses from the Quran daubed on its walls. Pious Nardaran is also home to a castle, more modest than the one at Ramana. Once, when the Caspian sea level was considerably higher, the town served as part of the Absheron peninsula's seaside defence system.

Ramana Castle.

INSIDE TRACK WORLD HERITAGE

Gobustan (*see p159*) was declared a National Monument in 1966 and a UNESCO World Heritage Site in 2007. Other UNESCO highlights in Azerbaijan include Baku's Old City, the Mugham musical tradition, the art of carpet weaving, the art of Ashiq, and the new year celebration of Novruz Bayrami.

An impressive collection of artefacts and carvings at the new **Gala Historical Reserve** demonstrates the area's rich history to great effect. In total, the open-air reserve covers 1.5 hectares and features more than 2,000 monuments and artefacts drawn from more than 25 locations across eastern Absheron. Artefacts date back to the third millennium BC, brought in from digs at the numerous ancient sites dotted around the peninsula. There is an extensive collection of prehistoric stone carvings, including a striking depiction of the Plough constellation made by prehistoric astronomers and some stone fetishes thought to represent the human form, perhaps used in lieu of a live body in stylised versions of rites that may once have featured human sacrifice.

Also of particular interest are the re-created homes and summer shelters of families from different income levels across various periods in the region's history, which give a great insight into how people lived. A small indoor display has a wonderful erotic relief, and some beautiful pots, beads and other jewellery recovered from the digs. A new indoor museum of Azeri metal-work and handicrafts, plus a restaurant, are due to open in late 2011. Just outside the main compound is an assortment of deep-water wells, still in use, and the fascinating partially excavated remains of a 12th-century hammam.

Other sites within easy reach of the capital include the Ateshgah Fire Temple at Surakhani, and the more visually impressive burning mountainside, Yanar Dag (*see p155*). Located a few miles east of Baku, the **Ateshgah Fire Temple** is one of the Absheron's most popular tourist destinations. Long thought to be a pre-Islamic Zoroastrian site dating back to the sixth or seventh century, the present Fire Temple was actually built by Indian fire worshippers in the early 18th century. There was, though, some form of temple already here. A natural eternal flame burned here for many years, but its natural fuel source – a gas pocket located deep in the rock beneath – has been used up. These days the flames, when lit, are fuelled by gas piped off the nearby mains supply.

Gala Historical Reserve.

Lying between the hamlets of Dilgah and Mammadli, **Yanar Dag** (literally 'Burning Mountain') may be rather tricky to find, but is definitely worth the effort. Azerbaijan, the 'Land of Fire', is home to quite a few other burning oddities – mountains, and even rivers and springs in the deep south – but none is as accessible as Yanar Dag. Here, natural gas escaping from the oil-rich soil has been burning constantly since its accidental ignition more than 50 years ago. The 'mountainside' is actually a strip of land around seven metres long and is best visited soon after nightfall, when the flames are at their most visually impressive. The adjacent café serves tea and all manner of sweet goodies for AZN8 per person.

INSIDE TRACK
GOING UNDERGROUND

Around a third of the items on display at the impressive new **Gala Historical Reserve** (*see p154*) are from Gala itself, whose ancient settlement covered 158 hectares in its prime and was the epicentre of a network of tunnels that linked the castles at Gala, Ramana and Mardakan. Some sources claim that it even reached the old mosque at Bibi Heybat, just south of Baku.

SALT LAKES

Seen from above, the amazing shades of pink, orange, maroon and vermilion that stain the salt lakes of the Absheron peninsula are a striking sight. These vivid hues are said to be the result of naturally occurring minerals, although the extensive pollution that the Absheron has been subjected to throughout the petrochemical era may well have played a part too. Attempting to find these salt lakes at ground level, though, can be something of a challenge. One of the most impressive – an other-worldly shocking pink – is unnamed and lies just to the right-hand side of the main Novkhani highway, beyond the larger Lake Masazyr.

Masazyr itself is home to one of Absheron's oldest industries: salt gathering. Here, the salty water that oozes up from the soil over the winter dries in the stultifying heat of summer, and the resultant salt crust is gathered and purified at a couple of lakeside plants.

To access the vivid pink lake, park at the petrol station at the top of the hill and backtrack, down the hill, crossing the waste ground on your left to reach the lakeside. Note that the greenish crust on the lakeside mud is not especially thick and gives way to a foot or so of warm oil-rich ooze that, while no doubt great for the skin, is surprisingly hard to rinse off.

THE BEST PLACES

For a day at the beach
Novkhani. *See p156.*

For a castle
Ramana. *See p154.*

For fire
Yanar Dag. *See p155.*

To explore the history of the region
Gala Historical Reserve. *See p154.*

Prehistoric relics
Gobustan Rock Art Cultural Landscape.
See p159.

BEACHES

Cleaner and more pleasant than the beaches at Shikhov south of Baku, those on the north side of the peninsula are the better choice for day-trippers heading out from the city. **Novkhani** and **Amburan** are arguably the best, but they are becoming increasingly built up, especially Amburan. If you're looking for a quiet beach, these may not be what you're after.

The **AF Hotel Aqua Park** at Novkhani (012 448 3043, www.afhotel.az) features the country's most extensive selection of waterslides, a private beach and family entertainment aplenty, and is situated near **Barbados Beach**, right at the end of the Baku–Novkhani highway. Expect to be charged around AZN5 for a lounger, and the same again for a sunshade.

Mardakan is also often mentioned as a beach destination, but while the public beach is passable, the best spots are the reserve of those wealthy and connected enough to have a private strip of sand. The town is a visibly wealthy

place that owes its status to being the summer resort of the nouveau riche oil barons of the late 19th century. These days, it is still home to many splendidly lavish summer *dachas*, including that of the current President of the Republic. The town features an attractive pleasure park in the centre, a couple of castles and a couple of modest hotel waterparks. The town beach lies a couple of miles to the north, between Buzovna and Primorskaya, which is these days almost a suburb of Mardakan.

HEADING SOUTH

Gobustan – or the Gobustan Rock Art Cultural Landscape, to give it its full title – lies about 65 kilometres (40 miles) south of Baku, beyond Shikhov beach. It is well signposted near the small, unremarkable oil-workers' settlement of the same name (*see p159* **Rock of Ages**).

As well as burning mountainsides, Azerbaijan is also home to more than half of the world's mud volcanoes, more than 400 in total. One of the most accessible outcrops lies some ten kilometres (six miles) south of Gobustan, on a hilltop off the road to Alat. At present it is not signposted, but if you turn off the main road at the sign for Dash il and park, the volcanoes are due west (inland) about 1.5km (one mile) up a steepish hill. Locals may be able to help or even guide you if you ask for '*vulkan*', or more properly, *palchyg vulkanlary* (literally 'dirty volcanoes').

There are six distinct forms of mud volcano: gryphons, mud cones, scoria cones, salse, springs and mud shields. The vast majority in Azerbaijan are gryphons, characterised by their shape – a steep-sided cone, less than three metres high – and the fact that they belch out mud from their crater. Anything taller than three metres is categorised as a 'mud cone' and often shoots out bits of rock along with the mud. One Azeri volcano hit the headlines in 2001 when it erupted, producing flames that shot some 15 metres

Beach.

A salt lake. See p155.

(50 feet) into the air. Don't be too alarmed, though – flame-producing mud volcanoes are very rare.

HEADING NORTH

On the main road north from Baku lies a spectacular range of unnamed hills and mountains, which have entered guidebook parlance as the **Candy Cane Mountains**. Here, visible layers of sedimentary rock littered with small bullet-shaped fossils swirl in enticing shades of pinks and creams, like – well – a candy cane, or raspberry ripple ice-cream.

To find them, look out for a precarious-looking Soviet-era behemoth of a building just before Gilazi at around the 85-kilometre mark from Baku. Here, turn off the main Guba road on to the road to Gizi and Alti Agach. The best of the mountains are visible 14 kilometres (nine miles) along the road, directly opposite the shrine to martyred poet and musician Mikail Mushvig, who was born in the area. There's a little café here too. You can happily scramble up the hillside and do a spot of fossil-hunting, and it makes an interesting detour on the way to Besh Barmaq beyond.

About 100 kilometres (60 miles) north of Baku on the Guba highway, **Besh Barmaq** (literally 'Five Fingers') juts majestically some 400 metres (1,300 feet) into the air above the flat coastal highway. At the summit of the mountain is an Islamic shrine, accessible by many steps and with stunning views down to the coastal plain and out over the Caspian Sea beyond. Families of refugees live at the foot of these steps in the hope of a handout from those who make the pilgrimage to what is a very holy site for Azeri Muslims. At the summit, women will pray for you, for a small donation, and give you a small piece of the holy rock, blessed to keep you safe.

At the foot of the steps is the main car park. Here, stalls sell more prosaic lucky charms, beads and key-rings featuring the ubiquitous blue-glass eye motif, as found across the eastern

INSIDE TRACK FIRE AWAY

Fire worship was practised by Zoroastrians long before Azerbaijan was converted to Islam. In fact, the name 'Azerbaijan' is a bastardisation of the Persian for 'Protector of Fire'. As well as sites such as **Yanar Dag** (see p155) and the **Ateshgah Fire Temple** (see p154), the importance of fire in Azeri culture can be seen in the annual celebration of Novruz (see p142), originally a Zoroastrian holiday and now included in the UNESCO List of Intangible Cultural Heritage of Humanity, and in traditional country weddings, when the bride must walk three times around a fire at her father's home before carrying the flame across to where she will live with her husband.

Mud volcano, Gobustan.

ESCAPES & EXCURSIONS

ESCAPES & EXCURSIONS

INSIDE TRACK PRAYER KNOTS

At Besh Barmaq, pilgrims leave little bundles of herbs tied in pink-ribbon prayer knots to bring luck, a custom thought to stem from the animist history of the site that pre-dates its current Islamic incarnation. These bundles bring to mind the tied prayer knots found at shrines in Tibet. Other animist touches can be found at the many *pirs*, or holy places, throughout Azerbaijan, such as little cairn-like piles of stones, also thought to bring luck.

Mediterranean. At this level there is another, smaller, shrine with a rather battered blue dome, around which families and coach parties of pilgrims have barbecues and play volleyball or ride horses, and where many a sacrificial lamb is

Besh Barmaq. *See p157.*

led to the slaughter. From here, the dedicated take the steps to the left of the lesser shrine to the top to pray, meditate, contemplate or just admire the view. The less dedicated can drive up the road to the right, where a smaller car park at a higher level misses out half of the steps.

To access the site, drive past it on the main Guba road for three kilometres beyond the roadside stop at Namazkah, with its eye-catching new mosque and views of the mountain behind. By the Qarabag Café, take a left up into the mountains and bear left again, doubling back to arrive at the car park, which lies behind Besh Barmaq as you first saw it from the main road.

WHERE TO EAT & STAY

Top-notch eating options are limited around the Absheron, although there are plenty of basic restaurants and cafés. Those listed here are a cut above, for one reason or another, and all the hotels serve reasonable food too.

There is a lot of new building going on along the strip around Shikhov beach, so be prepared for some new spots to dine and drink over the next couple of years. Near **Novkhani**, **Barbados Beach** is awash with beachfront restaurants. Two stand-outs here are the curious **Sindibad**, shaped like a pirate ship, and **Sama** ('Sky'), which offers a marginally more peaceful beach experience than most of the competition, along with decent food. Crowds also still flock to the completely rebuilt **Retro Resort** (012 553 5900). Formerly the Retro Café, it is now more of a holiday camp but still features a collection of vintage cars in the car park outside.

As most of the sites in this chapter are only a short hop from Baku and generally considered day trips, we've only listed the best beachside properties. **Amburan** is probably the liveliest beach of the lot, with the new **Jumeirah** (www.jumeirah.com) at nearby Bilgah likely to add a more chic element, with its wave-like design created by local architect Nazim Valiyev, huge spa complex and two rooftop restaurants. Until this opens, the glitziest hotel in the area is undoubtedly the **Khazar Golden Beach** (012 554 0739, www.khazarbeachhotel.com, doubles AZN200), although in the height of summer the thumping disco does little to engender a relaxing atmosphere. A quieter option near **Mardakan** is the very pleasant **Hillside** at Buzovna (Beynalmilal 33, 012 453 1661).

Shikhov has two hotels, both with outdoor pools for those not feeling brave enough to risk the sometimes rather oily-looking depths of the Caspian. The original **Crescent Beach** is now looking a little dated, but is comfortable enough (Salyan highway, 012 497 4777, www.cbh.az, doubles AZN120), while the **Ramada Baku**

(Salyan highway, 012 491 7303, www.ramada baku.com; doubles AZN200) is shiny but rather soulless.

GETTING THERE & AROUND

The Absheron peninsula is not large and even the furthest places mentioned in this section are no more than 90 minutes or so from Baku by car. If you happen to encounter a taxi driver you trust, he will most probably be happy to act as chauffeur. Expect to pay about AZN80 for a full day's driving. It is, of course, also quite possible to go it alone, although navigating the Absheron can be complex and a good map is essential.

Public transport is reasonable, although the language barrier may prove discouraging. Baku's enormous new bus terminal out on the Guba road

should be your port of call for most long-distance destinations, but the following are served by buses that depart from elsewhere in Baku:

Gobustan Bus 105 to Alat from Bayil region, along the street from the Crown hotel.
Mardakan town Bus 36 from Vurgun Gardens.
Mardakan beach Bus 341 from Neftchilar metro station.
Novkhani & Yanar Dag Various services from Ganjlik metro station.

Tourist information

Detailed tourist information is difficult to come by, but some useful titbits can be gleaned from the official Ministry of Culture and Tourism website (www.azerbaijan.tourism.az).

Rock of Ages

Prehistoric art and Roman inscriptions.

The **Gobustan Rock Art Cultural Landscape** (*see p156*) sprawls across a vast 540 hectares, but the most visited part of the site is a far more manageable and clearly labelled hectare. This features some of the most impressive of the more than 6,000 carvings, or petroglyphs that have so far been discovered among Gobustan's natural caves and shelters. They date back to at least the second millennium BC – some sources suggest they're much older.

Archaeological digs, some by the celebrated Norwegian archaeologist Thor Heyerdahl, have found signs of human habitation here from prehistoric times – and up until the Middle Ages. The carvings themselves depict men hunting and fishing and some of the many animals and fishes that were their prey, along with images of pregnant women and various aspects of everyday life.

Also at the site is a resonating drum stone, or *gaval dash*, thought to have been used for communicating with distant tribes

and hunters. When struck with a stone, the highly resonant rock produces a note that carries for miles around.

A solitary whiteish rock lies behind an iron railing. Its Latin inscription dates from the first century AD and is the easternmost evidence of the Roman Empire yet discovered. It reads: 'IMP DOMITIANO CAESARE AVG GERMANICO LVCIVS IVLIVS MAXIMVS LEGIONIS XII FVL', which translates as: 'Under the Emperor Domitian Caesar Augustus Germanicus, Lucius Julius Maximus of the 12th Legion Fulminata was here'. The Legio XII Fulminata was a legion of crack troops formed by Julius Caesar in 58 BC and veterans of many great campaigns up until the third, and possibly the fifth, century AD. They are known, courtesy of this inscription, to have been stationed in the Caucasus in the latter half of the first century and may even have founded the settlement of Ramana (*see p154*) on the Absheron peninsula.

ESCAPES & EXCURSIONS

The Great Western Route

Meet the Udis, eat hash and see the world's first Christian church.

In 1858 the great French writer Alexandre Dumas was accompanied by an escort of armed Cossacks as he traversed the lawless Caucasus, a journey he was to immortalise in his *Travels in the Caucasus*, published the following year. These days, the Cossacks are rather superfluous to requirements and the fast new highway from Baku to Ganja via Alat and Yevlakh allows you to break the back of the journey in a single day. But the Great Western Route, done as a whole or in part, remains one of Azerbaijan's finest journeys. One of the few true circuit routes in Azerbaijan (as opposed to the more normal there-and-back trips along the same road), it allows you to get to **Sheki** comfortably in a day, via **Yevlakh** on the new highway, and even to push on to Azerbaijan's often over-looked second city of **Ganja** and make your way back up to Sheki via Mingachevir.

MORE EXPLORATION

Once you've taken the Great Western route as far as the town as Sheki, you can even head further on into the far north-west into stunning mountainous countryside, exploring atmospheric Albanian ruins, encountering curious isolated ethnic groups and visiting the beautiful villages around Gakh and Zagatala. From here, the option to push on into Georgia is a great enticement for those with multiple-visa entry to Azerbaijan.

Alternatively, head back to Baku through Sheki along the older, slower route through the foothills of the Greater Caucasus via Gabala, Ismayilli and Shamakhi, which offers side trips into some of the more interesting and historic little villages and communities that Azerbaijan has to offer.

WEST FROM BAKU

The road to **Yevlakh** (*see right*) is paved with, well, not very much actually, other than plenty of police speed traps. As you head south out of Baku past the reconstructed grand mosque at **Bibi Heybat**, residential suburban sprawl

Road to **Yevlakh** and **Ganja**

INSIDE TRACK DRIVE TIMES

Baku to Ganja 5hrs (360km/225 miles)
Ganja to Sheki (via Mingachevir) 3hrs
(150km/93 miles)
Baku to Sheki (via Yevlakh) 6hrs
(360km/225 miles)
Sheki to Zagatala 90mins (80km/
50 miles)
Zagatala to Gakh 70mins (50km/
30 miles)
Ilisu (Gakh) to Sheki 70mins (50km/
30 miles)
Sheki to Gabala 90mins (65km/40 miles)
Gabala to Ismayilli 90mins (65km/
40 miles)
Ismayilli to Shamakhi 90mins (65km/
40 miles)

gives way to the grand bazaars and
warehouses of the outskirts of the capital,
which in turn give way to a landscape stunning
in its bleakness. Lion's-paw mountains shimmer
through the heat haze beyond sterile salt lakes
to your right, the burnt umber hillocks studded
with leakily capped test wells. Along the road,
multi-hued pipelines lie across the landscape.
To your left, the Caspian shimmers in a more
enticing light, but the increasing density of the
vast space-age machinery of the oil and gas
industry puts paid to any real attractiveness,
and even the sparkling mosaics of the roadside
bus stops fail to add much in the way of colour
to an otherwise desolate landscape, almost
dazzling in its emptiness.

Around a kilometre before Alat, the road
veers sharply to the right and you'll leave
the coast, heading inland on the fast new
highway towards **Yevlakh** and **Ganja**
(*see p162*). Here, your journey into the arid
heartland of Azerbaijan's flat central plain
begins. The lush Greater Caucasus looms
large beyond the mountains across the train
tracks, which follow the road at a respectful
distance and along which an occasional oily
freight train lumbers slowly by. Groves of
persimmons line the road, a mass of pretty
red flowers in early summer and laden with
beguilingly honey-sweet, heavy orange fruits
in winter. The ubiquitous irrigation channels
are edged with banks of rushes and pink-
fronded tamarisk, which provide the only
other hints of colour against the burnt earth
and golden cornfields all around. Storks are
a common sight, their vast, chaotic nests
perched precariously atop telegraph poles
and often providing tenement-style
accommodation for a whole host of other
smaller birds flitting around nearby.

Where to eat & stay

There are no hotel options to speak of on this
road and those in the one-horse towns along
the way are limited, to say the least. A few
of the unremarkable roadside restaurants
offer dingy rooms; none are recommended.

Food-wise, you may prefer to push on
towards Sheki or Ganja, but the lakeside
Qarabag Restaurant, just beyond **Kurdamir**,
with its stilt-top deck shaded by mulberry trees
and its peculiarly mosque-like main dining hall,
is easily identifiable. At around three hours
from Baku, it makes an ideal lunch stop.

YEVLAKH

Around 90 minutes beyond Kurdamir,
industrial **Yevlakh** has little to recommend it,
but is worth a brief stop to check out the pink-
granite-bisected **Lenin**, a one-man walking –
well, half-standing – metaphor for the death of
the Soviet Union, left to crumble in a rubbish
dump on the outskirts of town. It makes for
a great photo opportunity. To find Vladimir
Ilyich (bisected), continue through Yevlakh
on the Ganja road, heading west. Just over
a kilometre beyond the Azpetrol station
roundabout, there is a series of new warehouses
belonging to Lala Tekstil on your right, each
with its own little slip road access. After the
last of these warehouses, and just as you come
on to a new bridge, a similar slip road, also to
the right, takes you over a disused train track.
Lenin's pink granite edifice should just be
visible around 50 metres (165 feet) further
on, behind a crumbling sand-coloured wall.

With Lenin ticked off, you are faced with a
choice. Double back on yourself, back over the

ESCAPES & EXCURSIONS

Yevlakh.

Main square, **Ganja**.

Azpetrol roundabout and on eastwards for just a few kilometres and over the river, before heading left up to Sheki (*see p164*) or continue west for another 45 minutes or so to Azerbaijan's second city, Ganja.

GANJA

Entering **Ganja** from the east, you will hit a few kilometres of roadworks – the Ganja bypass, yet to open at the time of writing – before spotting the 20-metre (65-foot) torpedo-shaped thrust of the modern **Nizami mausoleum**, resting place of Ganja's most famous son and father of Azeri literature, the poet Nizami, on a bridge over the road. Although broodingly impressive from afar, this modern structure doesn't really merit closer examination. In a field adjacent to the mausoleum – now a military encampment – lies the site of **Old Ganja**, where the city stood until the river changed its course and the town's inhabitants followed suit. Sadly, these days there is little to see and what remains is out of bounds for security reasons (*see p176* **Nagorno-Karabakh**).

Ganja's main feature is its Stalin-era main square, lined with pillars of stout Communist construction and dominated by the façade of

INSIDE TRACK ON THE BEAT

Ganja is close to the territory occupied by Armenia and the local police presence is significant. Although they're almost invariably friendly, the police are quite likely to stop you and ask your business, and photographs are not always welcome.

City Hall, where any hammers and sickles have long since been painstakingly replaced with the red, light blue and green of the Azerbaijani flag. The square is home to a couple of grand fountains – the display at the southern end is set to music each night; the performance generally takes place at around 9pm.

South from the main square, the twin minarets of the 17th-century **Juma Mosque** lean slightly in a Pisa-esque fashion, dominating a small park. Nearby, the similarly aged **Chokek Hammam** is currently undergoing fairly extensive renovation, but may yet continue to be home to its uninspiring collection of 20th-century decorative arts. Further south from here, the tall trees of **Khan Baghi**, or the Khan's Gardens, has several nicely shaded cafés, although none serve beer. The park is a pleasant place to while away a few hours people-watching and searching out strange Soviet-era statues. An **outdoor theatre** on the south-western edge of the park hosts musical recitals during the summer.

Just east of the fountain, all that remains of the 18th-century caravanserai is an arched red brick façade with a statue, home to nesting swifts upstairs and an internet café below. A block west of the musical fountain, the well-kept 19th-century **Russian church** is one of the few remaining consecrated places of worship for Ganja's once-prominent Christian community. It is set within well-maintained rose gardens and has a charming, peaceful interior.

Half a block north from here, up Ataturk Avenue, lies the reasonably diverting **Historical Museum**. The streets behind it are filled with highly photogenic crumbling red brick façades of traditional Ganja architecture, though the police do not always

Juma Mosque.

ESCAPES & EXCURSIONS

INSIDE TRACK THE WILD EAST

In the early 19th century, when bad harvests and a widespread famine back home had made life intolerably difficult, impoverished Germans were given a substantial sum of money and a horse as incentive to trek east. Only about a third of the first group of families survived the terrible journey to the Causasus and, rather as it was for the pioneers of the Wild West to whom they have been compared, life on arrival proved no less difficult for the survivors. The Helenendorf Germans were ultimately deported en masse by Stalin during World War II, but their legacy remains in the village of **Helenendorf** and in the foundation of the now rejuvenated Ganja wine trade.

take kindly to foreigners snapping pictures of any building not in a visibly perfect state of repair.

Ganja's quirkiest attraction is undoubtedly the recently renovated **Bottle House** on Huseyn Cavid, just around the corner from the Historical Museum. Owner Ibrahim Jaffarov has made mosaics on the façade of his two-storey home with thousands of empty bottles, bits of glass and pebbles as a monument to his brother, who never came back from World War II – that's him in the slightly Mao-esque murals under the eaves. The family received a mysterious letter from the errant brother in 1957, but he has yet to show his face.

Where to eat & stay

Situated opposite City Hall, the **Grand Hotel** (022 565 106, doubles AZN60) looks grand, for sure, and would be grander still if someone switched all the lights on. Rooms are basic, with decidedly cosy en-suite bathrooms. Wi-Fi comes free of charge, but breakfast is extra. A better option is the **Hotel Emon** (022 572 280, doubles AZN50). At the western end of town,

INSIDE TRACK
I BELONG TO GANJA

Ganja's citizens enjoy a similar reputation with other Azeris as Glaswegians do with other Scots: a Ganja kiss is Azeri slang for a head-butt. But the truth is that, with the exception of the odd over-zealous policeman, the citizens of Ganja are extremely welcoming.

the all-new **Ramada Plaza** (022 569 029, doubles AZN120-AZN160) offers the best accommodation in town.

A few doors up from the Grand, **Café Zalatoy** has a decent menu and a fully stocked bar, and also makes a good spot for breakfast (including the famous local speciality *hash*, see *p165* **Regional Dishes of the Great Western Route**). Unusually, there is also a menu printed in English. The aptly named gold-toothed owner ('*zalatoy*' means 'golden' in Russian) and his staff are very friendly.

Russian church.

INSIDE TRACK
GANJA'S 15 MINUTES

In 1918, in the aftermath of the demise of Tsarist Russia, **Ganja** (*see p162*) briefly enjoyed fame as capital of the world's first democratic Islamic nation. The Azerbaijan Democratic Republic declared itself on 28 May, as immortalised in street names around Azerbaijan, and excluded Baku, which was then under Communist control, from its ranks. In less than two years, however, the whole of Azerbaijan would fall to the Communists and Ganja's 15 minutes of glory would be over.

Directly opposite the Russian Church, an unnamed restaurant also offers friendly service, reasonable food and serves alcohol, something that the pleasant cafés in the Khan Baghi gardens fail to do.

Most visitors to Ganja follow the lead of 19th-century travellers, and both eat and stay out of town in the shaded, tree-lined gorges of the pretty former German village of Helenendorf (now known as Khanlar or, officially, Goygol, *see p163* **Inside Track**) and Hajikand, both of which lie a few kilometres to the south. A series of identikit restaurants (**Flamingo** is good, likewise **Kapaz**) and basic cabin-style rest stops line the road as it winds on towards the majestic Lake Goygol. Do check the prices of the guesthouse rest stops, as cabins can be

expensive and, to be honest, none of them is anything other than very basic indeed. Sadly, Lake Goygol and the other six lakes that make up the beautiful 'Tears of Kapaz' are currently off-limits to travellers due to their proximity to the territory occupied by Armenia. The lakes take their name from Mount Kapaz, and are said to have been formed when it was cracked open by a 12th-century earthquake.

SHEKI

Even the merest mention of **Sheki** is likely to cause your average Bakuvian to go all misty-eyed, and when the occasionally unpredictable mountain weather holds out, it is easy to see why. With its aged tile rooftops, verdant mountain backdrop and prettily meandering little streets of houses with unrestored wooden balconies on stilts, Sheki is one of the most beautiful towns in Azerbaijan. Its citizens are also famously relaxed, and the cold and often foggy winter notwithstanding, it is among the best getaways the country has to offer.

Sheki's main attraction is the heavily restored 18th-century **Khan Sarayi** ('Khan's Palace' – in fact his summer residence) at the top, eastern end of Akhundov. The Khan Saray's miniaturist fresco work is breathtaking, as are its famous *shabaka* stained-glass windows (*see p166* **Inside Track**). Interestingly, one of the rooms of the surprisingly modest, six-room palace is undecorated. This is where the Khan's scribes worked, undistracted by the finery

Bottle House. *See p163.*

Regional Dishes of the Great Western Route

Eat hash in Ganja, halva in Sheki and Avarian pancakes in Jar.

Hash.

Makhar.

Jamaican patois has yet to penetrate deep into the consciousness of your average Ganja citizen, and so the comedic value of eating *hash* in Ganja will be lost on most of that city's natives. *Hash* (or *khash*) is, in fact, popular across Azerbaijan, although it is considered a particular speciality in Ganja. The simple dish of stewed head, feet and tripe of (generally) cow – although other regions replicate its charms with sheep or even goats – is traditionally served in winter to men only, with lashings of minced raw garlic and a shot or three of vodka. Oh, and did we mention it's also a breakfast dish? For those strong enough to give it a go, they say it sets you up for the day and you won't have to eat again until nightfall.

Sheki halva is actually not a halva as you might know it, but rather a form of layered pastry interleaved with chopped nuts and soaked in clear honey, very like the baklava of the eastern Mediterranean. Sheki is justly famous for its halva, which is on sale all over the city and at roadside stalls around the region, often with little boxes of super-sweet *mindal* (sugar-coated hazelnuts that look a little like dayglo popcorn) and other sweetmeats. The best halva in town comes from Ali Mamad, about halfway up Akhundov on the south side of the storm drain. The red liquid used to stain a criss-cross pattern across the sweet is a syrup made with either red food colouring or, if you are lucky, concentrated essence of rose petals. This rose syrup is also sometimes served in a shot glass, to be poured into your tea. Try it if given the chance – it is a delicious alternative to the more normal lemon.

The Avar people (*see p172* **Family Tree**) originate from Dagestan and are just one of the myriad ethnic groups that dot the landscape of north-western Azerbaijan. Azerbaijani Avars are concentrated in and around the village of Jar, just outside Zagatala. They have their own unique cuisine, including the Avarian breakfast dish of *makhar*: a giant pancake made with long, fronded edges and served with preserved quince and fresh honey on a raised dish, so the fronds drape down to the table. This makes a delicious breakfast and is perhaps a little more forgiving on your average western stomach than a bowl of *hash*. The Lazzat Guest House (*see p171*) in Jar makes a particularly splendid *makhar*.

Sheki halva.

INSIDE TRACK SHABAKA

Shabaka is the name given to the stained-glass work that characterises the façade of the **Khan Sarayi** (*see p164*) in Sheki. It is made from hand-cut pieces of stained glass that are fitted into a complex, wooden-slatted frame, traditionally without the use of nails.

Khan Sarayi.

that characterises the interior of the rest of the palace.

In the palace precinct, there is a fascinating working *shabaka* workshop and a fairly unremarkable history museum, housed in a 19th-century church, whose unusual shape marks it out as Russian. Sheki's second-biggest draw is also its most popular hotel – the last of the three caravanserais that lie almost side by side as Akhundov climbs towards the Khan Sarayi precinct. The **Caravanserai Hotel** (*see right*) is also home to the city's biggest concentration of gift shops, selling traditional hats and costumes, earthenware and metalwork and shawls, engraved boxes and the like. Other local souvenirs include Sheki halva (*see p165* **Regional Dishes of the Great Western Route**) and silks, which can be viewed and bought at a decent price from the shop attached to the old Kombinat silk factory, at the junction of Razulzade and Fatalikhan.

A few blocks north-west of the Caravanserai Hotel, **Khan Evi** ('Khan's House') clearly dates from the same period as the Sarai and is also a six-room construction, though of far more modest proportions. It is now thought to be the Khan's winter residence, as evidenced by the beautiful fireplaces, and makes a fascinating counterpoint to the arguably over-restored palace up the hill. Only one room is frescoed, although *shabaka* windows feature throughout. It's not officially open to the public, but you might just get a look in if you can persuade local Ministry of Culture & Tourism contact Ismail (050 506 3840 mobile) that you are a visitor in need. You'll have to have an Azeri or Russian speaker to help you, though.

Around Sheki

A few kilometres north of Sheki, the attractive, traditionally built stone village of **Kish** is most famous for the intact, heavily restored **church** that stands at its centre. Thought to be first-century, it is considered by some as a fair candidate for the Church of St Eliseus. Founded in 78 AD and mentioned in the New Testament, St Eliseus was the very first Christian church in the world. Fairly extensive archaeological digs have been unable to prove this, but have uncovered human remains dating to the first century BC (viewable under perspex covers in the churchyard), including the remains of a giantess who was almost seven feet tall. The current structure is thought to date from around the 12th century and houses an informative little museum about the early Albanian church. The key is held by the lady who lives opposite, and a small donation (or the purchase of handicrafts from the museum) seems a fair trade for access to such a fascinating place.

Caravanserai Hotel.

Where to eat & stay

Staying at the **Caravanserai Hotel** (0177 44814, doubles AZN20-AZN80) during summer is a great and unusual experience, but be aware that there is little or no heating in winter and your visit can be remarkably chilly as the temperature plummets. The restaurant is very unpredictable and its tea (AZN20) is unfeasibly expensive, although it does include quite a decent spread of sweets treats and one order is more than enough for a small group.

The charmingly simple **Panorama Guesthouse** (050 216 6241 mobile, doubles AZN40 with breakfast) overlooks Sheki's rooftops from the south side of Akhundov, and is accessed by following signs to the still-unfinished Green Inn Hotel and continuing past this rambling behemoth after turning right at the war memorial. Owner Elchin even speaks some English, although his business partner, the pleasingly laconic Azer, relies on his Russian. Rooms are good but basic, and share clean western-style facilities, although water for the shower can be unreliable. A tasty home-cooked evening meal, served in the overgrown orchard with the signature roof tiles down below, can be arranged if you let them know in the morning.

For a touch of luxury, the **Sheki Sarayi** (0177 48181, doubles AZN80-AZN100 with breakfast) is unrivalled in town and its **Shabaka** restaurant is good and reasonably priced. The hotel's **Buta Bar** has an extensive snack menu with some western varieties and is Sheki's only real option for nightlife. **Chelabi Khan** (0177 42920), the unmistakable modern Khan Sarayi-style building in the main town square, serves excellent food at reasonable prices.

GAKH & AROUND

Heading north-west towards the Georgian border, the next town of any size is **Gakh**. The fastest route in this direction, the new highway directly to Zagatala (*see p169*) and beyond, loops south of the old Sheki-Gakh road and bypasses Gakh entirely. If you're ultimately returning to Baku, this is the most obvious route to take, heading straight to Zagatala and then meandering back on the old road to Gakh. Along the way, you'll dawdle behind herds of sheep and

Kish.

goats, and horse-drawn carriages laden with food for livestock, as the road trundles along through pretty groves of ancient walnut trees with white-washed trunks, which in places have grown so large as to all but form a tunnel.

After Gakh, you can continue on via Sheki to Gabala, Ismayilli and Shamakhi. Note that at the time of writing, the Gakh–Zagatala road is impassable due to a bridge down on the outskirts of Gakh, near the Lakit turn. However, repair work is well under way and the road should be clear by the time you read this.

Gakh itself largely centres around the pleasant main square, with a metal-domed, modern *chaykhana* (teahouse) at its north-eastern edge. Along the southern edge of the square, Azerbaijan Prospekt winds its way to Icheri Bazaar küc; with its handful of old-fashioned houses with wooden hanging balconies on stilts, this street constitutes a sort of miniature old town. Gakh is known for its bottled spring water and there's a free spring just outside town, at the bottling plant on the Zagatala road.

Just beyond the plant, the village of **Gum** is home to the impressively large ruins of a fifth-century Albanian church. It is accessed to the left of the main strip, by a long green metal gate next to a couple of blue metal kiosk buildings. Beyond the village and through the next hamlet of **Chinarli**, there are a couple of other, more-neglected ruins from the same period to explore.

Ulu Dag.

Albanian ruins in **Gum**.

On the other side of Gakh, above the old Sheki road, the restored Georgian-style **Kümük Church** was built in the 18th century. It surveys the fertile plain from its spot among the trees, some of which are tied with strips of coloured cloth as a prayer token – a practice linked to animist worship that long predates Christianity in the region (*see p158* **Inside Track**). It is marked from the road and lies a kilometre or so beyond an unmarked bridge just outside town, near a double roundabout and up a track to your left. Note that it's only accessible in dry weather.

A similar period and style of church lies at the northern edge of Gakh on the road to **Ilisu**, a pretty village accessible through a dramatically steep, tree-lined gorge. Ilisu is arranged along a single, wide track, lined with photogenic tumbledown stone cottages, many of which still have traditional stone arches over the side entrance steps. The village's three-arched 17th-century **mosque** is currently undergoing restoration and some clearly older graves can be seen around and behind it. Hanging balconies on the larger houses are also widespread, as are little plaques with verses from the Koran inscribed in Arabic on the corners of the staunchly built stone houses. Off this wide track, little alleyways lead past nut groves straight into the forest behind. If you can shake off the pack of local kids likely to latch on to you the moment you arrive, there are some lovely secluded hikes here.

Where to eat & stay

Zagatala.

Gakh itself hasn't got much in the way of room or board, but magical **Ilisu**, 30 minutes up the valley, is packed with little restaurants and resorts offering cabin-style accommodation. The best of the bunch remains the now greatly extended **Ulu Dag** (0144 93425, double cabins AZN25), which, as the last resort in the village, has stunning views up the glacial valley to the mountains beyond. Ulu Dag is ever-expanding, and its Olympic-sized pool (open mid June to mid September) and disco with 'animators' hired for the summer season does mean that it runs the risk of being a little noisy, but the cottages are far enough away from the action not to be disturbed.

No longer enjoying the views it once had, thanks to flashy new-builds with indoor pools and astronomically expensive 'luxury' cabins, the quieter **Yashil Park** (0144 54575, double cabins from AZN25), is the village's original resort. There's also the more modest **Ilisu Pensionat** (050 328 5616 mobile, double cabins AZN25) and the **Eden Resort** (050 223 0073 mobile, double cabins AZN25), although staying at the foot of the village somewhat misses the point of visiting here in the first place.

ZAGATALA

As the road winds it way up beneath the lush forested slopes of the lesser mountains of the Greater Caucasus and on towards the Georgian border, the last town you will encounter is **Zagatala**.

Zagatala town is laid out around a pretty central park, with a handful of enormous 700-year-old plane trees, a couple of *chaykhana* (teahouses) and a café that, unusually for the region, offers western food. At the eastern end of the square is a rather kitsch monument to Dada Gorgud, or Dede Korkut ('Grandfather Korkut'), the fictional narrator of a book of folkloric stories that was one of the foundations of the oral storytelling traditions of the Oghuz Turkic people of the Caucasus and Central Asia. Behind this monument and off to the right are some of the town's oldest houses, with their pretty, two-tone grey stone walls and red brick corners. Tucked away off the main square, behind the library (Kitabxana), lies the unreconstructed shell of a once magnificent Georgian-style **church** that is said by local historians to date from the fifth century. Above the square and accessed by steps, the old citadel wall encompasses an area of 11 hectares and was built by Tsar Nicholas I in 1830 to protect Russian settlers from marauding Lezghian mountain tribes (*see p151*). The wall was rather enthusiastically renovated in 2009.

ESCAPES & EXCURSIONS

Albanian church. *See p169.*

Perigala rock fortress.

An intriguing side trip from Zagatala is to the **Perigala rock fortress**. Said to date from the third century, it clings precariously to a sheer mountainside some 400 metres (1,300 feet) above a meadow a few kilometres east of town, north of Mukhakh village. Views of the unreachable fortress can be enjoyed over a cup of tea at the seasonal summer-only *chaykhana* in the pretty meadow below. The fortress has not been fully excavated, perhaps due to its astonishingly inaccessible location, but takes the form of a fortified natural cave with a series of window openings beneath and to the side of the more visible main 'gate'. Russian-speaking

Seyid (050 627 7744 mobile) is a native of Mukhakh and will happily arrange transport to and from Zagatala.

Mukhakh village itself is interesting for its fine examples of traditional village architecture, sturdily built stone-walled houses with red-brick corners and architraves over the windows. Heading back into Zagatala from Mukhakh, a pair of **ancient graves** of uncertain age is visible just off the road, marking the resting places of two unnamed holy men. Nearby is an ornate brick **spring-water pavilion** that dates from the same period.

Family Tree The Avars

Sunnis with roots in Dagestan.

The Caucasian Avars are a Sunni Islamic people who originated in Dagestan. Their name probably means 'highlanders', and they can trace their history back to at least the fifth century AD. There are around a million ethnic Avars left, mainly concentrated in Dagestan, although there is a significant Avar population of around 40,000 in Azerbaijan; many of them live in villages such as **Jar** (*see p171*) in the Zagatala region.

Their distinct language is part of the Alarodian north-east Caucasian or Nakh-Dagestanian language group, now written in the Cyrillic script, having previously been Latinised between 1927 and 1938, and written in Arabic script before that. Their culture is lively, and includes distinctive carpet-making styles, unique national dishes and energetic traditional dances.

Also north of Zagatala is the pretty Avar village of **Jar**, with its mossy, dry-stone walls and Georgian mountain dwelling-style tower house, the **Chingiz Gala**, which dates back to the 16th century. Jar is nestled in an ancient beech forest with beautiful hiking and walking opportunities, and is also home to the delightful Lazzat guesthouse (*see below*).

Where to eat & stay

The **Turgut Motel** (0174 56229, doubles AZN15-AZN50) has basic but comfortable rooms in Zagatala town and serves decent food in its pretty rose garden. Just across the street, the eccentrically bottle-faced front of the **Gagash** restaurant has an equally eccentric interior and back garden dining pavilions, and is another good option for food. The best place in the area, however, is **Lazzat** (050 313 3199 mobile, double cabins AZN40) in the village of Jar, where you can dine in a treehouse, sleep in a cabin in the forest and, if you're lucky, be treated to a display of traditional Avarian dancing in the remarkably fun hotel bar by the friendly staff. The food is outstanding – especially the Avarian special breakfast of *makhar* pancakes (*see p165* **Regional Dishes of the Great Western Route**) – and, almost uniquely in rural Azerbaijan, English is spoken. The **Dashliq** restaurant next door is also recommended.

GABALA

Heading back towards Baku from Zagatala and Gakh, you must turn off the main (fast) highway and head into the outskirts of Sheki (*see p164*) to access the rather slower old road towards **Oghuz** and **Gabala**. The pretty road winds its way along the foot of the mountains, offering splendid views up to the snowy summits to the north and over the plains to the south through the ancient walnut trees that line the road.

Just before the Oghuz turn, enterprising refugees displaced from Nagorno-Karabakh (*see p176*) have set up roadside *tandir* ovens and sell delicious fresh bread to passing motorists. It's worth stopping and buying a loaf to help these visibly needy folk, to say nothing of getting some of the best bread you'll ever taste.

Just beyond the refugees is a large roundabout with an Azpetrol station where you should bear right to continue towards Gabala, via the unremarkable villages of **Bayan**, where the roadside Palma restaurant sports an impressive fountain, and **Karimli**. Meadows on either side of the road here are a mass of wild flowers in May and June, and buffalo are a common sight, along with herds of cattle and mixed flocks of sheep and goats. At the next junction, a smart-looking hotel and

Quixotic Gabala

A wonderfully random collection.

The **Gabala Historical Museum** (*see p174*) is home to a cornucopia of objects, with artefacts from Old Galaba, a re-creation of the old town in model form, and lots more.

A display case in the second room holds three pottery spheres with small openings – 14th-century hand grenades. Filled with gunpowder and lit by a fuse, they would have exploded, shattering the ceramic outer casing into shrapnel. Other highlights include a 19th-century safe with a hidden key mechanism, a Soviet-era wind-up record player complete with vintage USSR discs, and, by the door into the little gallery at the end of the museum, a photo of an apple upon which the face of Imam Ali spontaneously and miraculously appeared.

Family Tree The Udi

An ancient Christian community, with its own – endangered – language.

The Udi people are the oldest Christian community in Azerbaijan, and probably one of the oldest in the world. Now thought to number only around 10,000, the Udi are direct descendants of the long-defunct Albanian civilisation (that's Caucasian AlbaNNia, which has nothing to do with the Balkan state, pronounced AlbAYnia). They were first mentioned by name by Herodotus in the fifth century BC, as well as by Pliny the Elder in the first century AD – around which time they adopted the new Christian faith.

The Udi, or Udin, speak their own language, also called Udi, which is related to the more widely spoken Lezghian (*see p191* **Family Tree**). Udi has its own alphabet of 53 letters, is only spoken by around 5,000 people in the world and is listed as a severely endangered language by UNESCO. The Udi mingle animism with their own brand of Christianity, swearing oaths by the sun, the explosively named *b'gh*, and holding fire sacred. Near Udi churches, holy stones known as bird stones are often found, frequently decked out with lit candles as a form of prayer. Another common practice is to tie bolts of cloth to trees near churches in prayer knots, as practised by other – sometimes even Islamicised – descendants of the Albanian civilisation across the region.

Just over a third of the world's population of Udi – 3,600 according to a recent census – lives in the village of **Nij** (*see right*). There were many more until the Armenian conflict of the early 1990s, but many Udi, whose traditional names, Christian faith and, indeed, language, are not dissimilar to Armenian, fled during the conflict. They have yet to return.

Nij is home to three large churches of the Udi faith, two of which lie derelict. The third, the 17th-century **Jotari Church**, has been impressively restored and acts as a de facto cathedral. Inscriptions above the doors of the derelict churches are in Armenian and date to the Udi church's alliance to the Armenian Orthodox Church in the 19th century, long before the current Azeri–Armenian hostilities. This has been mooted as a reason why these churches have been left to crumble, as the Udi are still – unsurprisingly – worried about any perceived association with modern Armenia.

The Udi pray without priest or pastor, although community elders lead regular Sunday services. Their faith is strong, as is their sense of Azerbaijani nationality, a loyalty that was put fiercely to the test in the 1990s when the perceived similarity between Udis and Armenians led to many Udi being unfairly persecuted by their Muslim brethren. Now, however, better times are expected for these people, who look to live peaceably among the Muslim minorities in their quiet village.

Jotari Church.

a garage mark the hard right turn to the village of **Nij**, home to the mysterious and ancient Udi people (*see left* **Family Tree**).

Nij remains a centre of nut production, as it has been for generations. It is visibly different from traditional Azeri villages in that houses are concealed behind nut groves, making them all but invisible from the road, as opposed to the walled plots of land set along the roadside seen in Azeri villages elsewhere in the country. The Udi were once renowned pig farmers, but their pigs were all but wiped out by a mystery virus some years back and they now mostly raise the same sheep and goats as their Muslim neighbours.

Old Gabala

A few kilometres beyond the Nij turn, a clearly signed dirt track to the right heads to the site of Old (Çukur) Gabala. Gabala is mentioned by Pliny as being a 'prominent town in Albania' and certainly dates back as far as the first century AD. It remained prominent for at least a millennium thereafter. The heavily pot-holed track trundles bumpily along for four kilometres, with hazelnut groves to either side. If in any doubt, the lads at the roadside Elçin café, with its curious streamside garden planted with roses and prettily edged with upturned beer bottles, will be happy to help you find the site of the Old City, which is bewilderingly unsigned. Take the left at the T-junction not far past the café, then down a steep slope to the riverside and over a bridge, where you double back on yourself, bearing hard left, to an official caravan that serves as the entrance to the site.

Beyond the caravan, the road forks left and right to a pair of gates. If these are locked, the keys are held at the caravan. The right fork takes you to **Gala**, home to Old Gabala's most visually impressive site, the stubby red-brick remains of the twin city gates and partial city wall of the citadel, which are thought to date from somewhere between the first and fourth centuries AD. Elsewhere, Gala, like Selbir, the part of the city accessed by the left-hand fork, bears a striking resemblance to an overgrown field. Despite being less than visually spectacular, it is worth a visit, if nothing else to admire the fact that at its peak, the city was home to no less than 17 towers.

The small covered excavation of the city wall at the far end of **Selbir**, with its intact graves, pot fragments and layers of the city wall itself, is fascinating and lies at the far, northerly end of the plot. Archaeological remains from Old Gabala feature prominently at the impressive, if rather tired-looking, Historical Museum at New Gabala, about 20 kilometres (12 miles) further down the main road.

Old Gabala.

ESCAPES & EXCURSIONS

Copper Craft

Lahij has a long heritage of metalwork.

The cobbled main drag of **Lahij** (*see right*) is lined with traditional houses, many of which function as open workshops, with hand- or foot-pumped bellows used in the heating of metal and the tapping of little metal hammers ringing out across the valley. Smiths still ply their trade here as they have done for centuries, stamping, burnishing, beating and etching pieces of copper into beautiful designs.

One of the most common motifs in Azeri metalwork and, indeed, silks and carpets, is the paisley-like *buta*, a ritualised flame symbol that dates back to ancient fire worship and is one of the national symbols of Azerbaijan. It also features in the name of many bars, restaurants and hotels across the country.

As well as selling bits of copperware to passing tourists in what are sadly these days becoming little more than glorified gift shops, the workshops do still service more traditional aspects of village life. In Lahij, you are still likely to see women – and men – making trips to roadside springs to draw water for home in large, engraved copper water jugs or *jujums*.

New Gabala

Continuing on the main road past the turn to Old Gabala, you'll see the Soviet-era **Radio Location Station** sitting prominently atop a hillside to the south of the road. Well and truly out of bounds to visitors, the RLS has long proved its worth as a missile-tracking system, much used during the Gulf War. Turn left at the T-junction, 15 or so kilometres beyond the Old Gabala turn, to get to New Gabala. As a town, it's unremarkable apart from the **Historical Museum** – worth a visit to see the wonderfully random collection of artefacts from Old Gabala (*see p171* **Quixotic Gabala**). The museum lies on the right-hand side of the main street, about halfway through the town and just beyond the ultra-modern **Heydar Aliyev Museum**. Its gate is an odd stone affair, which leads to a pretty courtyard with the sort of old carved ram figures and grave markers commonly seen at historical museums and sculpture gardens throughout the country. Inside, the lighting is dim and the museum could use a makeover, but there are some real gems on display.

Some four kilometres north-west of Gabala, the village of **Bum** (pronounced 'boom') draws in the puerile for its obvious photo opportunity but has little else to recommend it. Take the Ismayilli road east from town, via the justly renowned roadside pickle and preserve stalls of the village of **Vandam**, through pretty beech forests, which make an excellent picnic spot.

Where to eat & stay

The glitziest bed in the area is undoubtedly to be found at the **Qafqaz Resort Hotel** (0160 54200, www.qafqazresorthotel.com, doubles AZN160), which offers a full range of facilities and a wide selection of outdoor activities. Under the same management, the recently renovated **Hotel Gabala** (0160 52407, doubles AZN40) is a more modest but rather drab affair. Better all round is the **Hotel Kotuklu** at the Nij roundabout (050 348 1161, doubles AZN40), which has just five spacious rooms, good food and Udi staff, who will be happy to tell you a bit about their culture, linguistic barriers permitting. Bizarrely, the hotel also keeps ostriches in its backyard.

ISMAYILLI & SURROUNDINGS

As you near Ismayilli, the forests give way to rolling hillsides, meadows and, of course, the famed vineyards of Ismayilli itself. Dusty Ismayilli has little to recommend it, but lies almost equidistant between the region's two biggest draws: Ivanovka, home of the Russian dissident Molokans (*see p175* **Family Tree**); and the coppersmiths' village of Lahij.

Ivanovka

Around 15 kilometres (nine miles) south-west of Ismayilli, the village of **Ivanovka** is situated on a fertile plateau surrounded by rolling hills. Uniquely in Azerbaijan, Ivanovka's population is almost entirely Russian, descended from the Molokans, who were exiled to the Caucasus in the mid 19th century for their perceived heretical beliefs, which ran contrary to the dogma of the Russian Orthodox Church. Today, the architecture of Ivanovka is different from any other community in Azerbaijan, with clearly Russian-style houses lined up directly on the road, rather than lying behind walled compounds. The Molokans do not believe in churches, so there is no ecclesiastical architectural draw, but the pretty village, stunning countryside and excellent produce more than make up for that. A few kilometres further down the road from Ivanovka is the village of **Hajihatamli**, which is home to the totally renovated Château Monolit winery, with tasting cave and excellent four-star hotel nearby.

Lahij

Accessed by a vertiginous road about 15 kilometres (nine miles) up into the mountains north-east of Ismayilli, the village of **Lahij** was founded well over 1,000 years ago by silk merchants from the town of Lahijan, meaning 'place of silk manufacture'. Lahijan lies on the Caspian coast of modern Iran and some words in the modern dialect of Lahij come from Farsi, clearly reflecting this history. Surprisingly, considering how quaint it looks now, Lahij is known from contemporary accounts to have been a substantial community some 400 years ago, when it was best known for the quality of its silk carpets. These days, the carpets are still renowned, but it is also famous for copperware, the metal hewn from the copper-rich mountains that surround the village (*see left* **Copper Craft**).

Lahij's chocolate-box looks and relative proximity to Baku have made it a popular summer day trip excursion for expats, but the increased presence of foreigners and their inevitable investment has been something of a double-edged sword. While you stand a good chance of encountering some English speakers – a rarity for rural Azerbaijan – and the influx of tourist money is having a beneficial effect on village life, the ongoing gentrification of the village has led to it losing some of its charm as necessary modernisation takes place. For now, though, traditionally built

ESCAPES & EXCURSIONS

Family Tree The Molokans

Christian rebels against the Orthodox Church.

In the 17th century, a group of Russian 'Spiritual Christian' peasants protested against the lavish nature of the Orthodox Church – specifically against what they perceived as the worship of the cross, which they believed was idolatry, and fasting for Lent, which they considered unnecessary. Then, as now, the cornerstone of their belief was a living God. They found no use for churches, married only among their own community and followed Old Testament food hygiene laws – so no pork, shellfish or 'unclean' foods. As they continued to drink milk throughout Lent, they were dubbed 'Molokane' ('milk drinkers'), a name they adopted for themselves.

Their difference in belief led to a long period of persecution for heresy and various mass deportations and emigrations to other lands. In 1830, Tsar Nicholas I exiled a large number to the Caucasus. Many more are thought to have followed voluntarily. One group founded the community of **Ivanovka**

(*see above*), named after Ivan Pershin, the peasant leader who led them to this 'promised land'. As it was for many 19th-century migrant settlers in the Caucasus (such as the Germans at Helenendorf, near Ganja, *see p164*), life was extremely difficult. However, by a combination of a well-chosen plot, a lot of hard work and their strength of belief, they founded what is considered Azerbaijan's most effective – and richest – farming community.

Long before the advent of Communism, the Molokans farmed collectively, so it should come as no surprise that in 1930 their community was designated a collective farm, or *kolkhoz*, by the Soviets, named after their leader Nikolai Nikitin. The *kolkhoz* **Nikitina** developed into the most prosperous farming community in Azerbaijan and, when the Soviet Union collapsed, its members voted unanimously to retain their designation as a *kolkhoz*, making it the only active Soviet collective farm today.

stone houses retain their horizontal wooden joists, inserted into the walls after every few courses of stone, which act as buffers against the area's not infrequent earthquakes. The forgiving wood compresses under the strain, preventing the walls from collapsing.

Where to eat & stay

A new option in pretty **Ivanovka** is the highly recommended, British-owned **Ivanovka Guest-House** (050 377 1273, 050 225 8861, both mobiles, double chalets with full English breakfast AZN50), which has five comfortable, modern chalets built in the kitchen garden of a traditional Russian-style house. You have the option of self-catering, half-board or full-board, with helpful advice on planning trips around the surrounding countryside.

The four-star **Monolit Winery Hotel** (070 289 8890, doubles with breakfast AZN100)

in **Hajihatamli** lies at the centre of a wine-production plant, which is itself at the centre of the resurrection of Azerbaijan's long-neglected 2,000-year-old history of viticulture. The hotel offers excellent tours of its impressive caves, tastings and an opportunity to buy some excellent wines at a very affordable price – arguably the only such place in the country.

Options in **Lahij** are limited, although it is a popular place for homestays, which offer a fascinating insight into village life and generally very good local food. A homestay can normally be arranged upon request in the village itself or via the local tourist office (0178 77303).

With so many more interesting options all around, few would elect to stay in **Ismayilli**, although if needs must, there are reasonable, basic cabins and good food at the **Makhsul Restaurant** (0178 51220, 0178 51520, doubles AZN40). Comfortable, although not exactly

Nagorno-Karabakh

Azerbaijan's spiritual heartland is still the setting for much inter-ethnic conflict.

Called Daghlig Garabagh by Azeris, the mountainous region of Nagorno-Karabakh, squeezed between Christian Armenia and Muslim Azerbaijan, was the theatre of a brutal war between the two during the period of the collapse of the USSR – the first conflict involving ex-Soviet republics.

Now occupied by Armenia, Nagorno-Karabakh is considered the spiritual heartland of Azerbaijan. Locals in Baku speak of it in painful, bitter tones the way that Serbs describe Kosovo. Mines still dot the landscape and snipers still carry out their fatal task despite a ceasefire brokered in 1994 after some 30,000 deaths. Nagorno-Karabakh has since been the subject of four UN resolutions for an immediate, unconditional Armenian withdrawal, none so far successful. Foreigners should treat any conversation about the region with respect and ideally avoid talking about it altogether.

As an unrecognised republic ruled from Yerevan, Armenia's capital, Nagorno-Karabakh is inaccessible from Azerbaijan. In fact, the presence of a Nagorno-Karabakh entry stamp in your passport would preclude you from having an Azeri visa in any case. Even the border area around the Araz river is out of bounds and dangerous.

Interpretations differ as to the region's history. From the early 19th century, it fell under the rule of Tsarist Russia. It was Stalin who made Nagorno-Karabakh semi-autonomous under the Soviet republic of Azerbaijan in the 1920s, tampering with the borders to include as many Armenian communities as possible. Divide and rule was always Moscow's policy in the Caucasus.

Armenians remained in the majority and by the late 1980s were staging demonstrations to unify with Yerevan. Inter-ethnic conflict broke out and Azeris fled in their thousands to Azerbaijan.

After Azerbaijan brought Nagorno-Karabakh under direct rule from Baku, Armenians living in the region voted for its independence, a referendum boycotted by local Azeris. With both of the rival states gaining independence from Moscow in 1991, aggression increased in the power vacuum and conflict was inevitable. Over one bloody night in February 1992, the mainly Azeri community of **Khojaly** was annihilated, with more than 600 civilians being killed. The city of **Agdam**, right on what was the front line, remains a scene of complete devastation, barely touched since 1994. All in all, it is estimated that some six cities, 12 towns and 800-plus communities were destroyed, and great swathes of forest and agricultural land rendered unusable.

built with any great sensitivity to the surrounding area's rural charm, is the **Green House Complex** (0178 51023, doubles AZN60) near the villages of Vandam and Istisu. Well signposted from the road, it sports an outdoor pool and reasonably modern cabins. There is also a row of little restaurants and cafés on the Ismayilli–Shamakhi road.

SHAMAKHI

Sadly, following several earthquakes, over-enthusiastic renovation and reconstruction has all but destroyed the charms of what is one of the oldest cities in Azerbaijan. Traces of a settlement have been found here that date from as long ago as the fourth century BC, and for centuries it was the capital of the Shirvan region, ruled by the Shirvanshahs who built their eponymous palace in Baku's Old City (*see p62*). In the 11th century, Shirvanshah Gubad

Hundreds of thousands of refugees remain stranded from their homes.

Yet perhaps, for Azeris, the most poignant loss is **Shusha**, an ancient capital and birthplace of many notable Azeris – musicians, writers, artists – and a major centre of carpet manufacture. The priceless collection here was gathered up at the last minute and dispatched to Baku before all Azeris fled the town in 1992. It is now displayed in the Letif Kerimov State Museum of Carpets & Applied Arts (*see p76*) in the Azeri capital.

Just nine kilometres away, the de facto capital of **Stepanakert** (Khankendi in Azerbaijani) bears witness to much recent investment, particularly from expatriate Armenians. New hotels and restaurants abound, as well as museums dedicated to the war – as seen from the Armenian side. An hour away, the 13th-century **Gandzasar Monastery** is thought to be the most significant Christian site in the area.

Two decades after war broke out, there is still no sign of reconciliation. Azerbaijan considers Nagorno-Karabakh to be its own land, 16 to 20 per cent of its overall territory, while Armenians in Nagorno-Karabakh believe in the right to self-determination. Casualties still occur – a dire impasse that seems unlikely to change in the near future.

constructed the citadel of **Gulustan** atop a hill fortress just to the north-west of modern **Shamakhi**. These days, all that remains are a few crumbling low walls reached by scrambling up from the village of **Khinishli**, although the views are good on a clear day. Across the valley from Shamakhi town, in a large graveyard, the 18th- and 19th-century **Yeddi Gumbaz** ('Seven Tombs') are the octagonal mausolea of the Khans of Shamakhi; they are surrounded by simpler but far older grave markers. The three intact *gumbaz* are open and contain beautifully painted and ornately carved gravestones in surprisingly good condition, preserved as they are from the elements.

It has been suggested that the *yeddi* of the Yeddi Gumbaz actually means 'many' in this context rather than its literal meaning of 'seven'. There are, however, seven tombs clearly discernible in the main grouping in the cemetery: in addition to the three intact tombs there are four ranging from basic foundations to roofless wall fragments. It is this grouping, and the perceived luckiness of the number seven, which perhaps gives the whole lot their popular name.

Around Shamakhi & on towards Baku

Thirty or so kilometres (around 19 miles) north of Shamakhi, the area around **Pirguli Observatory** used to offer great rural accommodation. Unfortunately, the observatory appears to no longer be open to visitors and the rest stops and guesthouses have largely gone to seed. The surrounding countryside is still attractive, though. The road from Shamakhi to Baku passes some beautiful scenery, with lush hillsides giving way to increasingly barren desert scrub and plains as you approach the Absheron Peninsula (*see pp153-159*). Along the way are some stunning views through gaps in the rolling hills out on to the arid central plain to the south.

Where to eat & stay

Great food, stunning views and attentive service are on offer at the charming lakeside **Khan Baghi** restaurant (0178 76606), far and away the best of the many little places along the high ridge about halfway between Shamakhi and Ismayilli. It's a shame it has yet to branch out into accommodation.

With the Pirguli area rather abandoned, options for overnight stays are extremely limited and you may choose to push on elsewhere. If you're intent on exploring the mountainous meadows around Pirguli,

ESCAPES & EXCURSIONS

THE BEST PLACES

For a spot of culture
Historical Museum of Gabala. *See p174.*

For a forest hike
Jar. *See p171.*

For getting away from it all
Perigala rock fortress. *See p170.*

For chocolate-box looks
Lahij. *See p175.*

For Soviet-era kitsch
Bisected Lenin at Yevlakh. *See p161.*

For sweet treats
Sheki halva. *See p165.*

For a glass of red
Château Monolit, Hajihatamli. *See p175.*

though, the **Khan Baghi** resort centre (050 530 3499 mobile, cabin AZN50) is one of the least run-down in the area.

If you're stuck in Shamakhi itself, the **Savalan Motel** (055 662 1838 mobile, doubles AZN25) and **Shamakhi Motel** (050 322 9808 mobile) offer unremarkable accommodation and food for a reasonable price by the busy roadside on the western edge of town.

GETTING THERE & AROUND

Buses to all major towns on the route leave several times a day from the **Central Bus Station**, on the Guba road on the outskirts of Baku. A less regulated network of minibuses and shared taxis also operates from here. This is a very affordable way to travel, although it can be punishingly cramped, especially with luggage. It is usually possible to purchase a second ticket for your bag, and this is generally affordable even on a relatively tight budget. Local minibuses from regional centres to outlying villages run at least daily in most cases. Taxis and paid hitchhiking can be a good way to supplement the local networks without breaking the bank too.

There are overnight trains from Baku Station, near 28 May metro station, which trundle slowly enough to give a decent night's sleep, even on shorter routes such as to **Ganja**. Others wind their way to **Sheki**, **Gakh**, **Zagatala** and beyond, although all stations are a fair way outside the towns themselves. Sleepers in three classes are safe, affordable and, for first class at least, relatively comfortable, although all can be stiflingly hot and hit-and-miss in terms of cleanliness. Lighting on trains is also variable, so as everywhere in the regions, be sure to pack a torch.

Internal flights operate to **Ganja** and **Zagatala** daily from the domestic terminal at **Heydar Aliyev Airport**. Tickets can be booked at travel agents or at the airport.

Yeddi Gumbaz. *See p177.*

Nakhchivan

Azerbaijan's exclave is home to mountains and mausoleums.

The Autonomous Republic of Nakhchivan is a small, land-locked exclave of Azerbaijan, surrounded by Armenia to the north and Iran to the south, with a small border with Turkey at its westernmost point. It is about 180 kilometres (112 miles) long by 90 kilometres (56 miles) wide and lies some 450 kilometres (280 miles) to the west of Baku, with the only practical access by one of the four daily flights to and from the capital.

Nakhchivan has a long history: the first reference to it in classical literature comes from Ptolemy's *Geography* in the second century AD, although local tradition dates its founding to the fourth millennium BC and archaeological evidence from the late Stone Age confirms there was a settlement here at that time.

WHAT'S IN A NAME?

Nakhchivan's name is said to mean either 'People of Noah' or the 'First Descent', both references to its being first populated by descendants of Noah, following the landing of the ark on nearby Mount Ararat, just across the border in modern-day Turkey. Another version has its name deriving from the old Persian Naqsh-e-jahan, meaning 'Image of the World', in reference to the region's beauty. Whichever version you subscribe to, Nakhchivan's age and beauty are undisputed and it is one of the most visually stunning, friendly and culturally rich regions of Azerbaijan – and thus well worth a visit.

Architectural highlights include the ancient **mausoleums** that feature heavily on tourist posters, and the delightful, if rather heavily restored, old town of **Ordubad**. Mountain-lovers will doubtless be seduced by the dramatically verdant landscapes around **Lake Batabat**, with its slightly anticlimactic floating islands, while the desert landscapes of the mountains en route to Ordubad provide stark contrast and a tantalising glimpse of Iran.

Unfortunately, the area's proximity to Armenia means that foreign travellers can fall under suspicion from the authorities, and reports of accusations of spying are relatively commonplace, especially for those using public transport. For this reason, it is a good idea to arrange a trip with the knowledge and support of the local Ministry of Culture and Tourism. Friendly young Atilla Shirkhan Oglu (070 784 8400 mobile) works for the department, speaks good English and will be happy to arrange a car and driver, homestays in villages, and may even be able to accompany you as translator and guide if time allows.

THE BEST PLACES

For desert views
Nakhchivan City to Ordubad road. *See p183.*

For historical treasures
Ordubad. *See p184.*

For Islamic pilgrims
Ashabi Kahf. *See p180.*

For mountain landscapes
Ganli Göl. *See p186.*

For a stunning fortress
Algadyz Citadel, Alinja. *See p182.*

For Old Testament beauty
Ilan Dag. *See p182.*

For a dose of salts
Duzdag. *See p181.*

For village life
Garabaghlar. *See p186.*

Duzdag.

NAKHCHIVAN CITY

Heavily restored, rebuilt and renovated in the 20th century, Nakhchivan City has little at first glance to betray its ancient history. It lies on the banks of the Araz river, which runs along the southern border of Nakhchivan and separates it from Iran, to the south.

As you set foot on the tarmac at the airport, Nakhchivan's dramatic mountainous scenery is immediately striking, with **Ilan Dag** and the peak that conceals the shrine of **Ashabi Kahf** both looming from the haze on the plain to the north. The airport is just three kilometres from the city itself, and once you have passed

INSIDE TRACK HUSEYN JAVID

Huseyn Javid wrote at an especially difficult time in Azerbaijan's history. In 1937, when he was living in Baku, Javid's anti-colonialist, pro-freedom stance ran foul of Stalin, allegedly by dint of a letter of denunciation from fellow poet Samed Vurgun. Javid was one of many of Baku's intelligentsia who were summarily rounded up and deported to Siberia by an increasingly paranoid Kremlin. Like many of his contemporaries who shared the same fate, Javid never saw his homeland again, dying and being buried in exile in 1941. In 1982, on the 100th anniversary of his birth, his remains were repatriated by yet another famous son of Nakhchivan – Heydar Aliyev – and re-interred near his home, with a beautiful white marble mausoleum (*see p181*) erected on the site in his honour.

security – and likely been greeted in broken English by every uniform at the airport (foreign visitors to Nakhchivan are still something of a rarity) – you will find smartly liveried, state-licensed taxi drivers waiting to whisk you on to your destination.

Taxi drivers in Nakhchivan all wear uniform, and prices here tend to be better fixed than elsewhere in Azerbaijan. They are also required to make an official log of all trips, so it is as well to arrange an itinerary with your driver in advance and then stick to this itinerary, in case of run-ins with officials who may frown upon unplanned detours.

The undisputed highlight of Nakhchivan City is the mausoleum, or *turba*, of **Momine Khatum**, which dates from 1186. It towers more than 25 metres (82 feet) above well-maintained rose gardens and contains what is probably Azerbaijan's best collection of stone rams and other carvings, most of them dating from the Middle Ages although some have origins in the pre-Christian era. The tower is an astonishing achievement and the small museum housed within is interesting, although sadly only labelled in Azeri.

The script that runs up the fluted sides of the mausoleum is Kufic and reads: 'Our time here is transient, but the world endures. We will die, but our legacy remains' – a forward-thinking motto for its time. In the centre of the stunning blue majolica-tiled rosettes in the tower's panels, the word 'Allah' is picked out in relief. The now-empty vault gives an insight into the construction of such an impressive example of the architecture of the period. Next to the tower's precinct is the old **Atabeg's Palace**, which bears more than a passing resemblance to the famous Khan Sarayi at Sheki (*see p163*),

Bazaar east of Nakhchivan City.

INSIDE TRACK TOWER OF LOVE

The exact identity of the great lady for whom the towering mausoleum of **Momine Khatum** was constructed is disputed. One rather romantic version has it that it was commissioned by her bereaved husband, the Atabeg (or Turkic Khan) Jahan Pehlevan, who died of a broken heart a month after her death. The tower's construction was then overseen by their son and heir, who had them both interred here upon its completion. The tombs were excavated by Soviet archaeologists in the 1950s and the treasures with which they were buried were transported to the Hermitage Museum in St Petersburg, where they remain to this day.

although it lacks the frescoes in its heavily restored interior. Once a carpet museum, it now houses a historical museum that is of some interest, although not a patch on the one at Ordubad (*see p184*).

On the south-eastern edge of the gardens is a statue of the mausoleum's architect, Ajami Abubekroglu Nakhchivani, whose slightly earlier effort was the more modest, pointy-roofed **Yusuf Ibn Kuseyir Turbasi**. This other mausoleum pre-dates its bigger sister by some 50 years and is located in another pretty rose garden in an otherwise unremarkable residential suburb on the south-eastern edge of town.

Another great son of Nakhchivan is the 20th-century poet and playwright Huseyn Javid, immortalised in the square named after him in Baku's university district. The modern **Huseyn Javid mausoleum** is Nakhchivan City's third and lies in the north-eastern quarter of town, adjacent to his house, now an interesting little museum to this great writer, thinker and advocate of freedom. For more about the writer, *see p180* **Inside Track**.

A fourth mausoleum that features heavily on posters around the city is the over-restored, blue-domed **Imamzade**, which marks the last resting place of Abu Mustafa Bahadur Khan, one of the khans who ruled Nakhchivan during a brief period of independence in the mid 18th century.

The fifth and final mausoleum in the city is an unremarkable modern structure built to commemorate **Noah**, allegedly marking the Old Testament patriarch's actual burial place. The claim, however, is not backed up by anything more substantial than popular belief.

A last word must go to the **bazaar** that lies to the east of Nakhchivan City, with its friendly, photogenic food market. Alongside,

the beautiful Turkish-style **Kazim Karabekir Pasha Mosque** is modern and undoubtedly Nakhchivan's finest, with its ornate gold on white decoration and slender, graceful minarets.

Around Nakhchivan City

On the northern outskirts of the city, **Duzdag** is a salt cave that has functioned as a mine, sanatorium and treatment centre for respiratory ailments since Soviet times. Visits to the cave are free to tourists, and treatments can be arranged by the management of Hotel Duzdag

Momine Khatum.

INSIDE TRACK
SPRINGS ETERNAL

Legend has it that local hero Naimi held off a siege from the marauding hordes of Tamburlaine for an incredible 14 years on top of **Alinja** (*see below*), thanks to the natural springs and a small but fertile plateau that fed and watered his people, and which remains near the top of the rock to this day. The story goes that Tamburlaine was so angry at being defied that he returned here in stealth some time after the siege and had Naimi summarily executed. After his death, the people of the valley had the mausoleum, known simply as Naimi Turbasi, erected in his honour.

(*see right*). It's a surreal experience to leave the arid, sun-baked outside world and walk for hundreds of yards into the cool heart of a mountain, surrounded by salt crystals that sparkle in the impressive floodlights. At the cave's end, some 400 metres in, unisex dormitories house patients unable to afford a more modern private room, who have been signed off work with a *putiovka* (*see p183* **Inside Track**) or treatments involving up to a month of confinement here.

Where to eat & stay

The local food scene is not highly developed, although there are a few decent Turkish eateries clustered along Heydar Aliyev Avenue, near the junction with Ataturk Avenue. Few of these

Yusuf Ibn Kuseyir Turbasi. *See p181.*

serve alcohol and the best of the bunch are **Urfa** (0136 400 263), by the Turkish Consulate, and **Ganclik**, right on the junction. Ganclik also has a basement bar, the **Marakesh Klub**, with access downstairs around the side of the restaurant on Ataturk Avenue. A few metres further along Ataturk on the left-hand side of the road, the **Alinca** restaurant serves good food in a pleasant courtyard setting, with beer on tap too. Just next to it and down a narrow alley marked '*Efes Fiçi bara*' are two little back-street drinking dens serving beer and snacks, with a shared pool table.

As a whole, Nakhchivan suffers from a dearth of decent hotels and its capital is sadly no exception. The heavily restored **Hotel Tabriz** (0136 447 701, doubles AZN80) has modern but rather poky rooms in the centre of town, overlooking the garishly renovated 18th-century hammam, now a lacklustre *chaykhana* teahouse. It is, with the Hotel Duzdag (*see below*), probably the only place in the exclave where English is widely spoken. The Tabriz serves reasonable food in its 13th-floor restaurant and, unusually for Nakhchivan City, also alcohol. More pleasant, even though the rooms are a little garish, is the **Nakshijahan Motel** (050 481 2442, doubles AZN50), just off the airport road, which also serves excellent food in a willow garden by the often almost-dry bed of the Nakhchivan river.

The glittering new **Hotel Duzdag** (0136 444 901, www.duzdag.com, doubles AZN130) looks for all the world as if it may have just landed on a brief pit stop on some inter-galactic voyage. It serves good food (and alcohol) and features all mod cons, plus an aqua park (AZN10 for non-guests), and can arrange treatments at the nearby salt cave sanatorium (*see p181*) for guests and non-guests alike. On the north-western outskirts of town, the clean but uninspiring **Hotel Ganclik** (0136 446 215, doubles AZN40) occupies the top floor above a commercial centre of the same name and has 16 bedrooms with a dreary view over the main road. Other, cheaper hotels in town range from the dubious to the downright unsanitary and are not recommended.

ALINJA

Alinja is a natural rock fortress that lies around 20 kilometres (12 miles) east of Nakhchivan City, accessed off the Ordubad road. The road that winds its way up to the fortress offers magnificent views of **Ilan Dag**, 'Snake Mountain', whose sheer cleft is said to have been gouged out by Noah's ark as it came to rest on A ri Dag, Mount Ararat, 100 kilometres (60 miles) or so to the west. On top of the fortress, booted eagles soar over the remains of a man-made castle called **Algadyz**, which crowned the rock from

Alinja.

ASHABI KAHF

The Koran recounts a tale of seven holy men said to have fallen asleep in a mountain cave for over 300 years, and legend has it that it was here at **Ashabi Kahf** that this act of over-sleeping took place. Religious scholars have cited similar tales in Christian and Jewish traditions, arguing that the tale is a parable and not based on actual events, but the large numbers of pilgrims who flock to Ashabi Kahf would disagree. A well-surfaced road takes you six kilometres off the main one to Ordubad and ends at a flight of steps, with cafés and souvenir stands set between mulberry trees on either flank. Up the steps to the left is the actual cave, with clearly discernible grooves allegedly made by at least five of the seven somnolent holy backs. Opposite the cave, pilgrims attempt to pile seven stones atop one another to bring luck. Students come here to pray for success in exams and return with thanks thereafter. As you climb the steps, a cool breeze fans past a modern shrine from the sprawling system of large caves and chasms behind, which are a mass of nesting swifts and sparrows. Authentic or not, it certainly feels like a spiritual place.

EAST OF NAKHCHIVAN CITY

The road to Ordubad snakes along the bed of the Araz river, with unforgettable, parched pink lion's-paw mountains rising dramatically on either side of the flat, green river plain. Across the Araz, the higher peaks of Iran remain dusted in dirty snow throughout the summer, as do the mountains to the north that mark the border

the seventh to the 11th centuries. Now just a few low walls remain and it is a punishing climb to reach them, but the views even from the base of the scarp are magnificent. The pretty, gold-domed **shrine** across the valley on the other side of atmospheric **Khanagar** village, with its walnut groves and cobbled streets, is the mausoleum of local hero Naimi (*see also p182* **Inside Track**). There is an especially sweet spring beside the heavily restored shrine, which also has an excellent view up to the castle remnants across the valley.

Even in midsummer, the spring water from the top of Alinja – which made the castle viable under siege – flows out of the little green plateau on top of the citadel, staining the rockface a deep charcoal grey and providing a scant water supply to heavily scented clumps of wild thyme and camomile. The loud clattering of the rare Caucasian black grouse rings out across the valley in late spring and early summer, when meadows of stunning wild flowers frame beautiful views of Alinja and back to Ilan Dag.

INSIDE TRACK
TAKING A CURE, SOVIET-STYLE

A *putiovka* is a Soviet-era throwback. Essentially, it's a form of doctor's note, enabling an Azeri citizen to be signed off work for up to a month to take a treatment at any one of a number of sanatoria, usually based around taking a natural cure – such as hot sulphur springs, mineral mud baths or, in the case of **Duzdag** (*see p181*), a spell underground in a salt cave.

Ashabi Kahf.

Batabat.

with Armenia, now out of bounds. Along the way you'll pass the dull Azerbaijani/Iranian border town of **Julfa**.

Beyond Julfa, the dramatic scenery continues, the road coming tantalisingly close to the Iranian border at times. The village of **Aza**, shortly before you reach Ordubad, has a moderately interesting five-arched bridge across the river that dates back to the 17th or 18th century – but little else.

Ordubad

Ordubad is a very old town, situated right in the corner of Nakhchivan, close to the borders with both Armenia and Iran. It is famed for its town squares, shaded by plane trees. Traditionally, each square in Ordubad features a mosque, a plane tree and a spring, and the older ones contain houses with male and female door knockers (*see p185* **Great Knockers**). It is also justly famous for its lemons, with which the French ethnographer Chopin is said to have been impressed when he visited in the 19th

century. Ordubadi lemons are so sweet that they can be eaten whole – pith, skin and all (admittedly with a sugar lump on top) – and taste like a sherbet lemon sweet.

Along the deep chasm of the riverbed, much of the traditional architecture has been cleared in the name of progress and renovation. Climbing up the hill that forms Ordubad's main drag, and leaving the steep-sided river bank to your left, you'll see two large, restored 18th-century buildings that sit prominently on either side of the road. On the right, the **Juma Mosque** operated the only *madrasa*, or Islamic seminary, to remain open in the whole of Azerbaijan during the Soviet era. Across the street, the rather gaudily restored **Zorkhana** is a sort of wrestling hall, where Sufi-style contests of strength and combat were once held. It now houses perhaps the most impressive regional **Historical Museum** in Azerbaijan, which reopened after extensive renovations in early 2011. If you're lucky, and Russian-speaking, the museum director, the voluble Vilayat Baghirov – or 'William Brown', as he styles himself – will

Ordubad.

Family life in **Bichanak**.

regale you in excellent Russian and great detail about Nakhchivan, and in particular Ordubad's rich heritage of academia and learning.

Indeed, Nakhchivan as a whole, and specifically Ordubad, has produced far more than its fair share of leaders, professors, academics, writers and artists, having led the field in Azerbaijan in many areas for centuries. The museum has worthwhile exhibits on all aspects of Ordubadi life, from ancient burial urns to traditional clothing, via tools, arts, crafts, scientific advancements, academic achievements and natural history. Particularly fascinating is a prehistoric apothecary's stone, with seven slots cut in a slab of rock to take seven daily doses of whichever medicine was ground in the central wheel.

Above the Juma Mosque, opposite the Historical Museum, is the town's main square, where men chew the fat and play *nard*, a local form of backgammon, over cups of tea by the fountainside, under a vast canopy of 500-year-old plane trees. Further up the hill and bearing to the right, steep streets contain some of the town's older buildings, with wood-panelled hanging balconies and mud-brick, arched doorways. This old town quarter also sports pretty town squares and a 19th-century hammam, now rather over-enthusiastically restored and functioning as a *chaykhana* teahouse.

At the top of the main drag lie a pair of conjoined ancient plane trees. From here, squeezing your way up the right-hand side of the garage with the peacock decoration on its gable leads to a path to the site of **Afkhan Castle**, now bare but with great views across Ordubad to Iran in the distant south beyond.

Where to eat & stay

Ordubad's few eateries fail to impress, although the lakeside **Qapiciq Restaurant** (060 401 111), just out of town on the Nakhchivan road, is worth a visit. Surprisingly, for a town of Ordubad's size and repute, there is no hotel. The unremarkable **Hotel Araz** (0136 461 807, doubles AZN50) back at Julfa is the nearest option, but you may prefer to head back to Nakhchivan City for the night or arrange a homestay.

NORTH OF NAKHCHIVAN CITY

Batabat is a pretty alpine valley, tucked high up in the mountains that form Nakhchivan's northern border with Armenia and accessed by a series of hairpin bends on the road above the woodland village of **Bichanak**, beyond the regional capital of **Shahbuz**. The valley is dotted with lakes and alpine meadows filled with clumps of wild fennel, orchids and other pretty wild flowers in the late spring and early summer. The mountains around Batabat have a softer silhouette than the dramatic scenery of the High Caucasus, but the higher peaks remain snow-capped even in midsummer. The most well known of the lakes is **Ganli Göl**, 'Blood Lake', famous for its floating islands of reed

Knock Twice

Gendered door knockers in Ordubad.

Traditionally built houses in Ordubad often have two door knockers – a long, heavy, pendulous one for the men, and a lighter, circular one for the women. A sanitised version is that these are representations of a man's nose and a woman's breast, but you don't have to be Freud to spot a more likely inspiration for the shapes. Men would knock with the heavier knocker and women with the lighter one, so that female inhabitants of the house would know whether to cover their hair or not.

beds that drift slowly across the surface to the accompaniment of a deafening chorus of frog song. This is not as dramatic as it sounds, as the islands' movement is so slow as to be indiscernible. **Ganli Göl**, also erroneously known as Lake Batabat, is surrounded by large summer *dachas* and a high-altitude military encampment. Above Ganli Göl, in the same valley, another glacial lake has a rest stop with built-in barbecue facilities, popular in summer with Nakhchivanis who want a day's escape from the stultifying heat of the arid plain below. There is an observatory just below Ganli Göl and some beautiful walking, although hiking too far up into the mountains may take you close to Armenia, causing suspicion and problems with the military.

Wildlife in much of the Shahbuz region is now protected, to the consternation of local villagers who have long supplemented their mainly self-sufficient farming with hunted

Jehan Kudi Xatun Turbasi.

meat. Visitors to the region are supposed to check in with the police at Shahbuz, although arranging a trip through the Ministry of Culture and Tourism – and perhaps a homestay in Bichanak – will bypass any problems this may present.

Where to eat & stay

The impressive new **Batabat Restaurant** (0136 402 111) is a large log cabin construction right on the road just beneath the hairpin bends. It serves excellent food, including honey from its own hives, home-made cheeses and a selection of wild salads, including the salted stems of wild fennel. The manager speaks a little English. The owners are building a dozen or so cottages for overnight stays in the wooded grove behind the restaurant, although at present there is nowhere to stay in the region other than the uninspiring **Hotel Shahbuz** (0136 455 383, doubles 50 AZN) or a delightful homestay i n Bichanak village.

WEST OF NAKHCHIVAN CITY

Around 30 kilometres (19 miles) north-west of Nakhchivan City is the turn-off to the quaint, traditional village of **Garabaghlar**, which lies about six kilometres north of the main road, which in turn winds on to Sadarak and on into Turkey beneath Agri Dag. Garabaghlar, 'Black Gardens', is home to the 14th-century mausoleum complex of **Jehan Kudi Xatun**, with its stunning and unique fluted tomb tower, partially renovated in 2008. Making key-turning gestures to any of the nearby villagers likely to gather curiously around you should result in the caretaker mysteriously appearing and letting you into the restored building with the twin minarets. To the left, as you stand with your back to the mausoleum tower, you can climb up and get a bird's eye view of the mausoleum complex and the low foundation walls of the structures that filled the courtyard when it was built in the early 14th century. Beyond Garabaghlar along the main road, Mount Ararat, Agri Dag to Azeris, becomes increasingly visible from the haze as you near Turkey.

Where to eat & stay

There are no options in the area to eat or stay, with **Hotel Duzdag** (*see p182*) and the other options in Nakhchivan City the closest alternatives. If you're heading westwards into Turkey, **Hotel Sharur** (0136 423 999) and **Hotel Aziz** (0136 455 383), both in the town of Sharur, make convenient stop-offs.

Heading North

Castle ruins, peerless peaks and Azerbaijan's very own Ibiza.

The main attraction of the north is to be able to follow in the footsteps of the Tsar's army, exploring the rolling, high-altitude plains of the **Greater Caucasus**, enclosed by majestic snow-capped peaks. Pushkin and Lermontov also trekked in this region, for the most part further east in the Georgian borderlands, but the scenery here is no less awe-inspiring and it is easy to see how this wild and dramatic landscape was such an inspiration for a generation of great writers.

Ancient villages perch precariously on crags and sit in hanging valleys by bottomless gorges. Villagers go about their quasi self-sufficient lives, making the most of the summer months to grow, harvest, hunt and store produce to last them through the long, cold winter, when many are almost cut off from the outside world.

Also in the region are the impressive ruins of **Chirag Castle**, from where you can reach the seaside resort of **Nabran**, then **Guba** – and the jaw-dropping scenery and curious villages of the Greater Caucasus.

CHIRAG CASTLE

The ruins of **Chirag Castle** sit atop a steep cliff face above the simple village of **Mashrif**, whose other claim to fame is the Gala Alti sanatorium, where prescriptions may include a stinking sulphurous mud bath and/or a punishing climb up to the castle ruin itself. A glance at a map shows Chirag to be a mere 20 kilometres (12 miles) from the main road, but be prepared: the two badly rutted roads that form this loop – one from **Siyazan** and one from **Shabran** – are in such a woeful state of disrepair that you should allow a good 40 minutes each way. If push comes to shove, the Shabran road is marginally easier. The name Chirag means 'lamp', after the beacon fires that were lit here when it formed part of a defensive loop of castles around the coastal zone – along with the castles dotted around the Absheron (*see p153-159*). These defences were built in the Middle Ages and remained in use right up until the 18th century, when the castle started to fall into disrepair.

NABRAN

Tucked away in the north-eastern corner of the country, on the Caspian Sea, Nabran is

Chirag Castle.

ESCAPES & EXCURSIONS

Qirmizi Qasaba.
Synagogue.

Birthing House.

considered by Azerbaijanis to be the finest beach destination in the country – although those more used to the beaches of the Med are likely to be rather disappointed. Nabran is, in essence, a town of grey sand and pebble beaches whose waterside is dotted with snake-ridden reed beds and oily effluent. The town itself has plenty of loud discos and some pleasant-enough restaurants set among the woodland just inland from the shore. If it's just a quick beach fix you're after, though, you're probably better off heading to the northern Absheron resorts (see p156). Nabran is packed

to the gills with Bakuvians in July and August and so, unusually for Azerbaijan, booking is pretty much obligatory.

Where to eat & stay

Any of the beachside joints in Nabran offer reasonable food at a standard price to non-residents and there are plenty of rather samey restaurants too, none of which stands out in any way really. Take your pick.

Room prices vary widely depending on season and availability. Those quoted here are based on the shoulder seasons of June and September, but the tariff soars in midsummer and plummets in winter, when many resorts shut up altogether and few are heated against the cold winds that periodically whistle in from the north. The **Green Ville Resort Complex** (050 225 5315, doubles AZN70) has a decent pool, a range of sporting activities and fairly comfortable rooms, and is set back from the strip in peaceful woodland. **Atlant** (012 441 5848, doubles AZN50) is the one with the giant pirate ship floating across its child-friendly pool complex that features heavily on tourist brochures. Its cabins are rather pokey and close together, and its cramped setting does mean you might feel a little over-run. **Mirvari** (050 380 7651, doubles AZN40) has basic accommodation but good sea views from its hilltop location.

THE BEST PLACES

For astounding views
Khinalig. See p190.

For traditional village life
Griz. See p191.

For natural wonders
Cloudcatcher Canyon. See p190.

For a beach holiday
Nabran. See p187.

For romantic ruins
Chirag Castle. See p187.

GUBA

In low-rise Guba town, prettily modest 19th-century brick houses date from its heyday as an administrative centre for Russian imperialists, keen to watch out for any resurgence of the warring khanate states that fought over the region throughout the 18th century. Guba is quite small and laid out on a handy grid, so all of the following sights can easily be taken in meandering around on foot. The central square links Heydar Aliyev Avenue and Fatalikhan Avenue, still also known by its former moniker of Kizil Askar, and is called the **Meydan**, a name and concept common across the whole Turkic and former Ottoman regions for a public square or park that serves as a meeting place. On its northern side, **Juma Mosque** has a traditional octagonal shape and an outsized dome made of leaf-shaped metal panels. Its strikingly tall minaret is a modern addition and visible from afar, making it useful for orientation. Other mosques of note include **Haji Jafar** and **Adebil**, which lie a couple of blocks west and east of the Meydan respectively, and

both just to the north of Fatalikhan Avenue. These two mosques owe their square shape to having been churches in a former life. Curiously, **Sakine Khanum** mosque has no such Christian history and yet shares the square shape, perhaps built by association with the other two. All of them sport the small brick construction that is characteristic of Guba architecture. On the corner of Musabayov and Ardabil, five blocks west and one north of Meydan, the two rather dilapidated beehive-shaped buildings are an ancient **hammam**, which was still in operation only 20 years ago.

Qirmizi Qasaba (Krasnaya Sloboda)

Just across the bridge to the north of Guba, **Qirmizi Qasaba** (Krasnaya Sloboda) sounds like a classic Soviet name. But the town long predates the USSR and, at around 3,500 inhabitants, is thought by some to be the world's largest all-Jewish settlement outside Israel, populated by a curious and isolated ethnic group known as the Mountain Jews

Family Tree Mountain Jews & Tats

Two religiously distinct ethnic groups, with similarities in language.

There has been a thriving Jewish population in northern Azerbaijan for almost three centuries, thanks to Fatali Khan's establishment of a safe haven for Jews at Qirmizi Qasaba back in 1735. In the mid 19th century, Russian Imperial census-takers gave them the name Mountain Jews, by which classification they are still known today. In the late 1800s, it was noted by the ethnographer Anisimov that the Mountain Jews spoke a language closely associated with that of the Tats, an Islamic ethnic group of Persians now dispersed across the Transcaucasus, including Azerbaijan. Since then, the name Tat has

erroneously been applied to the Mountain Jews, often even by themselves, although they have no common root with the true Tats, who live wholly integrated into other Islamic communities across the the former Persian Empire.

One popular theory of the origin of the Mountain Jews is that they are descended from one of the lost tribes of Israel, who fled the sacking of Jerusalem in around 720 BC. Another theory has them descending from an itinerant tribe of Persian Jews, who are in turn said to have descended from one of the lost tribes. No one, it seems, can be quite sure.

(*see p189* **Family Tree**). In Soviet times, this community suffered terribly when Stalin banned the learning of Hebrew and, in a particularly cruel twist to the knife, forced the populace to farm pigs. Mass emigration to Israel, predominantly in the 1980s, halved the population, but these émigrés have since provided a financial lifeline to their relatives back home – it is very apparent that Qirmizi Qasaba is far more affluent than neighbouring Guba. It has two large synagogues – the newer **Grand Synagogue** is more visually impressive, while the **Old Synagogue** has a larger congregation. The attractive façade of the **Birthing House** towards the western end of town is also worth a visit and functions as a sort of community records office, in addition to containing a police station, post office and, of course, maternity hospital.

Around Guba

The best way to see the mountains around Guba is to arrange a jeep safari or do it by quad bike with a jeep escort. This can be arranged by the management of the Hale Kai hotel (*see p97*) in Baku, whose American owner also has plans for a permanent mountain base. Guba-based Kheyraddin Jabbarov (www.xinaliq.com) is a native of the nearby village of Khinalig who

speaks English and offers a range of services to tourists, including accommodation, jeeps with an English-speaking guide/driver and a horseback safari. Check out his highly informative website for more details and to contact him. Another Guba-based guide is Russian-speaking A Ali Muradov (050 642 6303 mobile, agacekli@yahoo.com), who can arrange homestays, a guided jeep safari for AZN80 per day and horses for AZN30 each, as well as guides speaking (limited) English.

Heading west out of Guba, towards Cloudcatcher Canyon and the road on to Khinalig, you pass through a dense forest of predominantly beech and birch, with hotels and eateries lining the road. **Cloudcatcher Canyon** is about 25 kilometres (15 miles) from Guba town, a sheer-sided chasm that does indeed trap clouds, often photogenically. At the near end of the canyon, a little restaurant lies beneath an enormous rock, wedged into a gap in the cliffside down by the bubbling river.

After Cloudcatcher, the new road continues through more and more dramatic scenery, skirting excellent locations for camping before crossing a glacial valley and passing through the remote village of **Jekh**. It then arrives at majestically beautiful and ancient **Khinalig**, set atop a smaller mountain, surrounded by breathtaking higher peaks. Khinalig's famed

Around Guba.

Cloudcather Canyon.

Juma Mosque, Guba. *See p189.*

ESCAPES & EXCURSIONS

beauty has led to an influx of tourist money and its houses are no longer as picturesque as they once were, many now sporting shiny corrugated iron roofs, but the views remain stunning. Nearby, itinerant shepherd families live in tents for the summer season, tending to vast flocks of sheep before repairing to accommodation in the lower-altitude villages in the icy winter.

Continuing up into the mountains will take you to the equally picturesque little village of **Griz**, cut off from the outside world for six months of the year and a wonderful place to do a homestay and experience traditional village life first-hand. Griz requires a four-wheel drive to access it, although it is reachable as a long hike from Khinalig. The villages of Khinalig, Jekh, Griz and others in the region all speak their own individual and ancient languages, which bear similarities to Lezghi and Georgian, but are generally thought by today's linguistic experts to be fundamentally unique.

Other similar villages of note in the mountains are the prettily whitewashed and little-visited **Budug**, around seven kilometres south-east of Cloudcatcher Canyon, and **Laza**, accessed from Guba via Qirmizi Qasaba and Gusar. Laza is also home to Azerbaijan's biggest new tourist draw, the ski resort nestling on the slopes of Azerbaijan's highest peak that it is named after, **Shah Dag**.

Where to eat & stay

The chances are that you have come to the Guba region to stay up in the mountains, and a glance around the town's accommodation options will only persuade you to get up into the fresh air as soon as possible. Near the bus station on the main drag, the **Oscar Hotel** (070 727 9607, doubles AZN30) is the best of the bunch, with seven mainly ensuite rooms that are comfortable if not exactly spacious. The **Hotel Khinalig** (0169 54445, doubles AZN10-AZN20), around the corner and actually inside the bus station and bazaar complex, is not as bad as it seems

---

Family Tree
The Lezghis

A mainly Sunni group.

One of the indigenous ethnic groups of the Caucasus region, the Lezghis or Lezghians live in villages across the mountainous regions of Azerbaijan and across the border in southern Dagestan. They are ancestrally linked with the Christian Udi (*see p167* **Family Tree**) and fellow Muslim Avars, Tabasarans, Rutuls and Tsakhurs. Unlike the majority of Azeris, the Lezghis are mainly Sunni, although with a minority who now adhere to the Shiite branch of Islam. Although Lezghi is still widely spoken within families, the language is considered 'vulnerable' by UNESCO's Atlas of the World's Languages in Danger. The centre of Lezghi population in Azerbaijan is the town of Gusar and its neighbouring mountain villages, although significant Lezghi minorities are found elsewhere in Azerbaijan.

Griz

at first glance, and is certainly cheap enough. More central, although equally fly-ridden, the **Shahdag Hotel** (0169 52927; AZN10) is a Soviet leftover with no showers.

Outside Guba, the best of the roadside cabin resorts in the birch forest are **Aynur** (070 649 4282 mobile, doubles AZN60), with excellent food and comfortable cabins; and **Afsana**

(050 517 1274 mobile, doubles AZN60), where rare attention to aesthetic detail seems to have been taken as it was being built, even if some of the original polish has now gone. The **Qachrash Bulaqi** restaurant doesn't look like much from the road, but it has tables in a pretty, natural amphitheatre in the forest, and food and service are both good. No rooms are available, though.

Heading on the northern loop from Guba, through Qirmizi Qasaba and on through the village of Alpan, **Long Forest** (050 526 4631 mobile, doubles AZN75) is the original mountain cabin resort in the area, but looks a little tired these days. This road leads on through some pretty villages, such as Susay and Geray, and then on up through beautiful high-altitude meadows, reliably accessed only with a four-wheel drive vehicle. Stunning **Laza** is home to the cabin resort of **Suvar** (0169 53671, doubles AZN50), the best of the higher-altitude options. Another excellent choice in these mountain villages would be a homestay, which can usually be arranged quite easily in

Taking to the Slopes

Skiing at Shah Dag.

It's not enough for Azerbaijan to put up the world's biggest flagpole, three towering buildings in the shape of flames and a new arena purely to accommodate the 2012 Eurovision Song Contest – now, in the wake of the 2011 Year of Tourism, it's opening the country's first ski centre.

When Azerbaijan President Ilham Aliyev laid the first stone by placing a time capsule into the foundations, it provided the formal start of a process that will see the state stumping up a sum of around $500 million-$700 million and Azerbaijan move into one of the world's most lucrative tourist markets: skiing.

Past the Cloudcatcher Canyon (*see p190*) and the beautifully picturesque village of Khinalig, nearly 30 kilometres (18.6 miles) north of Gusar, the new ski resort of **Shah Dag** sits on the slopes of Azerbaijan's highest peak, from which it takes its name, towering over the Greater Caucasus.

This was the original gateway to Azerbaijan, a forbidding landscape of high passes and cascading waterfalls that challenged many a trading party in Marco Polo's day.

Today the first of four stages in developing this site is set to be complete

by February 2012, when some 400-plus visitors can be accommodated. By 2020, this figure is set to be 10,000.

In the resort's initial phase, guests will be staying at a four-star, five-storey hotel and have access to a spa centre, pool and ski school. Chairlifts will take them up to a selection of five courses some 2,000 metres (6,560 feet) above sea level. By 2020, there will be at least ten hotels, around 170 chalets, an aqua park, tennis courts, football pitches, basketball and sports courts, climbing facilities and family-friendly entertainment – in fact, a complete leisure complex that also offers hikers and horse riders use of the canyons, ravines and mountain passes of the surrounding and stunningly beautiful **Shah Dag National Park**. Six to eight skiers at a time will be whisked up to the slopes in gondolas, with state-of-the-art snowmaking machines allowing for the season to be extended way past winter.

Meanwhile, a new road will ford the rushing mountain rivers of this dramatic part of the Caucasus and shorten the driving distance from Gusar to the complex, where underground parking will be provided.

For details on all facilities and developments, see www.shahdag.az.

Khinalig. *See p190.*

summer simply by arriving in your chosen village – ideally Khinalig, Griz, Laza or Budug – and asking around. Expect to pay about AZN15-AZN25 per person, including an evening meal and breakfast. Kheyraddin Jabbarov (*see p190*) will also arrange homestays or a bed in his little guesthouse in Khinalig.

GETTING THERE & AROUND

Buses, minibuses and shared taxis leave for Nabran and Guba regularly throughout the day from the central bus station in Baku (*see p205*). Although a new road makes Khinalig and Jekh

accessible in a normal vehicle, you are strongly advised to rent a four-wheel drive to explore the mountains properly.

From Baku, the road north follows the flat coastal plain, with the rolling desert hills around the Candy Cane Mountains and Besh Barmaq (*see pp153-159*) rising to your left. An extremely bumpy track from Siyazan heads to Chirag Castle, from where another only marginally less bumpy track will take you back to the main road at Shabran. From here it is a straight road until you get to Gandov, where a right fork takes you up to Nabran. Bearing left takes you on to Guba and the majesty of the Greater Caucasus mountains.

Heading South

Take a walk on the wild side.

As you head south from Baku, the semi-arid central plain gives way to the fertile lowlands beyond Bilasuvar, where cornfields lie alongside swathes of vines, sunflowers, tomatoes, watermelons and all manner of other crops. The town of **Masalli** marks the start of the surprisingly green rolling hills and mountainous gorges of Azerbaijan's wettest zone, the **Talysh** region, which, along with **Shirvan National Park**, with its huge variety of birds and herds of gazelle, is the main reason to venture southwards.

The protected area of **Hirkan National Park**, and in particular Lake Khanbulan, is the place to experience the verdant landscape of the Talysh region. It's also home to most of the last few remaining Caucasian leopards in Azerbaijan – although your chances of seeing one are very slim. Other routes of note within the Talysh region take you from Masalli to the barren hills of Iran beyond **Yardimli**, and from **Lankaran** through more beautiful forested gorges to **Lerik**, home to some of the longest-living people on the planet. Other major attractions of the deep south include two burning water features: **Yanar Bulag**, near Astara, and **Yanar Da**, on the Yardimli road.

TALYSH CUISINE AND ARCHITECTURE

Talysh cuisine and hospitality are rated as the best in Azerbaijan, particularly in the area around **Lankaran**. Talysh architecture, especially of mosques, is distinct from that of the rest of Azerbaijan, and the villages of **Pensar** and **Archivan**, near Astara, contain some of the finest examples.

SHIRVAN NATIONAL PARK

Clearly signposted from the main road just north of **Salyan**, Shirvan National Park was established in 1961, making it the oldest state reserve in Azerbaijan. Its 280 squre kilometres (108 square miles) are home to large populations of goitered gazelle (*see pp40-43*) and other indigenous mammals, as well as a bewildering array of over 200 mainly migrant bird species. At first glance, the flat landscape seems plain in the extreme, but subtle shades of pink, grey, green and blue scrub, punctuated by skeletal trees and stilted viewing platforms, actually make for stunning views (and photo opportunities). At the eastern edge of the park are some lovely deserted beaches, accessed by

30 kilometres (19 miles) of rough track, where camping is permitted. There is allegedly a submerged city offshore here, as well as shipwrecks that cry out for scuba exploration.

At the heart of the park, the rush-lined **Flamingo Lake** reservoir is a magnet for migrating birds, with up to 1,000 eagles feeding on tens of thousands of waders in winter, which is the best time to visit the park. There is a pontoon out to a hide on the water's edge so you can get close to the action. Near Flamingo Lake is the park headquarters and wardens' accommodation, where an overnight stay can be arranged for AZN10 per person in the one twin bedroom. Be prepared to be kept awake by an astonishing frog chorus and battalions of mosquitoes, though – stock up on repellent. You may also hear the eerie nocturnal howls of the park's extremely shy wolf population, the barking of the odd golden jackal, and, if you're very lucky, a mewing jungle cat.

There are no organised tours of the park, although most of it is accessible without a four-wheel drive in good weather. Unofficial guide Hikmet (050 381 1890 mobile), who speaks a smattering of English, and his park ranger brother Fouad (070 929 1530 mobile) will help you out with your stay and bring breakfast in for you, for a small fee. Entry to the park costs AZN4, payable at the gate. Overnight stays are supposed to be pre-arranged with the Ministry of Ecology in Baku, although ad hoc paying visitors are unlikely to be turned away.

Where to eat & stay

Salyan town is a pleasant enough place for a meal stop, although it has no recommendable hotel options. For those not feeling intrepid enough to overnight in Shirvan Park itself, there is little option but to push on south to Bilasuvar or Masalli, or head back north to Shikhov Beach or Baku.

Just at the northern city limit of Salyan is the impressive Kur bridge, with its lion statues at either end. At the southern end of the bridge, the curious stilt-top wigwam canopies of the **Golustu Restaurant** (050 678 4748 mobile) annoyingly all but mask the views of the lake upon which the restaurant sits, but it's a convenient enough stop. The restaurant was reportedly popular in Soviet times, but the grand renovation misfired and these days locals prefer the more traditional identikit places a kilometre or so further south along the main road. A better option altogether is **Ba İçi** (no phone) on Tabriz Khalinbayli in Salyan itself. On the southern edge of Bilasuvar, **Zirva Restaurant** (0159 32515; AZN50) serves great food and offers reasonable rooms.

MASALLI

Heading south from Salyan, a left fork takes you to dull, Soviet-style **Neftchala**, where plans for an eco-tourist camp seem to be foundering. Neftchala would seem the obvious base for a visit to the strictly protected

THE BEST PLACES

Dramatic roadside scenery
Yardimli Road, Lerik Road. See p196, p198.

A forested lake
Lake Khanbulan, Hirkan National Park. See p199.

A gazelle safari
Shirvan National Park. See p194.

Talysh architecture
Pensar, Archivan. For both, see p201.

A tree-lined gorge
Lerik Road. See p198.

A waterfall
Shalala, Yardimli Road. See p196.

reserve of **Gizil Agaj bay**, whose migrating birdlife reputedly includes vast flocks of flamingos that put even impressive Shirvan Park to shame. Sadly, though, this reserve is largely out of bounds to tourists, but an enquiry at the Ministry of Ecology in Baku may help.

A right fork at Salyan takes you on to Masalli, via the towns of **Bilasuvar, Jalilabad** and **Goytepe** (aka Priship), where a mildly interesting 19th-century Russian church sits in a schoolyard by the side of the road.

Masalli marks the start of the Talysh region proper and features a typical southern-style mosque and rather run-down 19th-century Hall of Culture, both of which can be visited in a few minutes as you drive through. Its real attractions lie outside the city limits, at **Lake Vilash**, on the road to Yardimli, and at the curious sanatorium of Masalli Istisu. The

Shirvan National Park.

ESCAPES & EXCURSIONS

attractive woodland around Lake Vilash is now awash with eateries of varying standards, some of which also have rooms, although the whole area has now become so busy you may prefer to push on a few kilometres to the quieter options recommended below.

Masalli Istisu (*istisu* being 'hot spring') lies beyond Lake Vilash, a few kilometres from the main Yardimli road and accessed via a well-signposted road that forks off to your left. It is a curious place, arranged on terraced groves of sycamore with beds of flowers and banana plants. Doctors in green scrubs prescribe baths in various sulphurous concoctions to cure a plethora of illnesses. The water here emerges from the ground scaldingly hot, although it is thankfully allowed to cool somewhat before being channelled into a series of private bathrooms, where ladies draped in tent-like floral housecoats disappear to take their cure. At the foot of the hill, families bathe and play in a stream, and you may well see camels being watered. It is possible to stay at the Istisu, although you may feel a little intrusive. It is far more pleasant to continue on to one of the recommended cabin resorts a little further along the Yardimli road.

A few kilometres beyond the Masalli turn, above the Yanar Da resort (*see p197*), there are several burning springs in the woods that are best visited by night. Another few kilometres beyond here, and only a few steps above the road, the pretty **Shalala waterfall** is at its most impressive in spring and early summer when the flow is swollen by meltwater; by late summer it dries up to little more than a trickle. There is a café here, but the drinks tend to be on the warm side and tea is the only real option. The name Shalala may well leave you humming an old Al Green tune to yourself, but it's actually Azeri for 'waterfall'.

Yardimli is a simple, traditional little village, remarkable in the main for the hiking and four-wheel drive possibilities that lie in the wild countryside beyond. Roadside tomatoes are sold out of aluminium buckets and there are stunning views over powdery blue thistle-clad hillsides on to the barren, pinkish desert landscape of Iran. Visitors are also welcome at the carpet-weaving factory at the far end of Yardimli village, although the end products are not for sale. The helpful

Meet Lerik's Supercentenarians

Happy 100th-plus birthday to Lerik's long-lived residents.

In 1963, a young photo-journalist for the Soviet TASS news agency, Kalman Kaspiyev, interviewed a Lerik shepherd called Shirali Muslimov, who claimed to be 158 years old. Muslimov went on to become something of a global celebrity, with interviews in the *New York Times* and *National Geographic*, and an obituary in *Time* magazine a decade later. Muslimov had five generations of descendants and remembered events that certainly placed him at well over 100 years old – even if, as gerontologists were sure, he had managed to add a decade or three to his real age.

The *New York Times* article spawned a flurry of interest in ancient Azeris, with Danone claiming the long lives of the region were down to a yoghurt-rich diet. In fact, when interviewed, Muslimov said he couldn't stand yoghurt, but did manage a healthy 100 grams of vodka a day.

These days, an impressive number of people in the Lerik region claim supercentenarian status, which is generally thought to be down to a combination of good genes, fresh air, a relatively healthy diet (vodka notwithstanding) and a stress-free lifestyle.

Masalli.

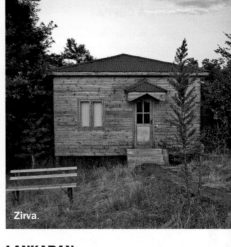
Zirva.

management of the **A&E Hotel** (*see below*) can help you find a jeep and driver to explore some of the more challenging routes in the surrounding countryside.

Where to eat & stay

The quietest spot in the Lake Vilash area is **Zirva** (050 578 2026 mobile, doubles AZN50), meaning 'summit'. It is perched on a hillside above the occasionally noisy road, just beyond the lake itself and before the Istisu turn. Zirva is arranged around a fibreglass mountain, complete with fibreglass goat, and has ten cabins that back on to a pretty, tree-lined gorge – No.1 has stunning views down to Lake Vilash. Food is simple but very good, and is served in little pavilions dotted among an ironwood grove. Right on the lake, and the best among the many restaurants with cabins clustered around here, is **Gulustan** (050 346 4686 mobile, doubles AZN50), which sports little displays of Azeri handicrafts on cradles among the woodland, and a bewildering collection of mossy African animal sculptures. Beyond Zirva, if you take the right fork across the valley and on towards Yardimli, **Yanar Dag** (050 325 5826 mobile, doubles AZN50) is rather more care-worn than Zirva, but is ideally situated for the burning water features of the hillside above that give it its name. The little **A&E Hotel** (0175 51246, doubles AZN40) in Yardimli has four simple but respectable rooms, and is the place to ask about off-roading around the village and, in good weather, even on the sketchy track to Lerik.

LANKARAN

The road from Masalli to Lankaran passes through the small town of Port Ilich, named in honour of Vladimir Ilich himself but now rebranded as **Leman** (Azeri for 'port'). Across a causeway from Leman, **Narimanabad**, formerly known as Sara, shimmers in the noon sun like a spectre hovering over the reed beds. Narimanabad was once an island, until the causeway was built in the 1950s when the Caspian Sea was at an especially low ebb. At the time, wealthy houses were built along the water's edge, despite warnings that the sea level might one day rise again. Unsurprisingly, rise it did and the houses at the end of Narimanov have since been reclaimed by the sea, adding to the ghost town feel of this eerie place. Narimanabad and Leman would be convenient places to base yourself for eco-tourism into the **Gizil Agaj Bay**, but until this promising region begins to truly open up it is a difficult trip indeed.

INSIDE TRACK
TALYSH IRONWOOD

Ironwood is a species of tree endemic to the Talysh region, characterised by its intense hardness and natural flame resistance. Traces of ironwood have been found in the foundations of settlements dating back at least 1,000 years and as far away as Mingachevir, giving firm evidence of a flourishing ancient lumber trade.

INSIDE TRACK
FANCY A CUPPA?

Azeri tea, as grown around Lankaran, is a low-altitude tea. The additional heat of the burning sunshine on the leaf tips increases tannin levels, making for a much stronger, tannin-rich variety once sought after in Azerbaijan. Now, though, milder-flavoured high-altitude Ceylon tea is becoming the preferred brew.

Lankaran is a mid-sized town and the de facto capital of the Talysh region. To Azeris, Lankaran means tea, and there are tea fields to be seen on both the Lerik and Astara roads, where huge fields of brambles look cultivated because they were once vineyards on a Soviet collective farm. In season, the berries are huge and juicy, as are all the fruits of this fertile region. This is where much of Azerbaijan's fruit, including all of its citrus and sub-tropical species, comes from.

Lankaran centres around a pretty town square with a memorial to local World War II hero Haji Aslanov. The memorial sits atop a stylised tank plinth behind the famous **Mayak lighthouse**, which was used as a prison for many years. Adjacent to the square is a moving memorial to Armenian atrocities perpetrated against the people of the region in both 1918 and 1992.

There is little to do in Lankaran by night, but a couple of blocks south-west of the Mayak is the **Heydar Aliyev Park** (still generally known by its old name of Dosa Park), which is packed with young couples, groups of friends and families having an evening walkabout. It is

a great place to make local friends among the notably hospitable people of the Talysh region. Next to Dosa Park is the little **Askar Aliyev Park** (also known by its old name of Druzhba Park), which contains a small sculpture garden with seven miniatures of famous buildings that each exemplify traditional architecture style of the seven main, historical regions of Azerbaijan. Dosa Park also contains some sculptures of note among its well-kept flowerbeds and illuminated fountains, in particular a vast Soviet-style war memorial of a soldier breaking free from a huge bronzed boulder.

Where to stay & eat

For restaurants and accommodation in and around Lankaran, *see p199*.

AROUND LANKARAN
Lerik

The road to **Lerik** passes the all-new Lankaran airport, which reopened after extensive renovation in 2008, and winds its way up a pretty, tree-lined gorge, where some of the region's best accommodation and food options are located. This gorge leads most of the way to the village of Lerik itself, via the village of **Guneshli**, once named Azerbaijan until the president himself decided that an address of Azerbaijan was inappropriate and the rebranding came about.

Lerik itself is not an exciting place, but the views along the way do not disappoint. As the road climbs beyond the gorge, the vista opens out into beautiful rolling hills, punctuated by small woods and hamlets all the way to the Iranian border and beyond.

Lake Khanbulan.

Lankaran.

Hirkan National Park

Densely wooded Hirkan National Park is a mid-sized reserve, covering around 10,000 beautifully wooded hectares, although the larger overall Hirkan area stretches all the way to the Iranian border. Entrance to the park costs AZN4 and is supposed to be by ticket only, although there are no barriers or ticket collectors and the great temptation is to do as many of the locals seem to do and push on ahead regardless. The park office and rather dreary visitors' centre (closed Sun), where you can buy the tickets, is on the Astara road, about halfway between Lankaran and the turn to Lake Khanbulan. Park deputy director Haji Safarov (050 687 1009 mobile) speaks some English and will be happy to advise on campsites, arrange horse-riding for AZN10 per person and provide other information. There are some lovely walks to be discovered across the whole region, but the real gem is pretty, forest-lined **Lake Khanbulan** – if you can turn a blind eye to the rubbish strewn around the lakeside picnic areas and roadside teahouses, many of which operate from the boot and roof of a Lada. About half of Lake Khanbulan is strictly off-limits, as it forms the compound of one of the presidential *dachas* – if you come to an electrified fence, steer well clear.

Where to eat & stay

Options in Lankaran itself are limited to the middle-of-the-road **Hotel Qala** (0171 50284, doubles AZN75), which has clean and respectable rooms, but not a great deal of character. The seaside **Qafqaz Sahil** (0171 26100, doubles AZN80) is the best option for long-term stays, offering decent service and

Family Tree The Talysh

A people of Persian origin.

The Talysh are an ancient Persian people whose homelands spread across the Talysh region of southern Azerbaijan and northern Iran. The Talysh claim descent from the even more ancient Cardusians, who were described around the time of Christ by the Greek writer and geographer Strabo as being 'a war-like tribe of mountaineers, fighting chiefly on foot, and well-skilled in the use of the short spear or javelin'. The Talysh language is related to Tati, the language of the true ethnic Tats, as well as to Judeo-Tati, the language of the Mountain Jews (see p189 **Family Tree**).

Lerik. *See p198.*

making the best of the grey sand beach. Just outside town, the **Palidli Sahil** (0171 52626, doubles AZN60) is universally known as the 'Titanic', due to its peculiar ship-shaped central restaurant building. Its cabins are closely packed and its pretty gardens filled with kitsch fibreglass sculptures of fishermen and the like. The 'beach' (about 30 feet of grey sand by the railway) is home to a solitary, jauntily striped parasol.

Options along the Lerik road are much better. **Relax** (0171 56068, doubles AZN95) is an all-inclusive resort with disco, whose troop of animators are shipped in from as far afield as Georgia and speak some English. The best places in the area, however, are both mainly restaurants, with a handful of clean but simple

cabins. **Tabassum** (0171 56150, doubles AZN50), where cabins and dining pavilions are arranged around a deep natural swimming pool at the foot of the gorge, is linked by a system of walkways. Owner Akif is quite a character and his food and welcome are simply superb. Also heartily recommended for both food and service is **Khanbulan Restaurant** (0171 57190, doubles AZN50), where you can dine in a birch forest on some of the best this culinarily rich region has to offer.

ASTARA

The tree-lined gorges of the Lankaran area end abruptly, giving way to a flattish plain of rice paddies studded by rocky outcrops that

ESCAPES & EXCURSIONS

Tabassum.

Astara.

vaguely resemble the mountainous rocky stacks of parts of south-east Asia. This landscape persists all the way to the Iranian border town of **Astara**. At first glance, the central square of Astara is straight out of 1960s cult series *The Prisoner*, and not for the first time in provincial Azerbaijan, you half expect Patrick McGoohan to leap out pursued by a giant weather balloon.

This notwithstanding, other than for those heading on into Iran, Astara offers little excitement. More interesting is the village of **Pensar**, a few kilometres back and just off the main road from Lankaran, which has several good examples of 19th-century mosque architecture and an old hammam that dates from the same period.

Easy to miss on the main road as it passes through **Archivan**, ahead of the giant radio tower, is a reconstructed 19th-century Talysh summerhouse. It is behind a hedge to your right as you head southwards towards Astara, just beyond the sprawl of Archivan itself and before Yanar Bulag.

Literally meaning 'Burning Spring', **Yanar Bulag** is another fire-themed Azeri oddity and well worth a quick stop, as it lies right on the main road. The standpipe, running from the spring nearby, is clearly signed and runs with water containing so much dissolved natural gas that it bursts spectacularly into flame when lit by a match. The pit around the tap is seasonally filled with watermelons, cooling photogenically in the run-off water from the spring.

Where to eat & stay

Options are limited. Just before the city limits and near the radio tower, **Savalan** (0195 33116) has a few lacklustre rooms behind what is primarily a massive wedding palace and restaurant serving good food. In town, the pleasant **Hotel Shindan** (0195 34177, doubles

AZN60) is convenience personified, lying right on the main square. The **Hotel Sahil** is reachable by taxi from the centre, and offers simple cabins and a reasonable restaurant, with a beachside location – just don't expect the Caribbean.

Getting there & around

Buses from the central bus station in Baku operate a regular service to the major towns in the region. Lankaran airport is up and running, with a daily service to and from Baku, although international flights still seem to be a pipe dream. The daily train from Baku is slow and subject to annoyingly suspicious staff.

Tea plant, Astara Road.

Yanar Bulag.

ESCAPES & EXCURSIONS

Your City Break doesn't have to cost the earth

Trees for Cities

Reduce the impact of your flight by donating to Trees for Cities

To donate, text
'TREE37' to 70070 or visit
www.treesforcities.org

Trees for Cities, Prince Consort Lodge, Kennington Park, Kennington Park Place, London SE11 4AS
Tel. +44 (0)20 7587 1320; Charity registration 1032154

Directory

Getting Around

ARRIVING & LEAVING

By air

Baku Heydar Aliyev International Airport (4972 732, http://baku-airport.com) is 20 kilometres (12 miles) north-east of the city centre. It has two terminals, North and South.

The arrivals process is reasonably straightforward, provided you have a valid visa (*see p210*) – without which you probably wouldn't have been allowed to board your flight in the first place.

Departure, on the other hand, is a long-winded and frustrating faff of protocol and security checks that starts with a first X-ray of your entire luggage as you enter the terminal. There then follows a series of queuing, stamping and inspecting. All kinds of foreign currencies are accepted in outlets – including the Cockpit Pub – as you wait for your flight, though your change will be in Azeri manats.

Most hotels, even three-star ones in the Old City, provide an airport shuttle service for a varying set of rates. A **taxi** (*see p205*) will cost AZN20-AZN25 but agree a price with the driver first. One leaving the domestic terminal may charge less. You could be canny and get a taxi as far as the first metro station – Azizbayov – but the hassle is probably only worth a few manats.

The very cheapest way of getting into the city is to walk a short distance from the terminal to the main road, and wave down communal minibus (*marshrutka*) No.36 to Samed Vurgun in town. This costs the same as other forms of public transport in town (20k). For more on public transport, *see right*.

Airlines

Flying time between London Heathrow and Baku is around 5.5hrs-6hrs. Two companies currently serve this route directly. **British Midland International** (www.fly bmi.com) flies daily, twice on Tuesday, Thursdays and Saturdays. The cheapest economy fare is currently between £400 and £500 each way, twice that for flexibility on flying times. **Azerbaijan Airlines** (www.azal.az) runs three times a week from Heathrow and twice weekly from Aberdeen – if you can be flexible with time you should be able to find a return flight for under £500.

There is currently no direct service to Azerbainjan from the USA or Canada.

A number of companies – most notably **Turkish Airlines** (www.turkish airlines.com), **Aeroflot** (www.aeroflot.ru) and **Lufthansa** (www.lufthansa. com) – offer affordable flights to Baku via their respective hubs, either Istanbul, Moscow or Frankfurt. The best stopover deals are usually with **Austrian Airlines** (www.austrian airlines.com) via Vienna and, quite often the cheapest, **Air Baltic** (www.airbaltic.com) via Riga.

By train

The main rail route into Baku is the affordable, overnight service from Tbilisi, Georgia. There is also a train three times a week from Moscow, though it is for Russian and Azeri nationals only. Baku's main train station (*see p79*) is by the metro hub of Jafar Jabbarli/ 28 May just north-east of the city centre.

By bus

A handful of companies provide a bus service from Istanbul, but with a journey time of 48 hours, the ticket price of around $70 seems steep. Baku's main bus terminal is located in the north-west of the city centre, with a stop, 20 Yanvar, on the red metro line.

By boat

Cargo ships regularly trawl across the Caspian between Turkmenistan/Kazakhstan and Azerbaijan, but schedules are non-existent and passenger comforts few. You will have to arrange your visa before you arrive.

PUBLIC TRANSPORT

Baku's city centre is compact, and walking is a good way to get around it (*see p205*). To travel further afield, you may need the following:

Metro

The easiest way to access the northern and eastern areas of town from the city centre is by metro. This is run on a simple chip-card system. First, buy the card itself (AZN2) at any main metro station, then charge it in one of the machines by placing it flat and face up before plonking in a bunch of 20k coins. Recharge once you start to run out.

Stations look very Soviet, with long, deep escalators and uniformed guards in little glass booths at the bottom. Signposting is poor and there's an impossibly confusing change at 28 May/Jafar Jabbarli – all trains but the one terminating one stop down the line at Khatai use the 28 May platform.

The stations you'll be using the most are **Icheri Sheher**, beneath a glass pyramid on the western edge of the Old City, and **Sahil**, just east of the city centre. Frustratingly, Fountains Square has no station.

Buses & minibuses

A baffling array of buses and minibuses (*marshrutki*) serves the Azeri capital, the former with fixed stops but no schedules or routes posted on them. First-time visitors simply have to see if their destination is posted above the driver's window as a bus approaches. In minibuses, passengers should shout '*Sakhla!*' when they want the driver to stop. All journeys have a set fair of 20k – simply pass your coin down to the driver.

TAXIS

A new fleet of 300 London taxis, painted purple, has arrived in Baku, though the bulk of cabs for hire are Ladas and other local cars. Agree a price first – most journeys across town should be in the AZN3-AZN5 range. The best service is provided by dialling 189. Your mobile receives a message when the driver is approaching.

DRIVING

Driving in Baku is not for the meek. Cars weave in and out of lanes, occasionally barked at by police vehicles with megaphones, and everyone honks at any every

opportunity. Parking is left to a fraternity of seemingly otherwise unemployable old locals who 'guard' your vehicle and help you back out into oncoming traffic, for a handful of coins.

The bureaucracy and cash deposits required for bringing your own vehicle into Azerbaijan make it a daunting proposition. Offices can deal with all paperwork, such as having your licence translated into Azeri, a local requirement. AzPetrol stations, seen throughout the country, stock the 95-octane fuel used by most vehicles.

Car & taxi hire

Most of the top international car-hire firms have a base in Baku – including **Avis** (www.avis.az) or **Hertz** (www.hertz.com) for details.

Note that taxis are not just for getting around the city – you can hire a driver for the day to go to a national park of place of interest a few hours' drive away, and pay a similar price to what you would have done had you hired a car yourself and paid for the petrol.

CYCLING

Baku is bereft of cycling lanes and bike-hire companies, although the waterfront Bulvar is crying out for a cycle path.

WALKING

Baku city centre is pretty compact: it shouldn't take you more than 15 minutes to walk from Fountains Square to the waterfront, or from Fountains Square to Sahil metro station. The Old City is even closer. Beware that crossing the street can be tricky from dawn to past dusk.

GUIDED TOURS

The only city-wide excursion generally available, and

promoted by the Baku Tourist Information Centre (*see p209*), is the five-hour Baku City Tour, which goes for a whopping AZN25 (598 4818, 418 9739, www.millenniumtour.az). Tickets are sold at the tourist office itself or at the Park Inn Hotel (*see p95*). Excursion buses leave daily at noon from Azadlig Square and finish at the Opera & Ballet Theatre at 5pm. In between, the route takes in Azneft Square, Martyrs' Alley, the funicular, the Old City and Black City.

The easiest, most affordable (AZN5) and the most recommended tour of Baku is the walking tour around the Old City, accompanied by an audio guide in English, which is available from the information office (Gulle Street, 417 7933, www.icheri sheher.gov.az; open 9am-6pm daily), on the Caspian side of the Maiden's Tower. You will need to leave your passport as a deposit, to be picked up at the end of the tour. The tour has 16 points, beginning and ending at the Maiden's Tower, featuring the Palace of the Shirvanshahs twice and including a jazz-*mugham* medley at the end. There are 23 push-button entries on your pocket-sized audio guide, which correspond to red-square headphone signs around the Old City, and a notional 60-minute limit on your tour. Each extra hour is will cost you another AZN1. *See p61* **Walk**.

One other enjoyable and affordable (AZN2) excursion is to take the 30-minute boat trip out on to the Caspian Sea. Although the cruise doesn't take you anywhere in particular, it does give you a different view of Baku, one that can't be glimpsed from the land. Boats leave from a jetty by the main harbour terminal building at the eastern end of Bulvar. *See p73* **Inside Track**.

DIRECTORY

Resources A-Z

DIRECTORY

ADDRESSES

In Baku, streets are known as *küçasi*, usually abbreviated to *küç*, and avenues *prospekti*, often abbreviated to *pr*. English transliterations vary, the q and g letters interchangeable: the many variations of Qala küç in the Old City may be rendered as Gala küç, which we use in this guide. There is also the upside-down Azeri 'e', rendered either as 'a' or 'e' in English.

Furthermore, major streets have been through three name changes in the last century: pre-Soviet; Soviet and post-independence. Certain major thoroughfares in the city, in particular the main avenue to the airport, have also been renamed at different points of the 1990s.

In this guide, we have tried to stick as much as possible to the street names used on the Heron street map. which is available at branches of the Ali & Nino book chain (*see p128*) in town.

Street signage, Downtown at least, is pretty reliable and set out in Latin script.

In smaller communities in the provinces, buildings are numbered after the name of the settlement: Jar 57, Ivanovka 22 and so on.

AGE RESTRICTIONS

The age of consent is 16 and the age of marital consent is 18 for men, 17 for women. Citizens legally become adults at 18.

ATTITUDE & ETIQUETTE

Azeri society is family-oriented and local hospitality is warm and friendly. If you are invited to a family home, it's a good idea to take gifts for all members of the household – and to err on the side of caution where alcohol is involved. Although the country is fairly secular (dress codes for women are liberal), it may always be best to play safe by offering flowers or chocolates rather than a good bottle of whisky. Remove your shoes once you are inside the house. Sharing a meal, particularly bread, builds up a sense of trust among the participants.

'Salam' is a catch-all greeting for 'hello'. Men greet each other with a handshake, old friends with air kisses to either cheek. Women greet each other with kisses to each cheek. Foreigners should play safe and use a simple handshake for both sexes. Eye contact is most important in all circumstances – particularly when greeting and raising a toast.

In business, phone calls are always preferred to emails, to suggest or arrange a meeting, to cancel one, and so on. Dress formally and expect to wait a while after the arranged meeting time. Have business cards printed up in English and Azeri and, if required, hire a translator fluent in English, Azeri and Russian.

BUSINESS

Baku looks and feels like an oil-rich city, although the quick wealth of the last ten years is not so evident in other areas of the country. While local wages remain low, prices for foreigners are artificially inflated – particularly when it comes to apartment rents. In the same ten-year period, start-up costs and bureaucracy for foreign companies have decreased significantly.

Nevertheless, many large Azeri concerns remain in state hands and doing business remains slower than in most countries in the West.

Many local entrepreneurs are aware that Azerbaijan's oil reserves are finite, and that diversification is essential if the economy is to remain strong over the next 20-30 years. There may be opportunities beyond ones confined to the energy industries.

Conventions & conferences

Most major hotels (*see pp86-99*) offer conference facilities. The major venue for trade fairs is the **Expo Centre** (*see p142*), out towards the airport in Surakhani. A shuttle bus is usually laid on from N Narimanov metro station.

Couriers & shippers

All major international dispatch companies have offices in Baku.

Be aware that the local customs authority will open all packages, sealing them back up again before they get to you.
DHL *Nobel prospekt 30, 1025 Baku (493 4714, www.dhl.com).* **Open** 9am-6pm Mon-Fri; 10am-3pm Sat.

Federal Express *M&M & Munch Baku, M Hadi Street 63A, 1029 Baku (464 4221, www.fedex.com).* **Open** 9am-8pm Mon-Sat.

Office services

Office Systems *Ahmad Rajabli Street 9 (448 4411, www.officesystems.az).*

Useful organisations

American Chamber of Commerce Azerbaijan *497 1333 www.amchamaz.org.*

British Azerbaijani Chamber of Commerce & Industry *+44 20 3174 1333, www.bazcci.com.*

British Business Group of Azerbaijan *www.britishbusiness groupazerbaijan.com.*

US-Azerbaijan Chamber of Commerce (USACC) *1212 Potomac Street, NW, Washington DC 20007 (+1 202 333 8702, www.usacc.org).*

CUSTOMS

Gone are the days when every Western visitor had to fill out a customs form upon arrival. If you are bringing a significant amount of Western currency into the country, in cash, then you must declare it at the border and produce the same form upon departure. The following items are free of import duty:
Up to 1,000 cigarettes
Up to 1kg of tobacco
Up to 1.5 litres of spirits
Up to 2 litres of wine
Goods up to a value of $10,000 or weighing up to 50kg.
Those wishing to take carpets, artworks or historical artefacts out of the country must have written permission from a special commission under the Ministry

of Culture and Tourism. The limit per person for exporting caviar is currently 250g.
See www.az-customs.net for more details.

DISABLED

Baku's facilities for disabled access are poor. Some of the city's better hotels (*see pp86-99*) have disabled-adapted rooms but none of Baku's public transport has been rendered disabled-friendly.

DRUGS

Azerbaijan is a major crossroads for drug trafficking and punishments for those involved are harsh.

ELECTRICITY

The current is 220V, which works with UK 240-V appliances – bring a two-pin adaptor. If you have US 110-V gadgets, bring transformers.

EMBASSIES & CONSULATES

Not all countries maintain embassies in Baku.
Australian consular assistance *MNG Building, 7th flr, Ugur Mumcu Cad 88, Gaziosmanpasa, Ankara, Turkey (+90 312 459 9500, www.turkey.embassy.gov.au).* In emergencies, Australian citizens may contact the British Embassy (*see below*) or call the 24-hour helpline +61 2 6261 3305 or 1300 555 135 within Australia.

British Embassy *Khagani Street 45 (437 7878, outside working hours 437 7864, http:// ukinazerbaijan.fco.gov.uk/en).* **Open** 9.30am-12.30pm Mon-Fri. *Telephone enquiries* 9.30am-12.30pm, 2.30-5pm Mon-Fri.

Canadian consular assistance *Cinnah Cad 58, Cankaya, Ankara, Turkey (+90 312 409 2700, www.canadainternational. gc.ca).* **Open** 8.30am-12.30pm, 1.30-5.45pm Mon-Thur; 8.30am-1pm Fri. *Visa & immigration* **Open** 9-11.30am Mon-Thur. *24-hour helpline* +1 613 996 8885.

Irish consular assistance *MNG Building, B Blok Kat 3, Ugur Mumcu Cad 88, Gaziosmanpasa, Ankara, Turkey (+90 312 459 1000, www. embassyofireland.org.tr).* **Open** 9.30am-1pm, 2-5pm Mon-Fri.

New Zealand consular assistance *Kizkulesi sok 11, Gaziosmanpasa, Ankara, Turkey (+90 312 446 3333, www.nz embassy.com/turkey).* **Open** 9.30am-noon Mon-Fri. *Inonu Cad 48/3, Taksim, Istanbul, Turkey (+90 212 244 0272). Emergency number +90 533 284 0888 mobile.*

US Embassy *Azadlig prospekt 83 (498 0335, http://azerbaijan. usembassy.gov).* **Open** 8.30am-5.30pm Mon-Fri. *Consular services* 2-5pm Mon-Thur; 9am-noon Fri.

EMERGENCIES

Emergency 103
Fire 101
Police 102

GAY & LESBIAN

Although homosexuality was decriminalised in 2000, open LGBT activity is rare in Baku and social attitudes are not generally liberal. The age of consent for homosexuals is 16. There are no officially recognised groups currently acting on behalf of homosexuals or LGBT rights.

HEALTH

EU citizens have the right to free emergency health care in Azerbaijan – although medical facilities outside Baku leave something to be desired. In Baku, there is an English-speaking medical consultancy service on 497 0911. *See also p208* **Insurance**.
Malaria is only present in the swampy area down by the Iranian border.

Accident & emergency

For emergency service numbers, *see above*.
Baku Medical Centre *Hasan Aliyev Street 101 (465 0606, www.bakumc.az).*

Clinical Hospital No.1
Mirgasimov Street 1 (495 5350).

Mediclub *Uzeyir Hajibeyov Street 45 (497 0911, www.mediclub.az).*

Opticians

Anar Optik *Neftchilar prospekt 85-87 (492 1449).*

Pharmacy

Asfarma *Ataturk prospekt 44 (440 1183).*

STDs, HIV & AIDS

Condoms are available at pharmacies and, sometimes, supermarkets. If you need an AIDS test, then the 24-hour Institute of Epidemiology (Jafar Jabbarli Street 34, 494 7353) can do one for you.

ID

You are legally obliged to carry photo ID or a passport at all times – but it will rarely be checked. If you lose your passport, report it to the nearest police station (*see p209*), then go to your embassy for an emergency replacement.

INSURANCE

All EU citizens are entitled to free emergency treatment – carry a valid European Health Insurance Card – but it's wise also to have medical cover in your travel insurance.

INTERNET

Of the local internet service providers, Bakinternet (www. bakinternet.net) is the most popular. Nearly all hotels of three-star and above, and flats rented out to high-paying foreigners, will have Wi-Fi installed. In Baku, there aretwo 24-hour internet cafés on the west side of Molokan Park, a short walk from Fountains Square.

LANGUAGE

While the official language is Azeri, many locals still speak Russian – conversations may even be a mix of the two. Most in Baku are fluent in both. English is widely spoken, especially by those under 40. Most signage in Baku is in Azeri, and most restaurant menus are in some kind of English. For language study, *see p209*. For vocabulary, *see pp212-213*.

LEFT LUGGAGE

There are left-luggage offices at Baku Railway Station (*see p79*). The fee per item is AZN2 for 24 hours.

LEGAL HELP

For legal assistance, contact your embassy (*see p207*) for referral to English-speaking lawyers. Or try **Baker & McKenzie** (www.baker mckenzie.com/Azerbaijan).

LIBRARIES

Azerbaijan University of Languages *R Behbudov Street 60 (421 2231, www.adu.edu.az).* Contains a free library with an extensive selection of volumes in English.

MAPS

There are two maps of Baku generally available: Heron, with a large-scale map of the city centre on one side, and an index and gazetteer of places of interest; and an inferior one produced by the Baki Kartografiya Fabriki (BKF), sold at Stanford's map shop in London, with no index but a lay-out of the metro network. Try and buy one locally – perhaps at a branch of Ali & Nino (*see p128*) in town – as the price there is five times cheaper.

MEDIA

Of the various dreadful English-language freesheets, monthly glossy *AZ Magazine* stands out, albeit with its over-emphasis on social hobnobbing. By far the most intelligent read, touching on culture, history and politics, is the quarterly *Azerbaijan* *International* (www.azer.com). Each edition since 1993 has featured a theme, explored from many viewpoints – the introduction of the Latin-based alphabet, the revival of local cinema, or literature under Stalin. Founded and edited by the indefatigable Betty Blair, it's a treasure trove of historical colour and cultural context. Great website, too.

Foreign newspapers are available at most top-class hotels, with a delay of at least a day.

MONEY

The Azeri unit of currency is the manat – in fact, the new manat – designated as AZN. There are 100 gapiks to a manat – keep 20 gapik coins for metro charge-card machines and bus journeys. There are notes for 1 (blueish-grey), 5 (orange), 10 (blue), 20 (green), 50 (yellow) and 100 (mauve) manats. At the time of writing, one manat was worth approximately €1, or $1.03.

Banks, ATMs & bureaux de change

There are ATMs and exchange offices all over central Baku. Exchange rates vary slightly between bureaux, so shop around if you're changing a large-ish sum. You can re-exchange excess manats without having to fill out any currency declaration forms. There's a bank of ATM machines on the northern side of Fountains Square near the Akademiya bookstore.

Credit cards

Credit cards are accepted in most restaurants and hotels around the city.

OPENING HOURS

Although office hours are officially 9am to 5pm, Mondays to Fridays, days seem to start quite late in Baku, and many bars and shops don't open until 9.30am or 10am. Banking hours are officially 9am-5.30pm,

Mondays to Fridays. Most shops close around 7pm, often later, and are open seven days a week. Bars and restaurants are open until at least until 11pm, often midnight, and some until the last guest leaves.

POLICE STATIONS

There are police stations dotted all over the city. Central ones include:
Neftchilar prospekt 129 (493 0202).
Nizami Street 22 (492 0202).
Nizami Street 44 (498 0202).
Samed Vurgun Street 16 (459 5502).

POSTAL SERVICES

Central Post Office *Uzeyir Hajibeyov Street 41 (498 8000).*

RELIGION

Churches

Baku International Fellowship
050 731 6445,
www.bakuchurch.org.
Evangelical. Meets at Baku International School.

Church of the Virgin Mary's Immaculate Conception
Orujev Street 10 (562 2255,
www.catholic.az). Roman Catholic.

St Archangel Michael's
Zargarpalan Street 38 (497 3596). Russian Orthodox.

Mosques

There are mosques throughout the city.

Synagogues

Ashkenazi *Dilara Aliyeva Street 171 (494 0288).*

Sefardskaya *Shamsi Badalbeyli Street 39 (494 0375, 495 5429).*

SAFETY & SECURITY

Baku is a relatively safe city, with little street crime. But there have been occasional muggings in recent years, so be as alert as you would be in any capital city.

In the provinces, be aware that the border area around Nagorno-Karabakh can be very sensitive – and that the province itself is out of bounds to foreigners.

SMOKING

Smoking is allowed in bars and restaurants, though some have designated no-smoking areas. The better hotels have no-smoking rooms.

STUDY

Language classes

The local English-language press (*see p208*) is full of ads for private lessons and part-time courses in Azeri. Private individuals charge around AZN10 per hour.
International Learning Center *Zargarpalan Street 12 (492 4643, 050 532 7889 mobile, www.azlearn.org).*
Three semesters (each AZN460) over the course of an academic year brings beginners to conversational level with lessons every weekday morning.

TELEPHONES

There are shops all over Baku that can provide a local SIM card for your mobile phone. Officially, you'll need a photocopy of your passport and have to fill out a pile of paperwork – **Azercell** is the most popular provider. Other dealers may bypass this process altogether. Note that UK visitors with a roaming facility contract with one of the international majors cannot necessarily use their phone in Azerbaijan – Vodafone, for one, have no such agreement with its Azeri counterpart. Your UK phone simply won't work here.

There are still a few public phones in Baku, a handful that work on the old, Soviet-era *zheton* system. These are for local calls only, and *zhetoni* are near impossible to obtain.

If you have no landline at home or in your hotel, and no mobile, go to the Central Post Office (*see above*) to make your call.

Phone numbers

Baku numbers all start with city code 012, which you do not need to dial from within the city – you only need the seven-digit number that follows it. If you're dialling from abroad, or using a foreign mobile, then +994 12 is the code. The international access code out of Azerbaijan is 00. Most local mobile numbers start with 050.

Operator services

International telephone communications 107.

TIME

Azerbaijan is four hours ahead of GMT in winter, five hours ahead in summer, so nine hours ahead of New York in winter, and 12 hours ahead of California. The system of daylight saving time is also used here, so clocks go forward on the last Sunday in March and back on the last Sunday in October.

TIPPING

Add an approximate ten per cent to your bill in restaurants and in taxi cabs unless the service provided has been particularly shoddy.

TOILETS

There are sets of new, clean. pay-for toilets at a few points along the Bulvar waterfront – *kişi* is for men, *qadin* for women. Note that in a number of local bars, restaurants and other public places that do not cater to high-spending foreigners, the toilet is unisex and is usually of the hole in the ground variety, with a jug or hose of water alongside. It may be wise to carry packs of tissues with you.

TOURIST INFORMATION

Baku Tourist Information Centre
Uzeyir Hajibeyov Street 6 (598 5519, www.tourism.az). **Open** 10am-1pm, 2-6pm Mon-Sat.

DIRECTORY

THE LOCAL CLIMATE

Average temperatures and monthly rainfall in Baku.

	High (°C/°F)	Low (°C/°F)	Rainfall (mm/in)
Jan	6 / 43	0 / 32	22 / 0.9
Feb	7 / 45	0 / 32	20 / 0.8
Mar	10 / 50	2 / 37	22 / 0.9
Apr	16 / 61	8 / 46	18 / 0.7
May	20 / 68	12 / 54	18 / 0.7
June	25 / 77	15 / 59	8 / 0.3
July	28 / 82	17 / 63	2 / 0.1
Aug	30 / 86	18 / 64	6 / 0.2
Sept	24 / 75	12 / 54	15 / 0.6
Oct	16 / 61	8 / 46	23 / 0.9
Nov	12 / 54	2 / 37	30 / 1.2
Dec	8 / 46	0 / 32	24 / 0.9

Near Government House, this little office has a few brochures and leaflets but the friendly staff are short on practical advice otherwise.

VISAS & IMMIGRATION

Nearly all foreigners, and certainly those from the EU, the US, Canada and Australia, require a visa to enter Azerbaijan. As of October 2010, visas are no longer issued at Baku Airport or at land borders; they must be obtained in advance. Passengers travelling without a visa are simply turned back.

As of June 2011, new rules apply to tourist visas. From now on, tourists must apply for their visa through a recognised travel agency licensed by the Azerbaijan Ministry of Culture & Tourism. The travel agency, in turn, must submit a number of documents in electronic form, including copies of the applicant's passport, documents outlining the tourist's purpose of visit and a tourist voucher. This voucher entitles the applicant to a reduced visa fee of $20 – before this recent introduction, the fee was around $100. The visa is electronic, and not stuck into passports, and is valid for 30 days. It is single-entry. There are also official letters of invitation that the travel agency needs to have stamped by the Azeri Embassy in the applicant's home country.

As one local online information portal, www.azerbaijan24.com

puts it: 'The complexity of the process is that there is no universal rule and every single Azerbaijan embassy interprets visa regulations with some variations of their own'. It goes on to list 25 countries with differing criteria and waiting times for their respective Azeri embassy. So it's a good idea to contact your nearest Azerbaijani Embassy in advance.

In addition to this, those intending to stay longer than 30 days must register with the nearest police station in Baku within three days of arrival, pay $10 and provide their passport, visa and proof of address. Those staying outside Baku must appear in person at the Passport Registration Department of the Ministry of Internal Affairs of Azerbaijan in the capital before they leave the capital. The fee for overstaying their official welcome is $50 each month.

In the UK, such was the volume of traffic and long (often month-long) waiting times for visa applications, the whole process has been outsourced to the **Azerbaijan Visa Centre** (Basement, 1 Star Street W2 1QD, no phone, www.azembassy.org.uk, www.visaforazerbaijan.org.uk, open 9am-noon Mon-Fri). The fee here for an ordinary tourist visa, with an unspecified 'normal' waiting time and collected in person, is £55 plus £24 VAT, ie £79. The voucher option, as opposed to the official guidelines laid out above, is calculated at £14 plus £60 VAT, in other words £74. The 'urgent' option

to have your visa processed more quickly demands a levy of £55 plus £86.40 VAT, ie £141 for an ordinary tourist visa and £14 plus £86.40 VAT for a voucher, ie £100.40.

There are also business visas, dealt with by the visitor's company; their cost ranges from £170 for a single-entry, short-term stay to £315 for a one-year, multiple-entry visa, express process.

US citizens must apply through the Azerbaijani Embassy in Washington DC (2741 34th Street, NW, 20008, consular section 202 337 5912, www.azembassy.us) or the Azerbaijani Consulate in Los Angeles (11766 Wilshire Boulevard, Suite 1410, Los Angeles, CA 90025, 310 444 9101, www.azconsulatela.org.

Application forms are available online, fee for a single-entry visa valid for 30 days is $131 for US citizens, waiting time ten working days.

WHEN TO GO

Weather-wise, the main thing to consider is that Baku is either windy or extremely windy, all year round. Winds come from the Caspian Sea to the south (known as *khazri*) or from inland areas to the west and north-west (known as *gilavar*). Winter is chilly but quite mild, and snow is rare in Baku, although temperatures can plunge seriously below zero in the mountainous areas to the north. Summer is hot and humid. Rain is heaviest in Azerbaijan's southern lowlands, by the Iranian border.

Public holidays

1 Jan New Year.
8 Mar Women's Day.
20-21 Mar Novruz
(*see p143* **Novruz Bayrami**).
9 May Victory Day.
28 May Republic Day.
15 June National Salvation Day.
26 June Armed Forces Day.
18 Oct National Independence Day.
12 Nov Constitution Day.
17 Nov National Revival Day.
31 Dec Day of Solidarity of Azerbaijanis Throughout the World.

DIRECTORY

Vocabulary

PRONUNCIATION

Azeri

Azeri shares great similarities with Turkish, the languages as close as, say, Italian and Spanish. A working knowledge of Turkish would go a long way here. Much like Turkish, Azeri was originally written in Arabic script but switched over to Latin. Under the Soviets, Cyrillic was used, but now Latin is once again the norm.

Azeri has a number of letters that require transliteration when rendered in English. The upside-down 'e' is, in fact, a short 'a'. As in Turkish, c with a cedilla is a 'ch' sound, while s with a cedilla is 'sh'. The soft, guttural 'g' with an accent can be rendered 'gh'. The q is a hard 'g', while umlauted ö's and ü's sound like their Turkish counterpart. The last syllable is usually lightly stressed.

Russian

In Baku, many locals still speak Russian, which is also used for business and dealing with foreigners, particularly those from the former Soviet Union. Anyone with a smattering of Russian would find it most useful during their stay here.

USEFUL WORDS & PHRASES

Greetings

Hello
Azeri *Salam*
Russian *Zdrastvuyte*

Good morning
Azeri *Sabahin xeyir*
Russian *Dobroye utro*

Good evening
Azeri *Akhshamin xeyir*
Russian *Dobriy vecher*

Good night
Azeri *Gejan kheyra galsin*
Russian *Spokoynoi Notchi*

Goodbye
Azeri *Sagh ol*
Russian *Dosvidanya*

Basic words

Yes
Azeri *Bali/ha* (inf)
Russian *Da*

No
Azeri *Kheyr/ yokh*
Russian *Nyet*

Please
Azeri *Lutfan*
Russian *Pazhalsta*

Thank you
Azeri *Saol/ tashakkur ediram*
Russian *Spasiba*

Sorry
Azeri *Baghishlayin*
Russian *Izvinitye*

Cheers!
Azeri *Saghligha*
Russian *Na zdarovye*

Here
Azeri *Burada*
Russian *Zdyes'*

There
Azeri *Orda*
Russian *Tam*

Cheap
Azeri *Daha ujuz*
Russian *Dyoshevo*

Cheaper
Azeri *Ujuz*
Russian *Padeshevlye*

Dear
Azeri *Baha*
Russian *Daragoi*

Good
Azeri *Yakhshi*
Russian *Kharasho*

Bad
Azeri *Pis*
Russian *Plokha*

Closed
Azeri *Baghli*
Russian *Zakrito*

Open
Azeri *Achig*
Russian *Otkrito*

Big
Azeri *Boyuk*
Russian *Bolshoi*

Small
Azeri *Kichik*
Russian *Malinki*

Hot
Azeri *Isti/gaynar*
Russian *Gariachi/ zharka*

Police
Azeri *Polis*
Russian *Palitsia*

Hospital
Azeri *Khastakhana*
Russian *Bal'nitsa*

Doctor
Azeri *Hakim*
Russian *Vratch*

Hotel
Azeri *Mehmankhana*
Russian *Gastinitsa*

Air-conditioning
Azeri *Kondisioner*
Russian *S Kondisiyonyerom*

Balcony
Azeri *Balkon*
Russian *Balkon*

Bath
Azeri *Vanna*
Russian *Vanna*

Breakfast
Azeri *Sahar Yemayi*
Russian *Zavtrak*

Room
Azeri *Otag*
Russian *Komnata*

Shower
Azeri *Dush*
Russian *Dush*

Restaurant
Azeri *Restoran*
Russian *Restaran*

Menu
Azeri *Menu*
Russian *Menu*

Vocabulary

Shop
Azeri *Maghaza/Dukan*
Russian *Magazin*

Market
Azeri *Bazar*
Russian *Rinok*

Post office
Azeri *Pocht*
Russian *Pochta*

Embassy
Azeri *Safirlik*
Russian *Pasolstva*

Toilet (men's/ladies')
Azeri *Ayag yolu (kishi/gadin)*
Russian *Tualet
(muzhchina/zhenshchina)*

Basic phrases

There is ...
Azeri *... Var*
Russian *Yest*

There isn't
Azeri *Yox*
Russian *Nyet*

Where?
Azeri *Harada?*
Russian *Gdye?*

Who?
Azeri *Kim?*
Russian *Kto?*

When?
Azeri *Na vaxt?*
Russian *Kagda?*

How much/many?
Azeri *Na gadar?*
Russian *Skol'ka?*

I don't understand
Azeri *Man anlamiram*
Russian *Ya nye ponimayu*

Do you speak English?
Azeri *Siz ingilizja danishirsiniz?*
Russian *Vi govoritye pa
angliski?*

I don't speak Azeri
Azeri *Man Azerbayjan dilinda
danishmiram*
Russian *Ya nye govoriyu pa
azerbaidzhanski*

My name is...
Azeri *Manim adim...*
Russian *Menya zavoot...*

How are you?
Azeri *Nejasan?*
Russian *Kak dyela?*

How much is?
Azeri *Bu nechayadir?*
Russian *Skol'ka stoyit?*

Can I have the bill, please?
Azeri *Hesabi zekhmet olmasa*
Russian *Shot pazhalsta*

I don't want this
Azeri *Bunu istamiram*
Russian *Ya nye hachoo eta*

Travel

Airport
Azeri *Hava limani*
Russian *Aeroport*

Bus
Azeri *Avtobus*
Russian *Avtobus*

Train
Azeri *Gatar*
Russian *Poyezd*

Ticket
Azeri *Bilyet*
Russian *Bilyet*

Which platform?
Azeri *Hansi platform?*
Russian *Kakaya platforma?*

When does it leave?
Azeri *Na vakht gedir?*
Russian *Kagda atpravlyaetsa?*

When does it arrive?
Azeri *Na vakht gelir?*
Russian *Kagda pribivayet?*

Fill up the tank
Azeri *Aghzina kimi dolu*
Russian *Polni*

Station
Azeri *Vaghzal*
Russian *Vakzal*

Bus stop
Azeri *Avtobus dayanajaghi*
Russian *Astanovka*

Left luggage
Azeri *Saxlama kamerasi*
Russian *Kamera khraneniya*

Ticket office
Azeri *Kassa*
Russian *Kassa*

Days & months

Monday to Sunday
Azeri *bazar ertasi;
charshanba akhshami;
charshanba gunu; juma*

*akhshami; juma gunu; shanba;
bazaar gunu*
Russian *ponyedyelnik; vtornik;
sreda; chetvyerk; pyatnitsa;
subota; vaskrisenye*

January to December
Azeri *yanvar; fevral; mart;
aprel; may; iyun; iyul; avgust;
sentyabr; oktyabr; noyabr;
dekabr*
Russian *yanvar'; fevral'; mart;
aprel'; mai; iyun'; iyul'; avgust;
sentyabr'; oktyabr'; noyabr';
dekabr'*

Today
Azeri *Bugun*
Russian *Sevodnya*

Tomorrow
Azeri *Sabah*
Russian *Zavtra*

Yesterday
Azeri *Dunan*
Russian *Vchera*

Day
Azeri *Gun*
Russian *Dyen*

Week
Azeri *Hafta*
Russian *Nedelya*

Month
Azeri *Ay*
Russian *Myesats*

Numbers

Azeri 0 *sifr*; 1 *bir*; 2 *iki*; 3 *uch*;
4 *dord*; 5 *besh*; 6 *alti*; 7 *yeddi*;
8 *sakkiz*; 9 *dogguz*; 10 *on*
Russian 0 *nol'*; 1 *adin*; 2 *dva*;
3 *tri*; 4 *ch'tiri*; 5 *pyat*; 6 *shest*;
7 *syem'*; 8 *vosem'*; 9 *devyet'*;
10 *dyeset'*

Content Index

INDEX

INDEX

Venue Index

INDEX

INDEX

INDEX

Maps

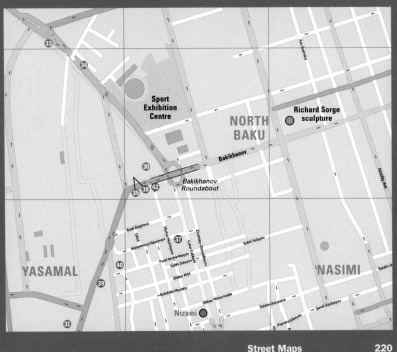

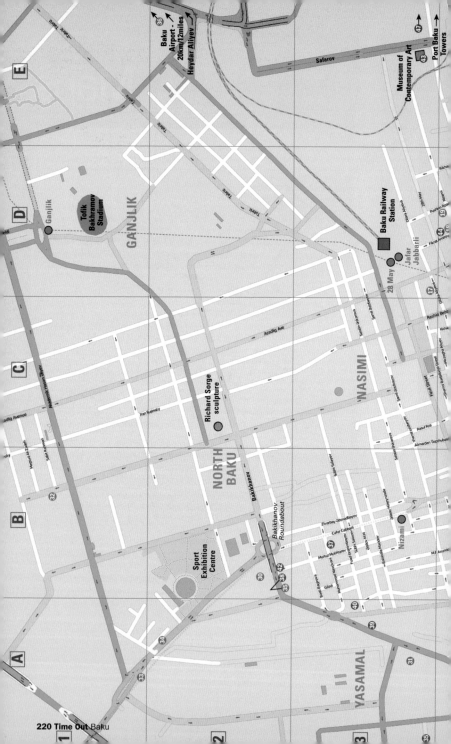

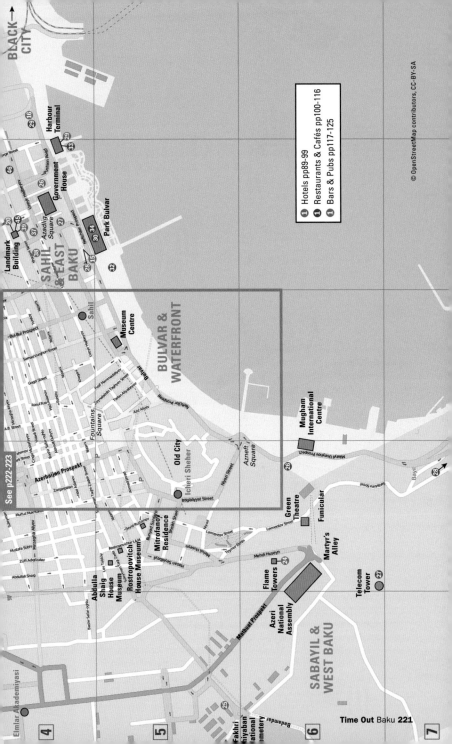

BLACK
CITY →

Harbour
Terminal

29 16

33 25

16

26 Government
House

27 Azadlig
Square

20 15
39
37 35

38
36

Landmark
Building

Park Bulvar

30 34

28
32

Sahil

SAHIL &
EAST BAKU

Museum
Centre

Bul-Bul Prospect

Azerbaijan Prospekt

BULVAR &
WATERFRONT

Bulvar

Fountains
Square

Old City
Icheri Sheher

Istiglaliyyat Street

Azneft
Square

Mugham
International
Centre

26

Green
Theatre

Funicular

Martyr's
Alley

28

Mitrofanov
Residence

Rostropovitch
House Museum

Abdulla
Shaig
House
Museum

Flame
Towers

24

Azeri
National
Assembly

Matbuat Prospekt

Telecom
Tower
27

Badamdar

SABAYIL &
WEST BAKU

25

Fakhri
Khiyaban
National
Cemetery

Elmlar Akademiyasi

See p222-223

4

5

6

7

Hotels pp89-99

Restaurants & Cafés pp100-116

Bars & Pubs pp117-125

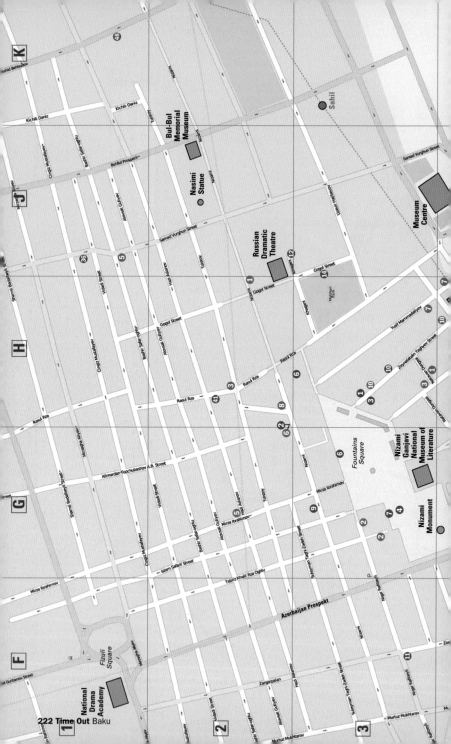

BULVAR &
WATERFRONT

Azerbaijan State Museum
of History

Bulvar

Children's
Puppet
Theatre

Azerbaijan
Cinema

Hajinski
Mansion

Sabir
Monument

Academy of
Sciences

Institute of
Manuscripts

Old City

Economics
University

City Hall

Wedding
Palace

Icheri Shaher

Philharmonia
Concert Hall

SOCAR
Building

Azneft
Square

State Museum
of Arts

See Old City map p58

- ❶ Hotels pp89-99
- ❶ Restaurants & Cafés pp100-116
- ❶ Bars & Pubs pp117-125

Baku Metro

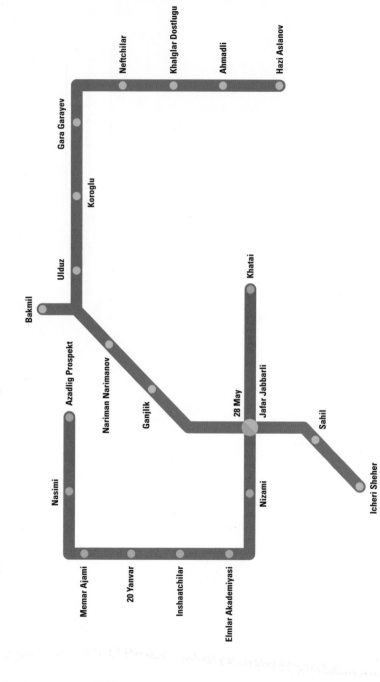

Neftchilar
Khalglar Dostlugu
Ahmadli
Hazi Aslanov
Gara Garayev
Koroglu
Ulduz
Bakmil
Azadlig Prospekt
Nariman Narimanov
Ganjlik
Khatai
Jafar Jabbarli
28 May
Sahil
Nasimi
Nizami
Icheri Sheher
Memar Ajami
20 Yanvar
Inshaatchilar
Elmlar Akademiyasi